CHOCOLATE

Editorial Director
Suzanne Tise-Isoré
Style & Design Collection

Editorial Coordinator
Boris Guilbert

Artistic Director
Philippe Marchand

Graphic Design and Layout
Emilie Greenberg
Thomas Hamel

Translation from the French
Stéphanie Curtis (recipes)
Philippa Bowe for mot.tiff inside (other texts)

Proofreading
Karolina Galluffo for mot.tiff inside

Production
Barbara Jaegy

Color Separation
Arciel Grafic, Paris

Printed in Spain by Indice, S.L.

Simultaneously published in French as *Chocolat*
© Flammarion, S.A., Paris, 2016

English-language edition
© Flammarion, S.A., Paris, 2016

editions.flammarion.com
styleetdesign-flammarion.com

16 17 18   3 2 1

ISBN: 978-2-08-020274-1

Legal Deposit: 10/2016

PIERRE HERMÉ

CHOCOLATE

PHOTOGRAPHS
SERGIO COIMBRA

RECIPES WRITTEN BY COCO JOBARD

Flammarion

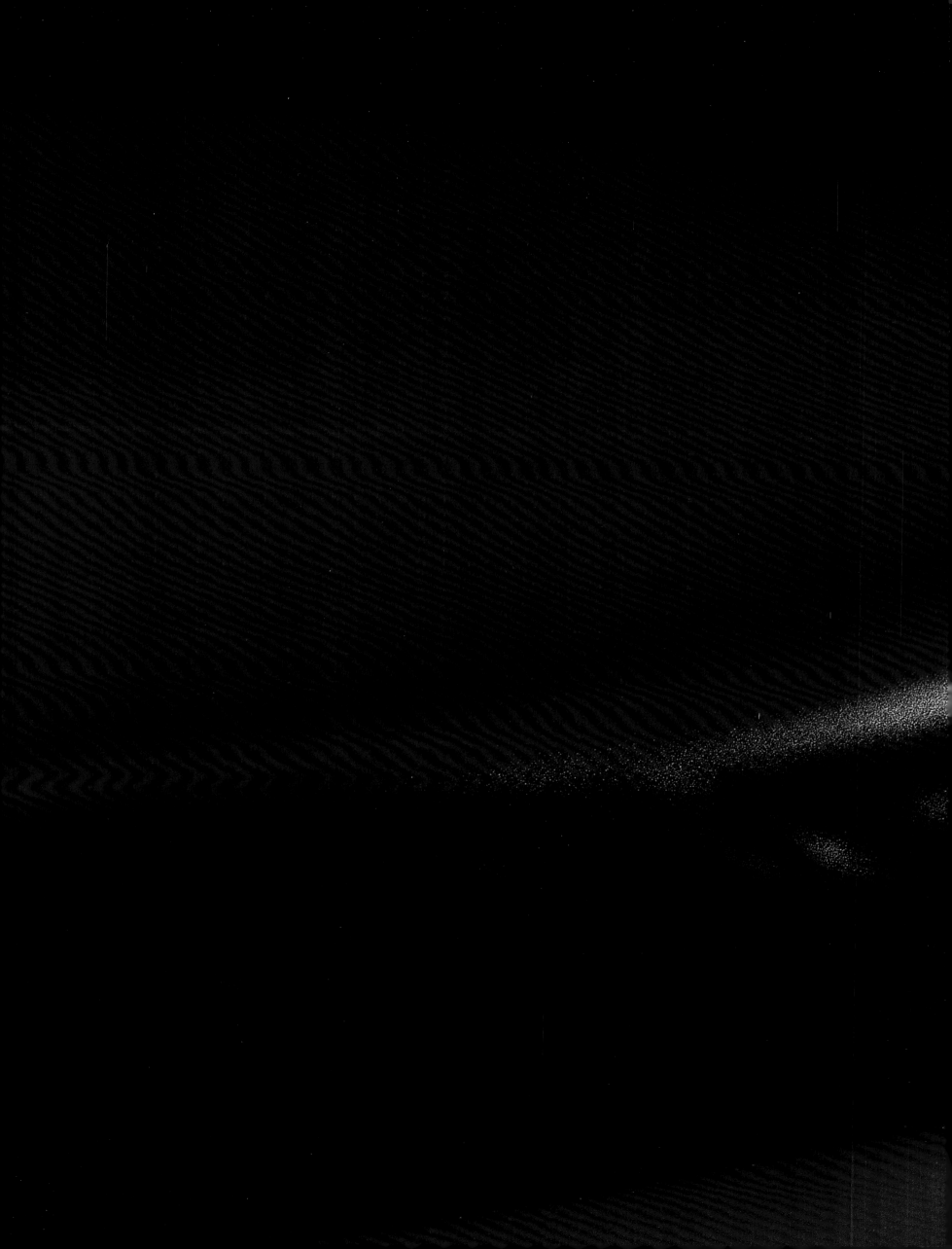

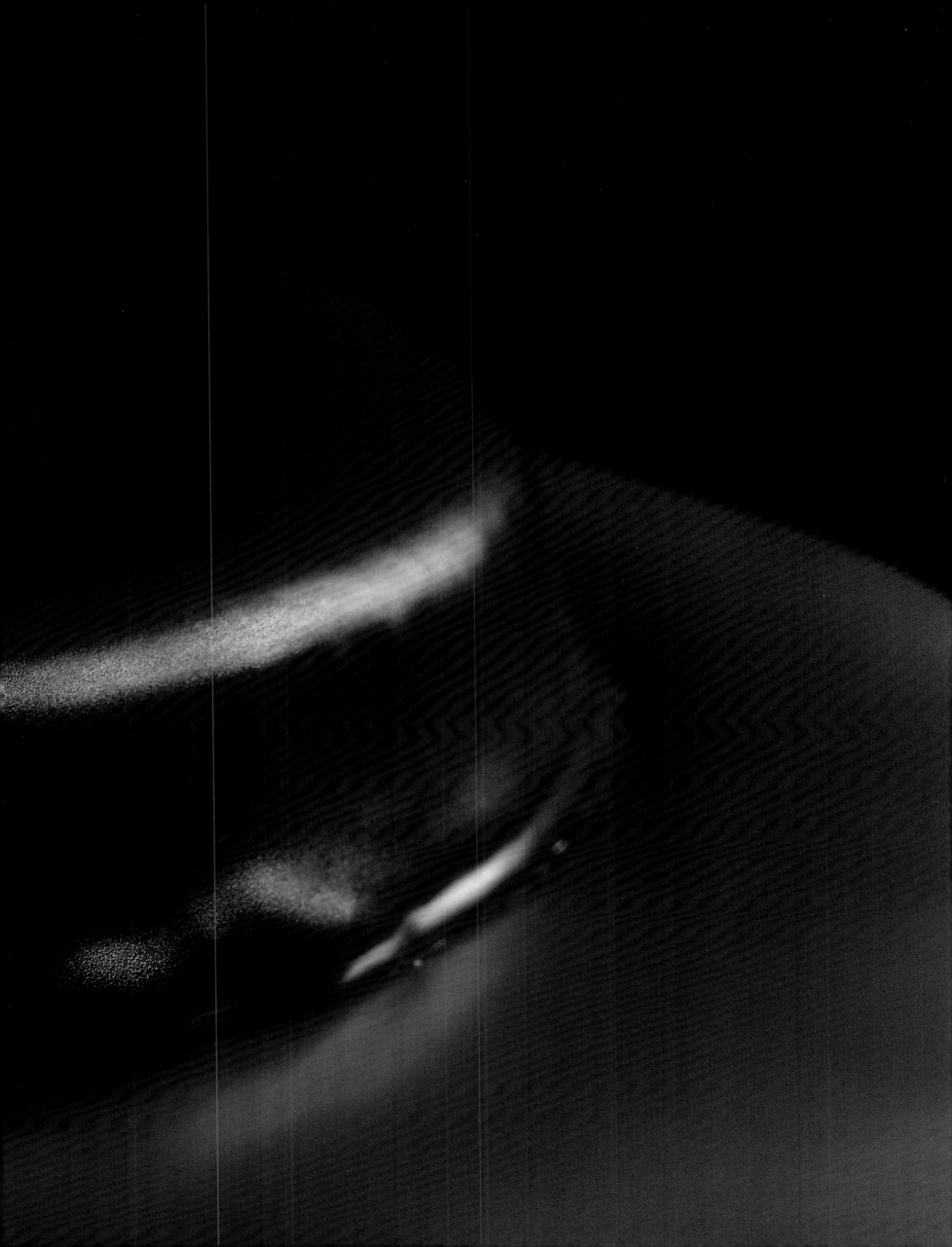

sergio coimbra

I am always surprised by the way some people enter our lives. Long before we ever worked together, Pierre Hermé was already on my professional radar. As I was still involved in another business, becoming a photographer was a dream I nurtured for the future. I strolled into Paris bookshops looking for food images that would resonate within me. Pierre Hermé's books were an inspiration. I collected nearly all of the volumes by the man called the "Picasso of Pastry." The variety of forms, the vibrantly colored macarons, chocolate delights, and other seemingly chiseled creations challenged the photographer in me. I will never forget my immense joy when, shortly after sending Pierre Hermé a copy of Studio SC's book, I received an invitation to visit his office.

I first met Pierre six years ago on Rue Bonaparte. During this brief interlude, we talked about working together some day. "Some day" came three years later. Charles Znaty, CEO of the Maison Pierre Hermé Paris, received me and quickly fostered a kind and considerate relationship. We held a test photo shoot from which a selection of images was chosen for the company's 2014 calendar, presented at the Grand Palais in Paris. Later, Pierre came to Brazil, discovered our studio, and spent some time in São Paulo. We quickly became friends.

Pierre told me he wanted to create a book with images of his work. Flammarion, a Paris-based publishing house, was interested in it, and Pierre asked me to author the photographs. You can imagine how delighted I was! The calendar had been an amuse-bouche, a palate teaser. I had cherished the hope of future meetings and of a book, which could one day join those that had for so long nourished my inspiration.

Working with someone as generous, professional, and respectful as Pierre Hermé is an exquisitely fulfilling experience. For two weeks, we worked together up to ten hours a day. He makes chocolates like a goldsmith crafts fine jewelry: with remarkable care and dedication. I strived to distill the soul of his creations while playing with light to reveal the personality of this reserved artist. Of the four hundred or so images taken, only a quarter made it into the book.

Throughout our collaboration, Pierre worked diligently and discreetly, allowing me to focus on photography. Never did he ask to see what I had shot or offer suggestions, no matter how natural that would have been. He trusted me as if we'd known each other for decades. As if the years I'd spent collecting his books had been part of the trip that had brought us to the time shared in creating this book together. We hope everyone will enjoy these pages as much as we did in bringing them to life.

May this volume pay tribute to the energy of our meeting.

pierre hermé

Capricious. Honorable. Obscure. Conceited. Obsessive. Luminous. Admirable. Tender. It fascinates me. Challenges me. I tame it. It coaxes me. I shape it. It resists me. Its law: perfection. My salvation: rigor. Protean, it defies my beliefs. Feline yet redolent with heavy aromas of tropical undergrowth. Sometimes just a fragile bean. Evanescence. Subtle fermentation. Drink of the gods. Amused by the idea that even though tamed, it throws back a somber look. To achieve my goals it is I who must bend to adapt to its demands. It remains a solid fortress that I take pleasure in constantly assailing with my epicurean thoughts.

In tribute to this Prince among ingredients, Sergio Coimbra has given me a gift that I have only dreamed of until now. Illumination. Colors. Shapes. Sergio seems to have slipped into my thoughts, capturing the essence of my imagination, to create visual scenarios that, through his lens, reflect all that fascinates and obsesses me. The result of his work is equal to the man I know: delightfully charming, thoroughly enchanting.

archi tec tures

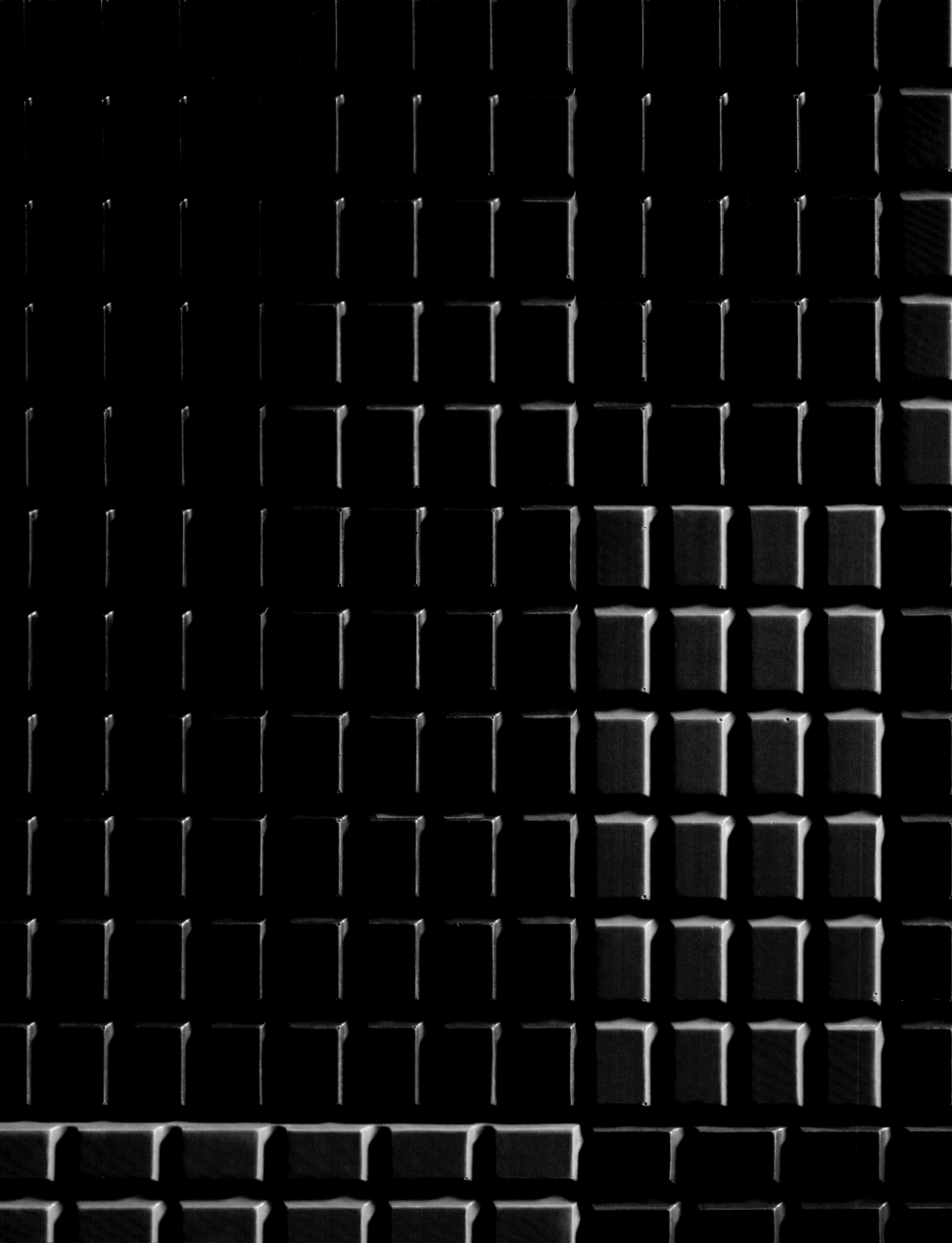

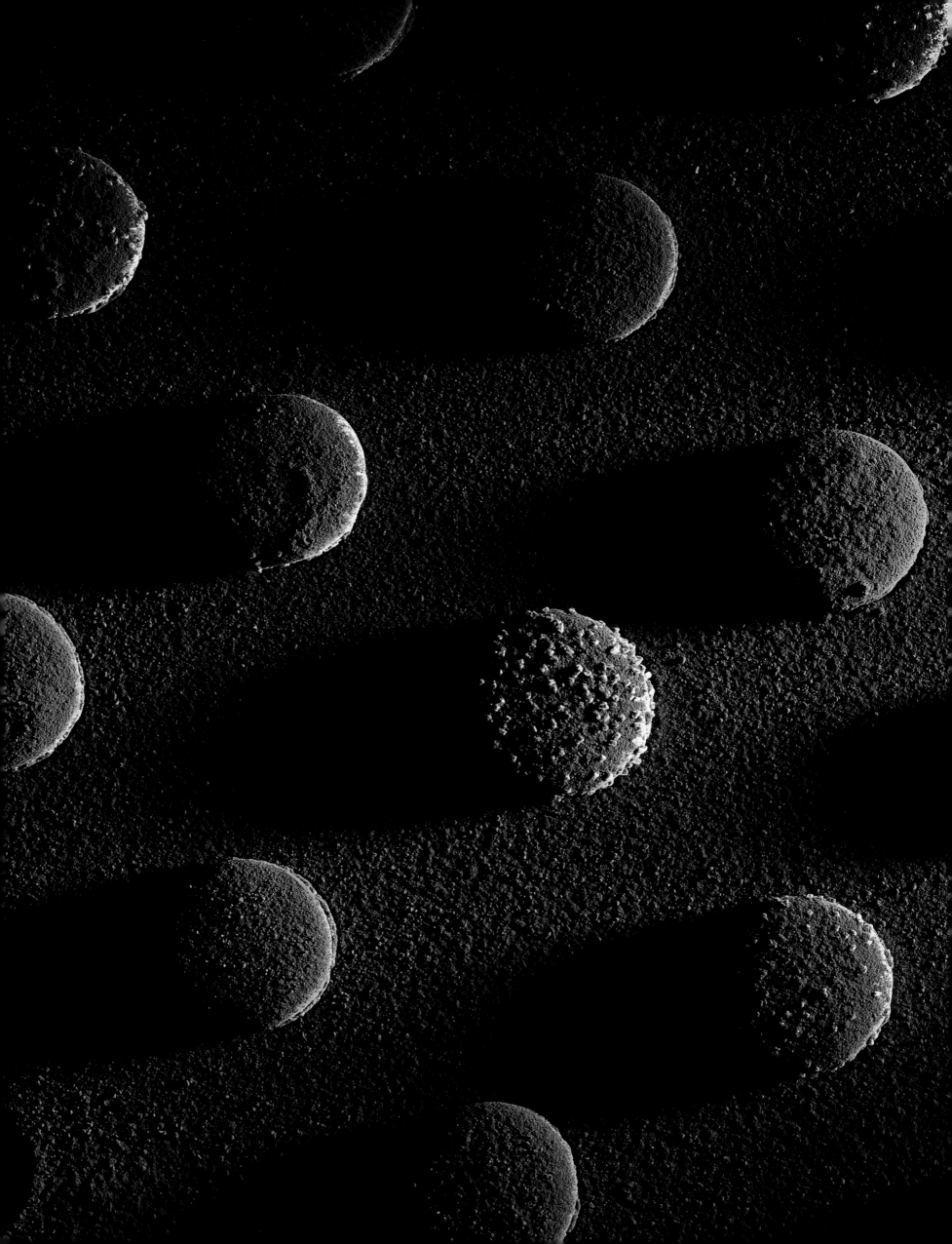

Éclair Azur

Azur Éclair

Makes about 20 éclairs

Ingredients:

Choux Pastry:

7 tablespoons + 2 teaspoons
(3 3/4 oz./110 g) butter
1/2 cup (4 1/3 oz./125 g) mineral
water
1/2 cup (4 1/3 oz./125 g) whole milk
1 teaspoon (5 g) superfine sugar
1 teaspoon (5 g) *Fleur de sel*,
preferably Guérande
1 1/2 cups (5 oz./140 g) flour
1 cup (8 3/4 oz./250 g) whole eggs

**Manjari Chocolate and Yuzu
Cream:**

2 teaspoons (1/3 oz./8 g) powdered
gelatin, or 4 gelatin sheets of 2 g
13 1/4 oz. (375 g) Manjari 64% dark
chocolate (Valrhona)
1 cup (8 oz./225 g) yuzu juice
1 cup (8 oz./225 g) egg yolks
1 cup (8 oz./225 g) superfine sugar
2/3 cup (5 3/4 oz./165 g) whole milk
2 cups (16 1/3 oz./465 g) liquid
cream

Chocolate Glaze:

1/3 cup (3 oz./90 g) mineral water
1/2 cup (3 1/2 oz./100 g) superfine
sugar
2 3/4 oz. (80 g) cocoa paste,
or 100% cocoa dark chocolate
17 2/3 oz. (500 g) fondant

Finishing:

80 small pieces candied yuzu rind

———

Preparation Time:

About 1 h.

Cooking Time:

About 25 mins.

Chilling Time:

30 mins.

Preparation:

Prepare the choux pastry:
Cut the butter into pieces.
Combine the water, milk,
sugar, *Fleur de sel* and
butter in a saucepan, and
bring to a boil. Add the flour
all at once, stirring briskly
for two or three minutes,
until the mixture is smooth
and pulls away from the
sides of the pan. Turn the
mixture into a bowl and add
the eggs, little by little,
stirring briskly to incorporate
the eggs well after each
addition. Preheat the oven
on convection setting to
395°F
(200°C/Gas Mark 6–7).
Spoon the mixture into a
pastry bag fitted with a
BF18 star pastry tip. Line a
pastry sheet with cooking
parchment and pipe the
dough out into even tube
shapes, about 6 in. (15 cm)
long, leaving space
between each. Place in the
preheated oven and turn off
the heat immediately. After
ten minutes, turn the oven
back on to 340°F
(170°C/Gas Mark 5–6) and
cook for an additional
ten minutes. After
ten minutes, open the oven
door very slightly (slide a
spoon into the door to keep
it ajar if necessary) and cook
for an additional ten minutes.
Remove from the oven and
transfer the éclairs to a
pastry rack to cool.

Prepare the Manjari chocolate and yuzu cream:
Sprinkle the powdered gelatin into a little warm water to
soften. (If using sheet gelatin, place in a bowl of cold
water for fifteen minutes to soften, then squeeze
between the palms of your hands to drain.) Chop the
chocolate with a serrated knife and place it in a bowl.
Heat the yuzu juice in a saucepan to 120°F (50°C).
Whisk the egg yolks and sugar together in a bowl. Bring
the milk and cream to a boil in a saucepan and pour,
whisking constantly, over the egg yolk–sugar mixture.
Add the warm yuzu juice. Pour the mixture back into the
saucepan and cook, whisking constantly, to 185°F
(85°C). Stir in the gelatin. Pour the mixture over the
chopped chocolate, stirring. Mix with a hand blender.
Press a sheet of plastic film directly on the surface of the
mixture and refrigerate until cooled.

———

With the point of a No. 6 plain pastry tip, pierce
three holes spaced evenly along the bottom side of each
éclair. Fill the pastry bag with the chocolate–yuzu cream,
and pipe the cream evenly and generously into the three
holes on the bottom of each éclair. Refrigerate.

———

Prepare the chocolate glaze: Combine the water and
sugar in a saucepan, and bring to a boil to make a sugar
syrup. Remove from the heat and let cool. Chop the
cocoa paste with a serrated knife and melt in a bowl
over a bain-marie of simmering water. Knead the
fondant between the palms of your hands until softened.
In a shallow bowl, combine the fondant with a few
tablespoons sugar syrup and the melted cocoa paste.
Add enough additional sugar syrup to obtain a supple,
fluid texture.

———

Place the glaze in a wide shallow bowl. Glaze the éclairs,
one at a time, holding each upside down over the glaze,
and dipping the top quickly in the chocolate. Remove,
turn the éclair right side up and run your index finger
around the glaze to make a neat edge, removing any
glaze that may have dripped down. Decorate the top of
each éclair with four pieces of candied yuzu rind and
refrigerate for thirty minutes before serving.

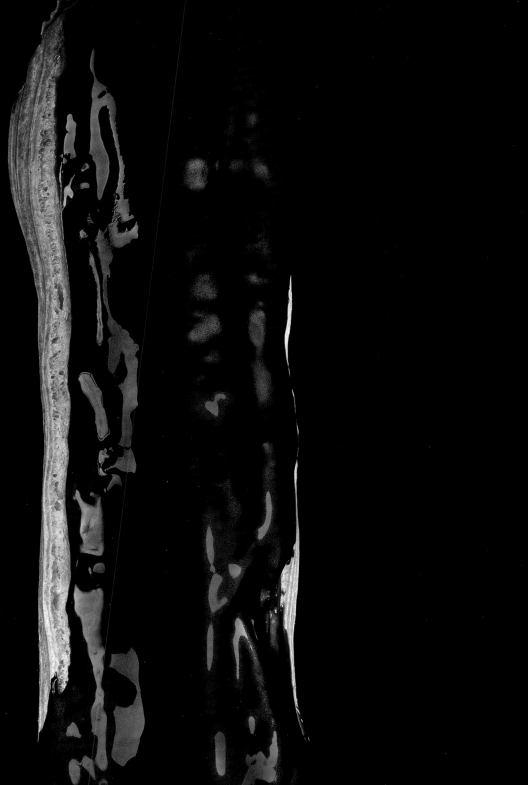

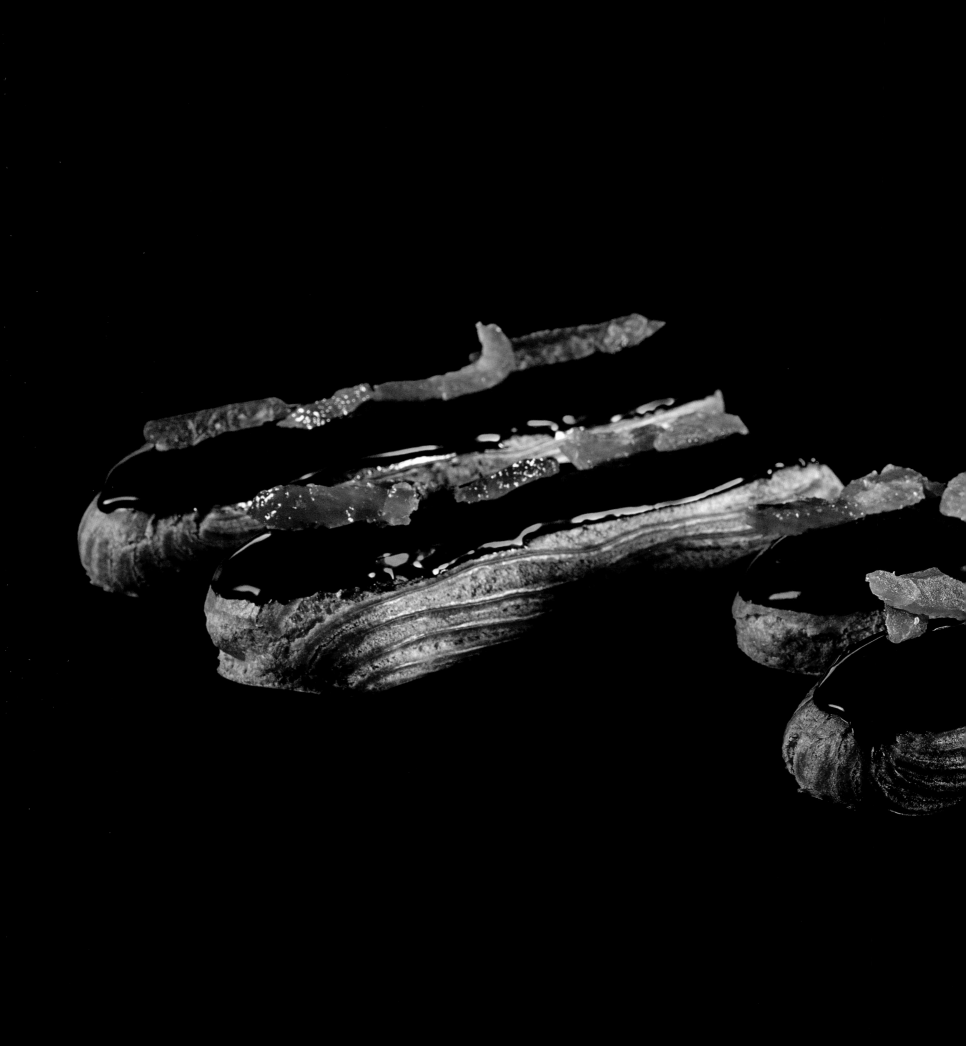

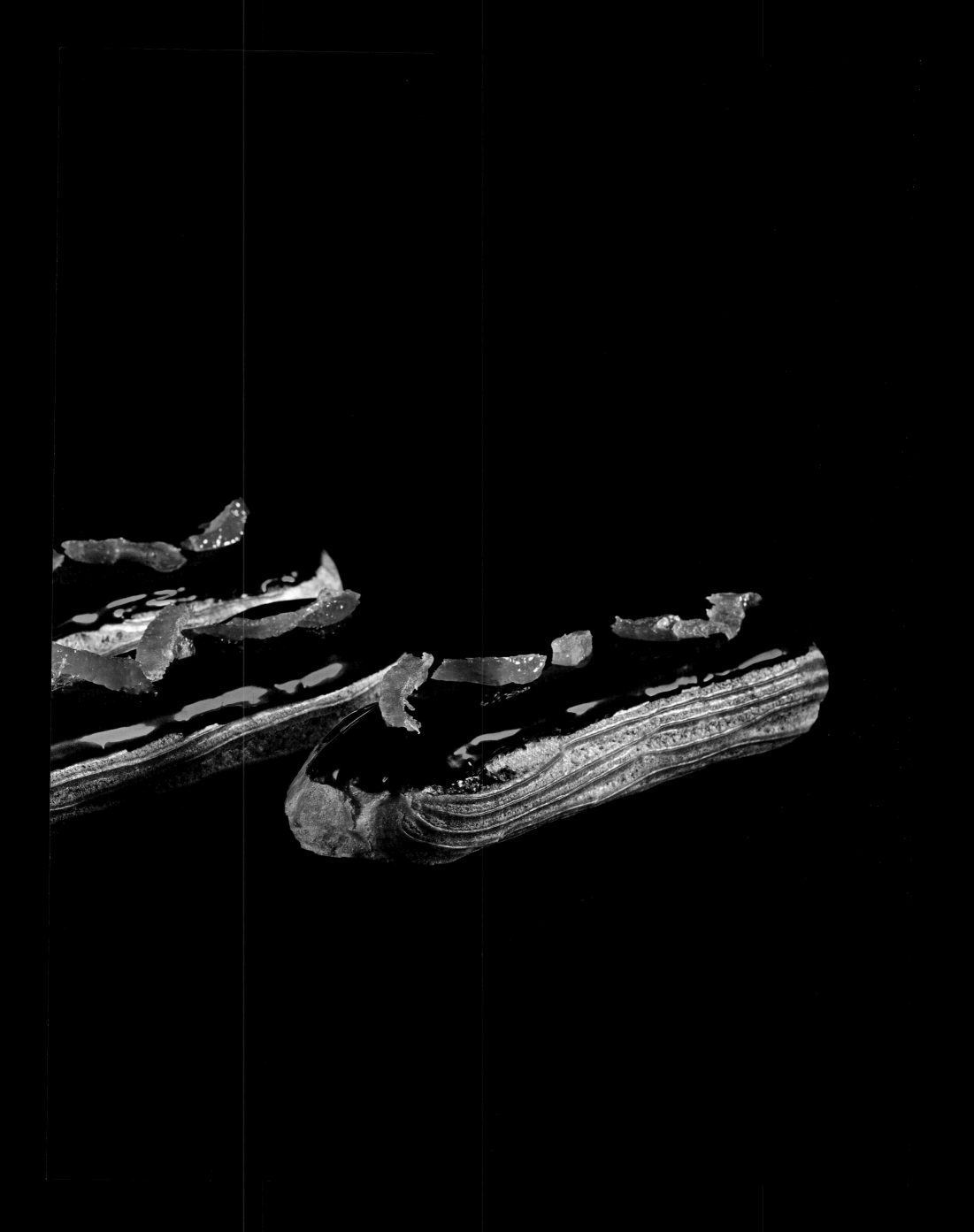

"My creative work is about projecting my fantasies. I like to really get to know the ingredients I use, including where they come from."

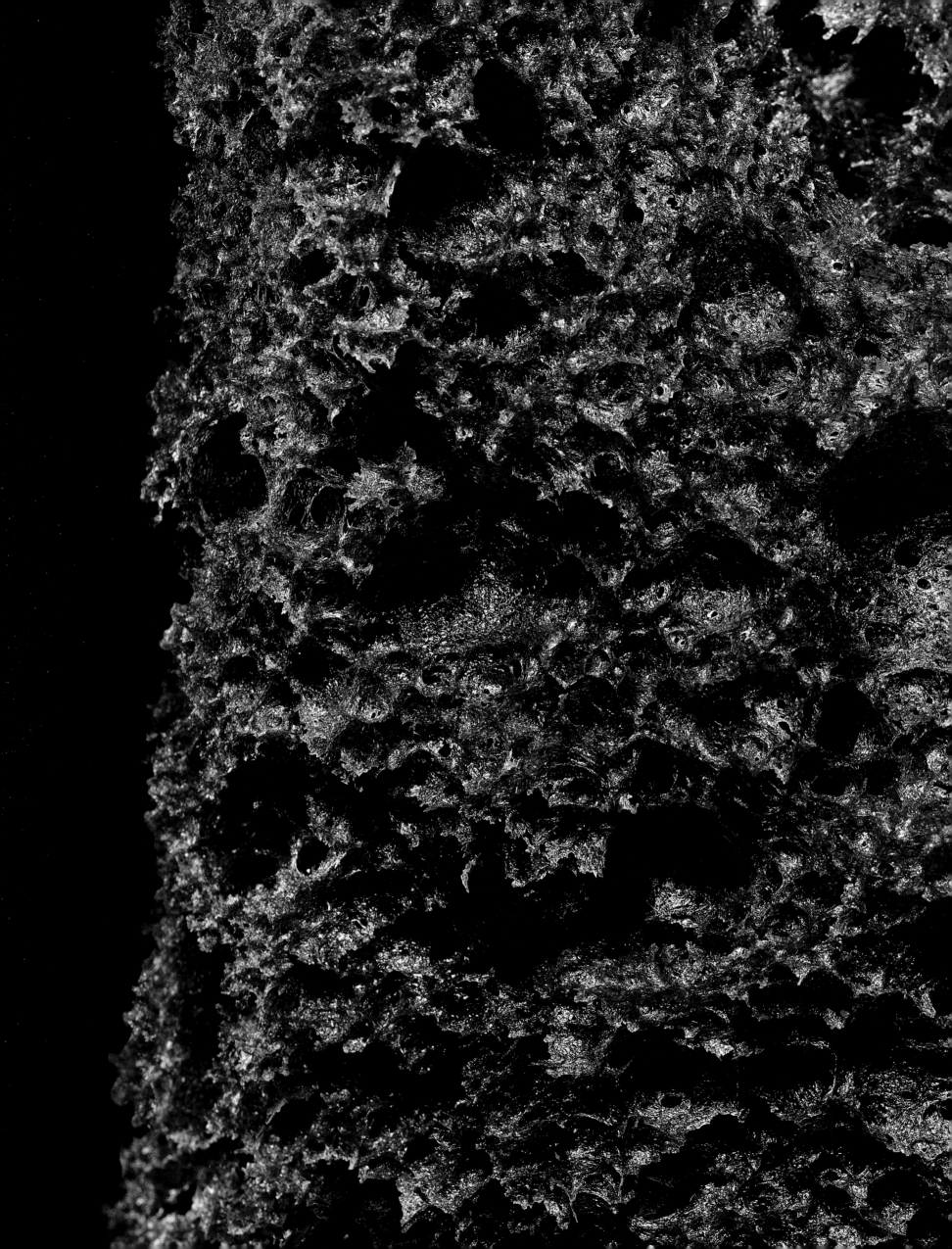

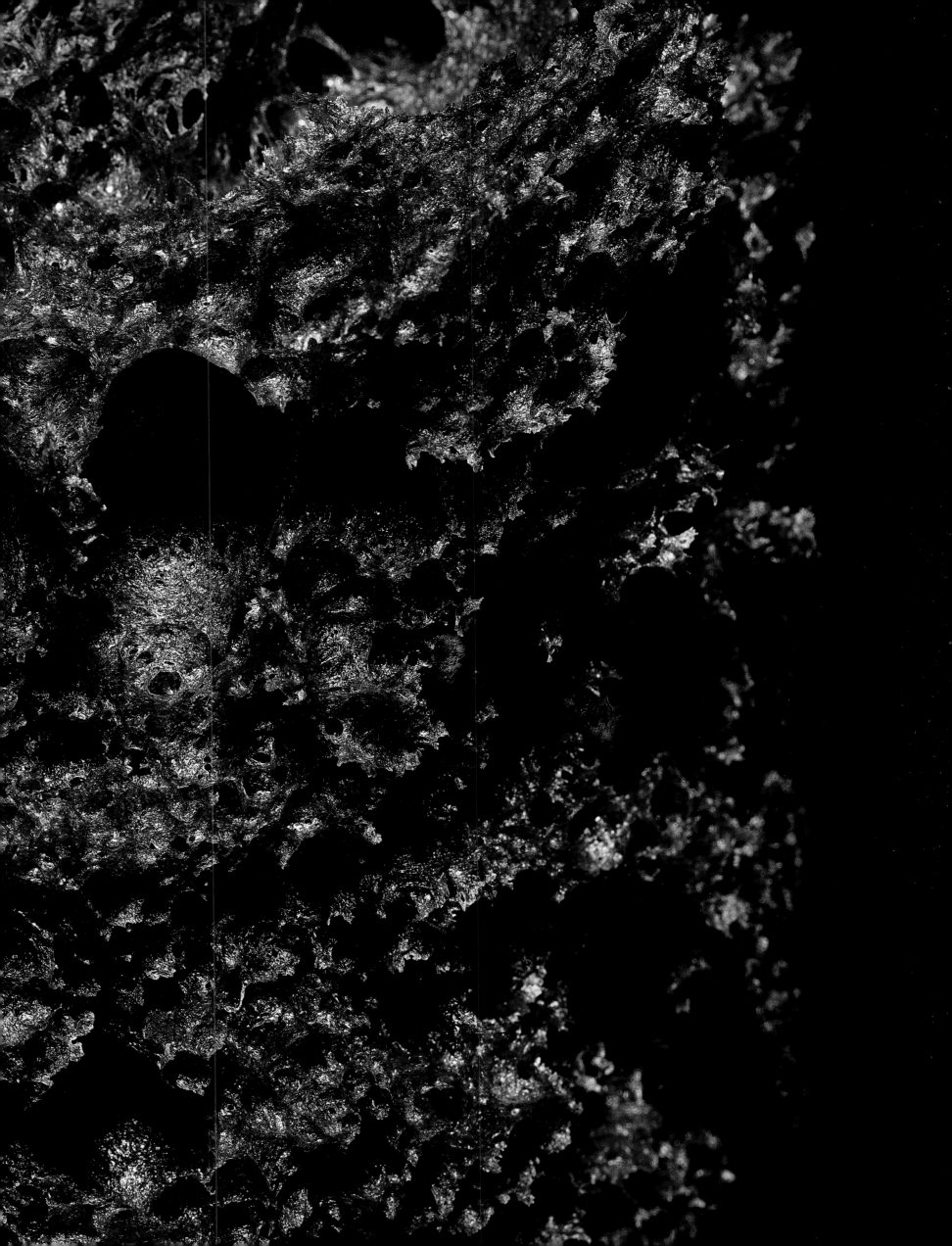

Barre Chocolat Intense

Intense Chocolate Bar

Makes about 60 bars

Ingredients:

Bitter Chocolate Ganache:

31 1/4 oz. (885 g) Araguani 72%
dark chocolate (Valrhona)
14 1/3 tablespoons (7 1/4 oz./205 g)
butter
3 cups (25 3/4 oz./730 g) liquid
cream

Pre-Coating:

10 1/2 oz. (300 g) Mexique 64%
dark chocolate (Valrhona)

Final Coating:

2 1/4 lb. (1 kg) Mexique 64%
dark chocolate (Valrhona)

—

Preparation Time:

3 x 1 h. (2 days in advance,
the following day and the same day).

Cooking Time:

A few minutes (2 days in advance, the
following day and the same day).

Resting Time:

2 x 24 h.

Preparation:

Two days in advance, prepare the bitter chocolate ganache: Chop the chocolate with a serrated knife and place it in a bowl. Cut the butter into cubes. Bring the cream to a boil in a saucepan. Pour the cream, one-third at a time, over the chocolate, stirring from the center out in small, then progressively larger concentric circles. When the temperature of the chocolate is at 104°F–113°F (40°C–45°C), add the cubes of butter and mix with a hand blender for two minutes. Pour the ganache into a shallow dish. Press a sheet of plastic film directly onto the surface of the ganache. Refrigerate until the texture is creamy. Place a square metal pastry frame, 13 x 13 x 1/2 in. (34 cm x 34 cm x 12 mm), on a baking sheet lined with a silicone pastry sheet. Use an elbow spatula to spread the chocolate ganache evenly over the silicone sheet. Smooth the top and leave at room temperature to set before placing in the refrigerator overnight.

One day in advance, prepare the pre-coating: Chop 10 1/2 oz. (300 g) chocolate with a serrated knife, place in a bowl over a bain-marie of simmering water to melt. Using an elbow spatula, spread a thin layer of the melted chocolate over the top of the ganache in the pastry frame. Let the chocolate dry at room temperature for twenty minutes. Invert the pastry frame on a sheet of silicon and spread a thin layer of the melted chocolate over the other side of the ganache. Let dry at room temperature for twenty minutes.
Remove the pastry frame, running the blade of a small knife dipped in hot water between the frame and the ganache. Cut the ganache into rectangles of about 3 x 1 in. (75 x 22 mm). Place the rectangles on a baking sheet, leaving a little space between each. Set aside at room temperature (about 60°F–64°F/16°C–18°C) overnight.

The following day, prepare the final coating: To temper the chocolate, chop 2 1/4 lb. (1 kg) chocolate with a serrated knife and place it in a bowl over a bain-marie of simmering water. Stir gently with a wooden spoon until it reaches 130°F (55°C). Once the temperature is reached, immediately remove the bowl of chocolate from the bain-marie and place it in a bowl of cold water with four or five ice cubes. Stir the melted chocolate from time to time, scraping it from the sides of the bowl toward the center as it begins to set. Once the melted chocolate has cooled to 80°F (27°C), return the bowl to the bain-marie over simmering water. Monitor the temperature carefully with a thermometer to ensure that it does not rise to more than 88°F–90°F (31°C–32°C).

Spread several sheets of rhodoid plastic* on a flat work surface. Dip a chocolate bar in the tempered chocolate, remove it with a three-tined chocolate dipping fork, lifting toward the edge of the bowl, then dipping the bar once again in the chocolate, lifting two or three times in a pumping motion to coat. Remove the bar with the fork, resting the fork on the edge of the bowl, tapping lightly to remove any excess chocolate. Finish by scraping the bottom of the fork along the edge of the bowl. Place the chocolate bar on the plastic. Continue in the same manner for the remaining chocolate bars, taking care to return the chocolate coating to the bain-marie of simmering water from time to time to maintain the temperature at 88°F–90°F (31°C–32°C). Let the chocolate bars dry at room temperature overnight.

The next day, arrange the chocolate bars in airtight container. Store in a dry, odor-free room at between 60°F–65°F (15°C–18°C).

* Transparent plastic celluloid used in pastry and confectionery.

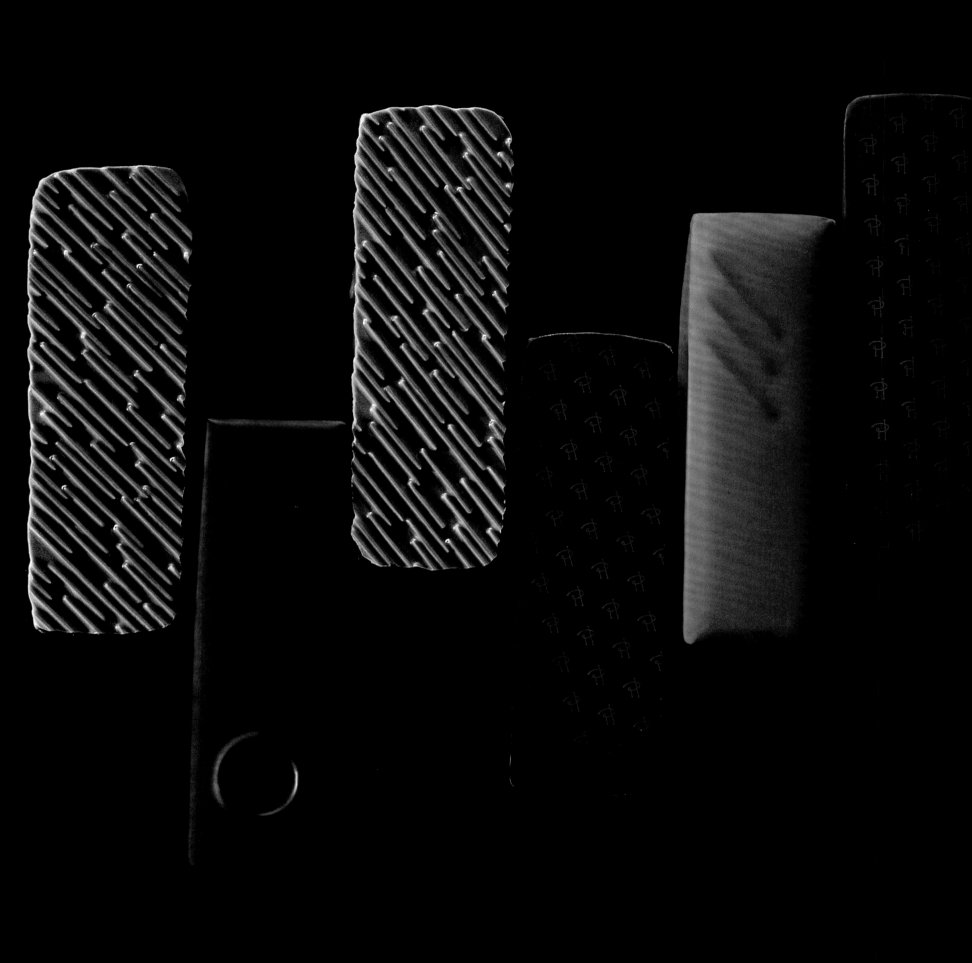

Barre Chocolat au Macaron Chloé

Chloé Macaron Chocolate Bar

Makes about 60 bars

Ingredients:

Chloé Macaron Shells:

1 cup (7 3/4 oz./220 g) or about
8 "liquefied" egg whites, divided
(see note)
3 1/2 cups (10 1/2 oz./300 g) ground
almonds
2 1/3 cups (10 1/2 oz./300 g)
confectioners' sugar
1 teaspoon strawberry red food
coloring
1 teaspoon carmine red food coloring
1 1/2 cups (10 1/2 oz./300 g)
superfine sugar
1/3 cup (2 2/3 oz./75 g) mineral water
Cocoa powder (Valrhona)

Raspberry Almond Paste:

16 oz. (1 lb./450 g) fresh raspberries
1 3/4 tablespoons (25 g) mineral
water
2 tablespoons (25 g) superfine sugar
7 oz. (200 g) Chloé Macaron shells
1 1/2 lb. (670 g) almond paste,
65% almond

Chocolate and Raspberry Ganache:

1 2/3 lb. (740 g) Caraibe 66%
dark chocolate (Valrhona)
3/4 cup (5 3/4 oz./165 g) butter
1 3/4 lb. (800 g) fresh raspberries

Pre-Coating of the Chloé Filling:

10 1/2 oz. (300 g) Mexique 64% dark
chocolate (Valrhona)

Final Coating of the Chocolate Bars:

2 1/4 lb. (1 kg) Mexique 64% dark
chocolate (Valrhona)

Preparation Time:

5 mins. (5 days in advance);
45 mins. (2 days in advance);
1 h. (the following day);
1 h. (the same day).

Cooking Time:

About 3 h. 10 mins. (2 days
in advance);
a few minutes (the following day
and the same day).

Resting Time:

12 h. + 30 mins. + 2 x 24 h.

Preparation:

Five days in advance, place the egg whites for the macaron shells in a bowl, cover the bowl tightly with plastic film, pierce a few holes in the film and refrigerate to liquefy. **Two days in advance, prepare the rectangles and the Chloé macaron shells:** Make two stencil templates for the macarons, cutting two 12 x 16-in. (30 cm x 40 cm) rectangles out of cardboard (about 1/16 in. thick). Draw a neat rectangle of about 2 3/4 x 1/2 in. (15 mm x 68 mm) in one corner of the first cardboard and cut out. Proceed in the same manner, cutting out a total of thirty rectangular stencils on each sheet of cardboard.

Sift the ground almonds and the confectioners' sugar together. Combine the two food colorings with 1/2 cup (110 g) of the egg whites. Pour onto the almond–sugar mixture without mixing. Combine the sugar and water in a saucepan, and bring to a boil, monitoring the temperature with a thermometer. Meanwhile place the remaining 1/2 cup (110 g) of liquefied egg whites in the bowl of a mixer fitted with a wire whisk. When the sugar syrup reaches 240°F (115°C), begin beating the egg whites on high speed. When the syrup reaches 245°F (118°C), reduce the mixer speed to medium and begin pouring the syrup in a steady stream into the egg whites. Continue beating until the mixture cools to 125°F (50°C). At this temperature, fold the meringue mixture into the almond–sugar mixture with a spatula. Spoon the batter into a pastry bag fitted with a No. 11 plain tip.

Place the first rectangular stencils on a baking sheet lined with a silicone pastry sheet. Pipe a little of the macaron batter into the rectangles, spread out in a thin layer, smoothing the top with a spatula and scraping off any excess batter. Carefully remove the stencils and proceed in the same manner with the remaining stencils to make a total of 60 rectangular macarons; reserve the remaining batter. Tap the baking sheets lightly on a work surface covered with a kitchen towel. Using a small sifter, sprinkle the top of the macaron rectangles with a mist of cocoa powder.
Let rest at room temperature for twelve hours to allow a "skin" to form. Preheat the oven on convection setting to 300°F (150°C/Gas Mark 5). Place the macaron rectangles in the oven to bake for ten minutes, opening and closing the oven door quickly twice during the baking to release steam. Remove from the oven and slide the macaron shells onto a rack on the work surface. With the remaining macaron batter, pipe rounds of about 1 1/3 in. (3.5 cm) diameter onto a pastry sheet lined with cooking parchment, being careful to space them about 3/4 in. apart. Tap the baking sheet lightly on the work surface lined with a kitchen towel and set aside to rest at room temperature for about thirty minutes

to allow a "skin" to form. Preheat the oven on convection setting to 355°F (180°C/Gas Mark 6). Place the baking sheets in the oven and bake for twelve minutes, opening and closing the oven door quickly twice during the baking to release steam. Remove from the oven and slide the macaron rounds onto a pastry rack.

Prepare the raspberry almond paste: Preheat the oven to 195°F (90°C/Gas Mark 3). Spread the raspberries out on a baking sheet lined with cooking parchment. Place in the oven to dry for three hours, stirring the raspberries every thirty minutes. Remove from the oven and let cool. Mix in a food processor until reduced to a powder. Bring the water and sugar to a boil. Let cool. Crush the Chloé macaron shells into coarse crumbs in a mixer or processor. Place the almond paste in the bowl of a mixer fitted with a paddle attachment and add the cooled sugar syrup. Add the raspberry powder and the crushed macaron shells, and process just long enough to obtain a smooth batter.

Prepare the chocolate and raspberry ganache: Chop the chocolate with a serrated knife and place it in a bowl. Cut the butter into cubes. Using a vegetable mill, press the raspberries to a puree. Strain the raspberry puree, place in a saucepan, cover and bring to a boil. Pour the raspberry puree, one-third at a time, over the chocolate, stirring from the center out in small, then progressively larger concentric circles. When the temperature of the chocolate reaches 104°F–113°F (40°C–45°C), incorporate the butter cubes. Mix for two minutes with a hand blender. Pour into a shallow baking dish and cover with a sheet of plastic film pressed directly onto the surface of the ganache. Refrigerate until the texture is creamy.

Place a stainless steel square pastry frame 13 1/2 x 13 1/2 x 1 1/2 in. (34 cm x 34 cm x 4 cm) on a silicon pastry sheet. Using an elbow spatula, spread a first layer of the raspberry almond paste in the frame. Place a sheet of plastic film on top of the almond paste and use a rolling pin to smooth the surface. Remove the plastic film. Pour the second filling, the chocolate raspberry ganache, evenly over the raspberry almond paste. Smooth the surface with an elbow spatula. Allow to set at room temperature, then store in the refrigerator overnight.

The next day, prepare the pre-coating: Chop 10 1/2 oz. (300 g) chocolate with a serrated knife, place in a bowl over a bain-marie of simmering water to melt. Using an elbow spatula, spread a thin, even layer of the melted chocolate over the top of the ganache in the pastry frame. Let the chocolate dry at room temperature for twenty minutes. Invert the pastry frame on a silicon pastry sheet and spread a thin layer of the melted

chocolate over the other side of the ganache. Let dry at room temperature for twenty minutes.

Run the blade of a small knife dipped in hot water around the inner edges of the pastry frame before carefully removing the frame. Cut the chocolate-raspberry preparation into rectangles of about 3 x 3/4 in. (75 x 22 mm), place them, well spaced out, on a pastry sheet. Store at room temperature (between 60°F and 65°F/16°C–18°C) overnight.

The following day, prepare the final coating of the bars: To temper the chocolate, chop 2 1/4 lb. chocolate with a serrated knife and place it in a bowl over a bain-marie of simmering water. Stir gently with a wooden spoon until it reaches 130°F (55°C). At this temperature, remove the bowl of chocolate immediately from the bain-marie and place it in a bowl of cold water with four or five ice cubes. Stir the melted chocolate from time to time, scraping it from the sides of the bowl toward the center as it begins to set. Once the melted chocolate has cooled to 80°F (27°C), return the bowl to the bain-marie over simmering water. Monitor the temperature carefully with a thermometer to ensure that it does not rise to more than 88°F–90°F (31°C–32°C).

Spread several sheets of rhodoid plastic* on a flat work surface. Dip a bar in the chocolate, remove it with a three-tined chocolate dipping fork, lifting toward the edge of the bowl, then dipping the bar once again in the chocolate, lifting two or three times in a pumping motion to coat. Remove the bar with the fork, resting it on the edge of the bowl, tapping lightly to remove any excess chocolate. Finish by scraping the bottom of the fork along the edge of the bowl. Place the chocolate bar on the plastic. Continue in the same manner for the remaining chocolate bars, taking care to return the chocolate coating to the bain-marie from time to time to maintain the temperature between 88°F–90°F (31°C–32°C). Let the chocolate bars dry at room temperature overnight.

The next day, arrange the chocolate bars in a well-sealed container. Store in a dry, odor-free room at between 60°F–65°F (15°C–18°C).

* Transparent plastic celluloid used in pastry and confectionery.

Note: "Liquefied" egg whites are egg whites that have been allowed to rest for several days to lose their elasticity. Simply place the egg whites in a bowl, cover with plastic film, pierce a few holes in the film and refrigerate for five to seven days.

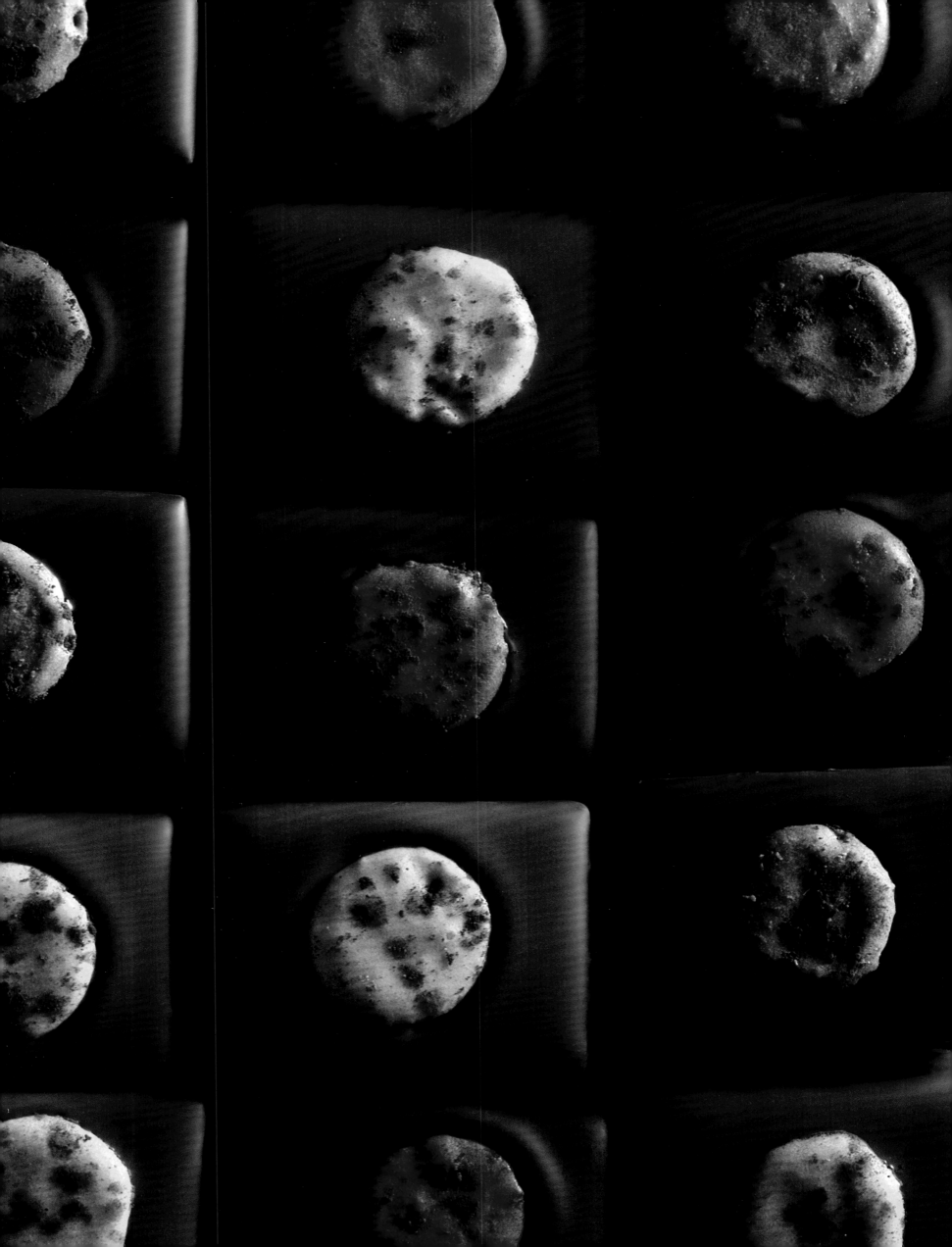

Bonbon Chocolat Infiniment Praliné Noisette

Infiniment Praliné Noisette Chocolate Bonbon

Makes about 130 chocolate bonbons

Ingredients:

Homemade Hazelnut Praline:

2 2/3 cups (15 3/4 oz./445 g) whole hazelnuts
4 used vanilla beans
1 1/2 cups (9 3/4 oz./280 g) superfine sugar
1/3 cup (3 oz./85 g) mineral water

Infiniment Praliné Noisette Praline:

4 oz. (115 g) Araguani 72% dark chocolate (Valrhona)
7 1/2 oz. (215 g) cocoa butter (Valrhona)
1 3/4 lb. (795 g) homemade hazelnut praline (recipe above)
1 3/4 lb. (795 g) hazelnut praline, 60% hazelnut (Valrhona)

Pre-Coating:

10 1/2 oz. (300 g) Jivara 40% milk chocolate (Valrhona) or milk chocolate, 40% cocoa

Final Coating:

2 1/4 lb. (1 kg) Manjari 64% dark chocolate (Valrhona)

Preparation Time:

40 mins. (2 days in advance);
1 h. 30 mins. (1 day in advance);
about 1 h. (the same day).

Cooking Time:

About 35 mins. (2 days in advance);
a few minutes (the following day).

Resting Time:

2 x 24 h.

Preparation:

Two days in advance, prepare the homemade hazelnut praline: Preheat the oven on convection setting to 300°F (150°C/Gas Mark 5). Spread the hazelnuts out on a pastry sheet lined with cooking parchment. Place in the oven and toast for fifteen minutes. Turn the hot hazelnuts onto a fine-mesh drum sieve, mixing and rubbing to remove the skins. Place the hazelnuts, still warm, in a saucepan with the vanilla pods. In a separate saucepan, combine the sugar and water, cook to 250°F (121°C), and pour this syrup onto the hazelnut–vanilla mixture, stirring and cooking until nicely caramelized. Turn immediately out onto a non-stick baking sheet and let cool. Chop the mixture coarsely, then place in a food processor and grind nearly to a paste, but with pieces of the praline remaining.

Prepare the Infiniment Praliné Noisette praline: To temper the chocolate and the cocoa butter, chop the chocolate and the cocoa butter with a serrated knife, and place in a bowl over a bain-marie of simmering water to melt. Stir gently with a wooden spoon until chocolate heats to 130°F (55°C). Once the chocolate has reached this temperature, remove the bowl immediately from the bain-marie and place it in a bowl of cold water with four or five ice cubes. Stir the chocolate from time to time, scraping it from the sides of the bowl toward the center as it begins to set. Once the chocolate has cooled to 80°F (27°C), return the bowl to the bain-marie, monitoring the temperature carefully with a thermometer until the chocolate warms to between 88°F and 90°F (31°C–32°C). Incorporate the homemade hazelnut praline and the 60% hazelnut praline.

Place a stainless steel square pastry frame of 13 1/2 x 13 1/2 x 1/2 in. (34 cm x 34 cm x 12 mm) on a silicon pastry sheet. Using an elbow spatula, spread the Infiniment Praliné Noisette praline evenly in the frame. Smooth the surface and let set at room temperature, at 60°F–65°F (16°C–18°C) overnight.

The following day, prepare the pre-coating of the bonbons: Chop the chocolate with a serrated knife and place in a bowl over a bain-marie of simmering water to melt. Spread a thin layer over the top of the hazelnut praline. Smooth the surface and let rest for twenty minutes at room temperature to set. Invert the pastry frame on the silicon sheet, then spread a thin layer of the melted chocolate over the bottom side of the hazelnut praline. Smooth the surface and let set at room temperature for twenty minutes.

Carefully remove the pastry frame, running the blade of a small knife dipped in hot water between the frame and the hazelnut praline mixture. Cut into rectangles of 1 1/4 x 1 in. (30 mm x 25 mm), separating them and placing them well spaced out on a pastry sheet. Keep at room temperature (60°F–65°F/16°C–18°C) overnight.

The next day, prepare the chocolate for the final coating: To temper the chocolate, chop the 2 1/4 lb. of chocolate with a serrated knife and place it in a bowl over a bain-marie of simmering water to melt, stirring gently with a wooden spoon until the temperature of the chocolate reaches 130°F (55°C). Once the chocolate has reached this temperature, remove the bowl immediately from the bain-marie and place it in a bowl of cold water with four or five ice cubes. Stir the chocolate from time to time, scraping it from the sides of the bowl as it begins to set. Once the chocolate has cooled to 80°F (27°C), return the bowl to the bain-marie, monitoring the temperature carefully with a thermometer until the chocolate warms to between 88°F and 90°F (31°C–32°C).

Spread several sheets of rhodoid plastic* on a flat work surface. Dip a first Infiniment Praliné Noisette chocolate bonbon in the chocolate, remove with a three-tined chocolate dipping fork, lifting toward the edge of the bowl, then dipping the bonbon once again in the chocolate, lifting two or three times in a pumping motion to coat. Remove the bonbon with the fork, resting it on the edge of the bowl and tapping lightly to remove any excess chocolate, and finish by scraping the bottom of the fork along the edge of the bowl. Place the bonbon on the plastic. Continue in the same manner for the remaining bonbons, taking care to return the chocolate to the bain-marie from time to time to maintain the temperature between 88°F–90°F (31°C–32°C). Let the bonbons dry at room temperature overnight.
Store the chocolate bonbons in an airtight container at between 60°F and 65°F (15°C–18°C), away from humidity and odors.

* Transparent plastic celluloid used in pastry and confectionery.

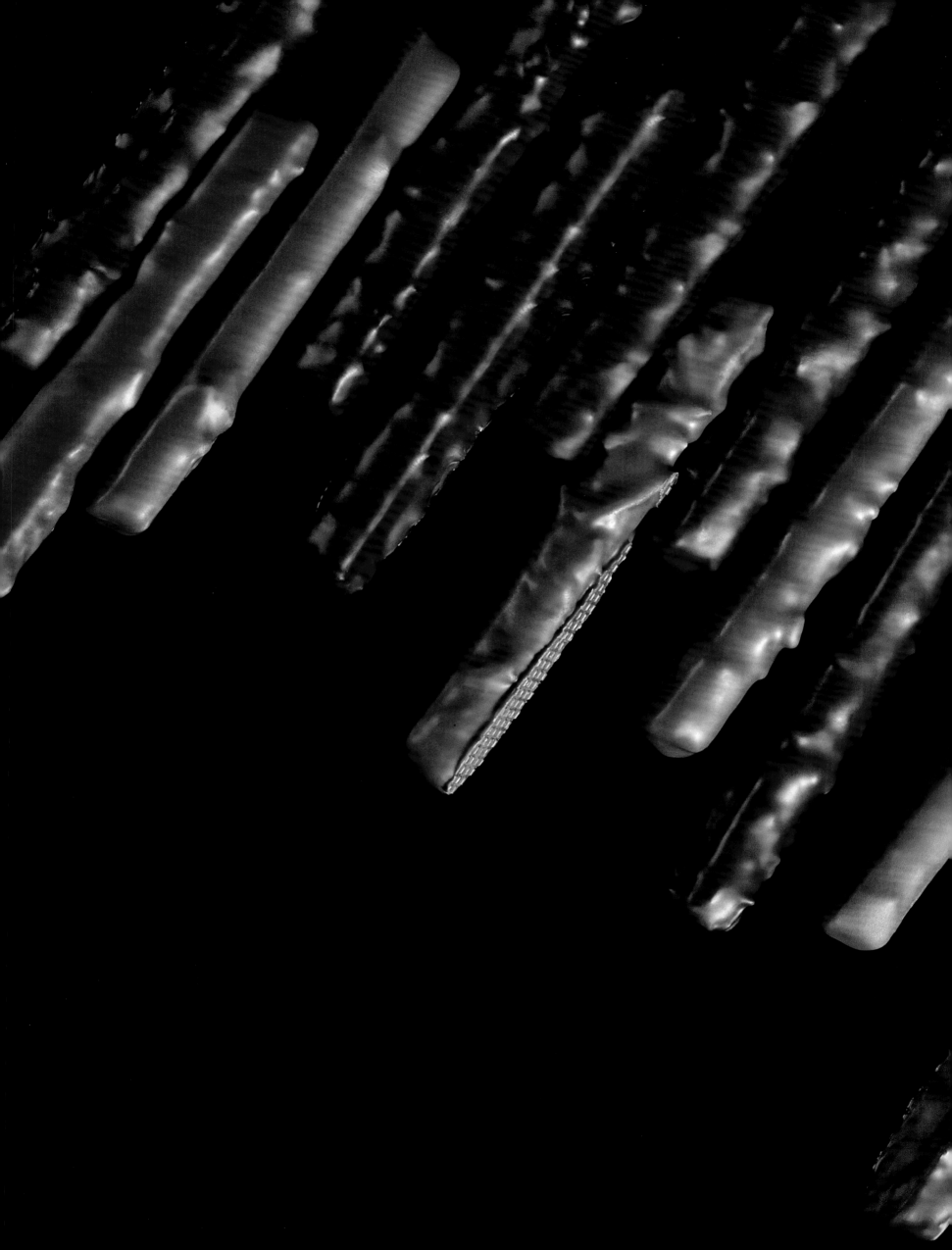

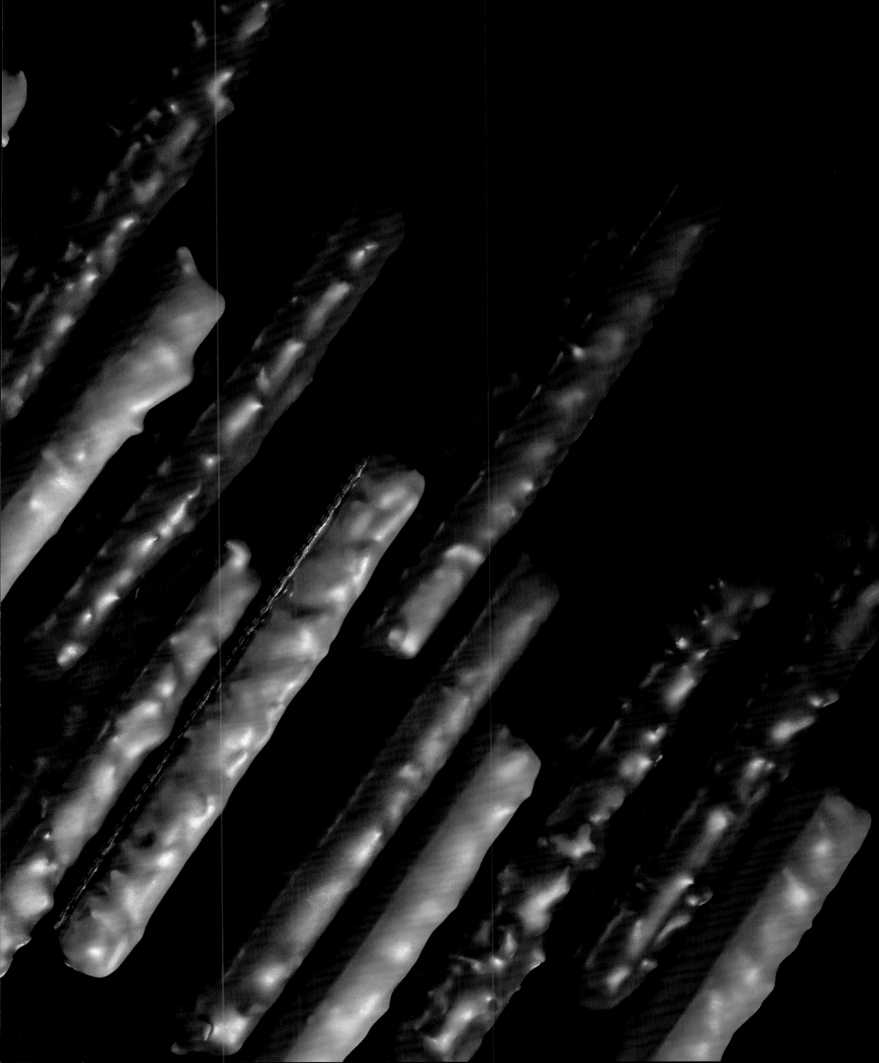

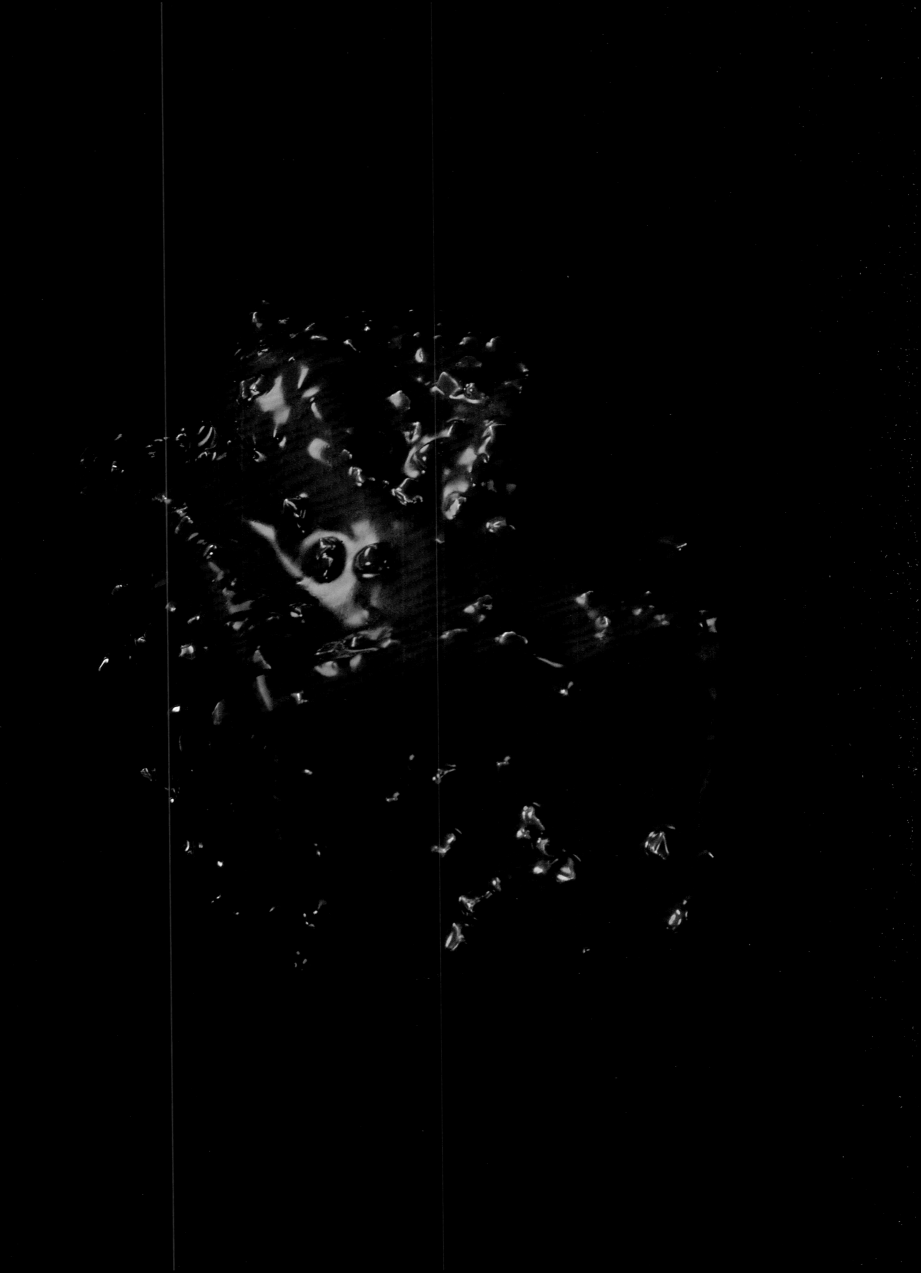

"This is an encounter between sculpture and flavor."

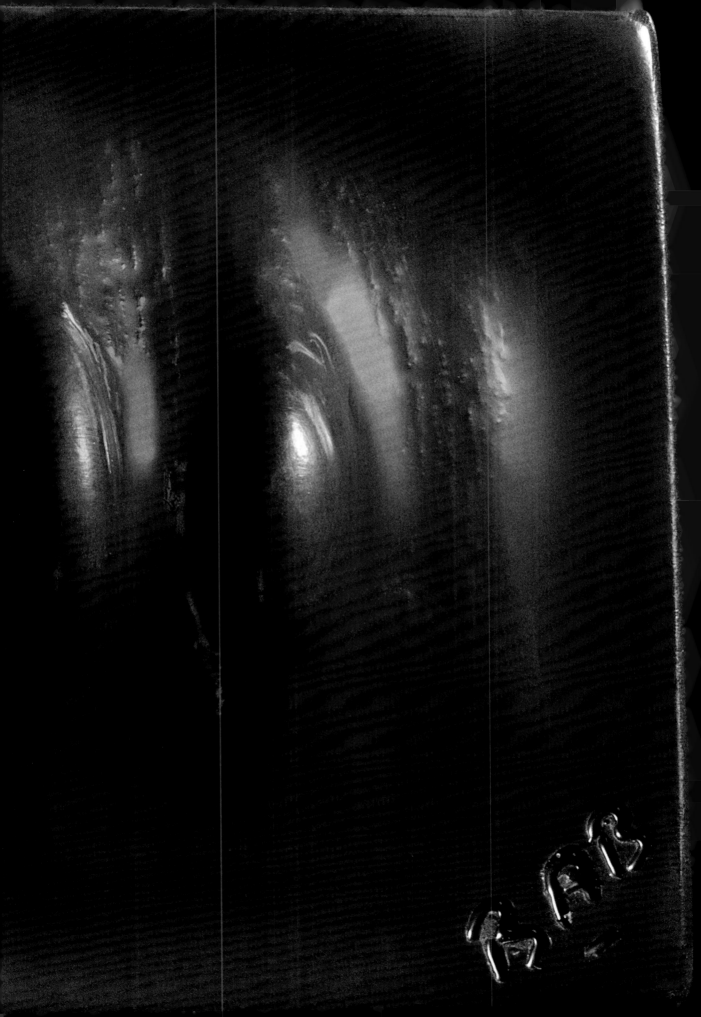

"Perpetua is the fruit
of my discovery of a great
artist's work."

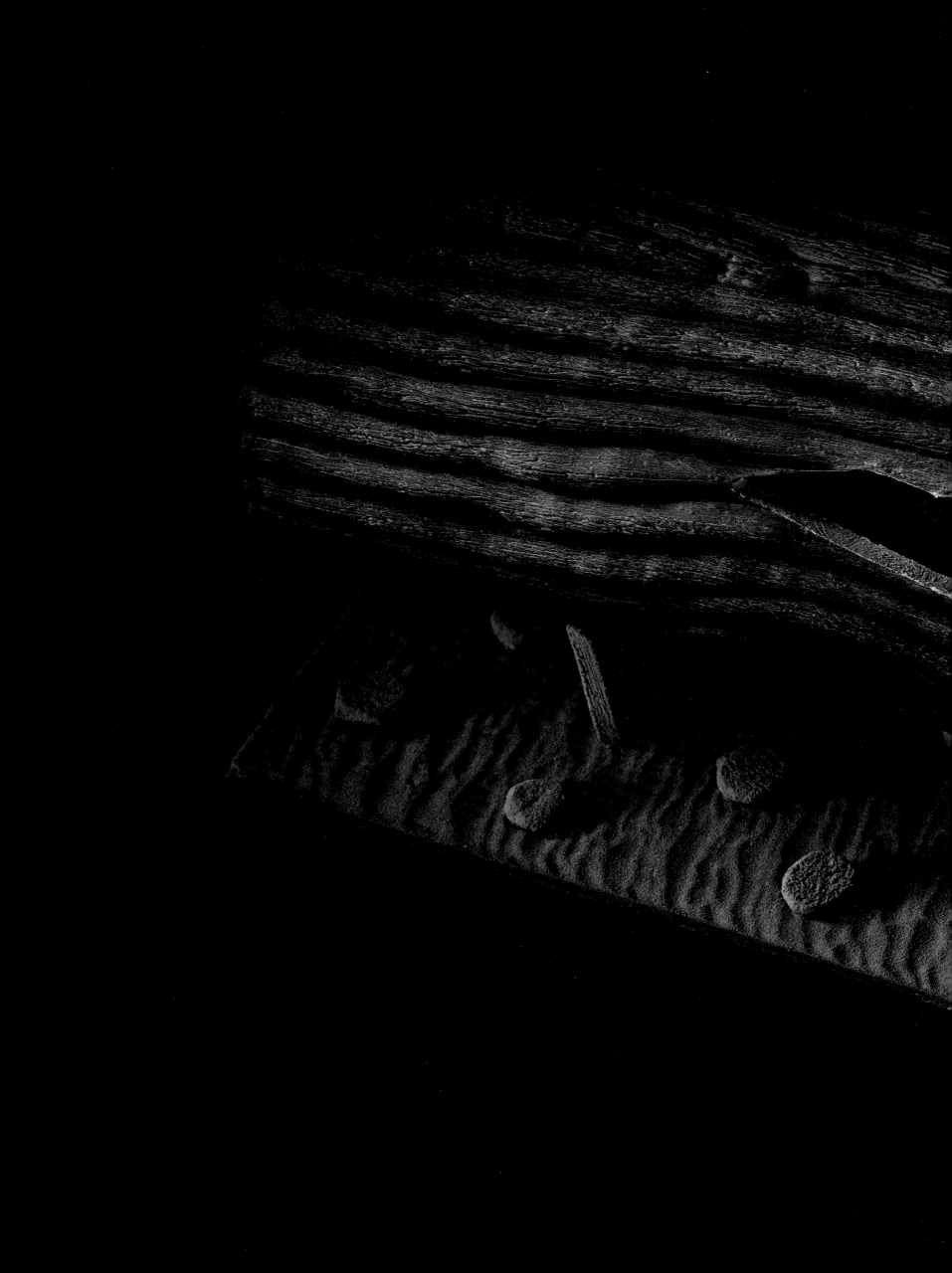

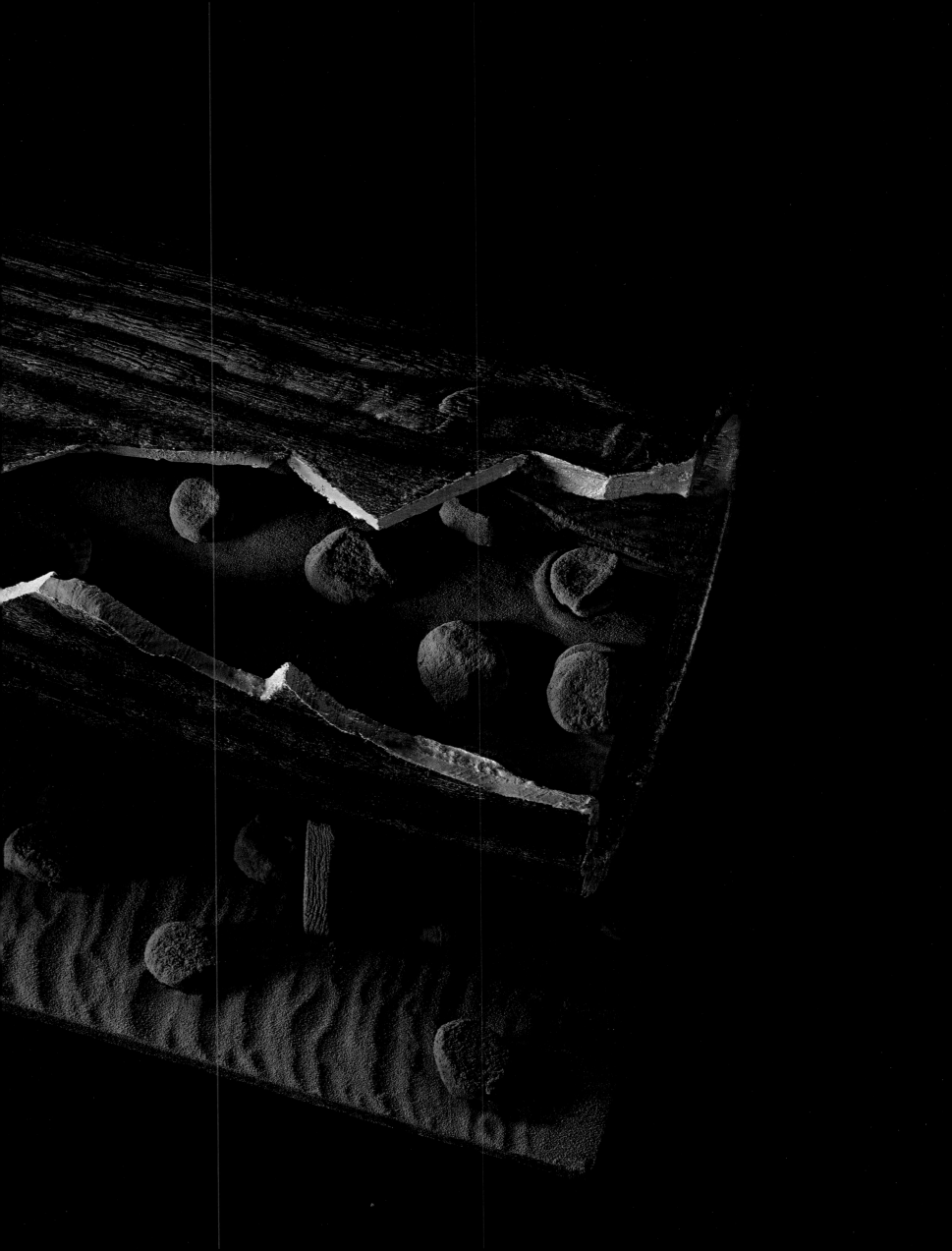

Millefeuille Infiniment Chocolat

Infiniment Chocolat Mille-Feuille

Serves 10

Ingredients:

Caramelized Inverted Puff Pastry:

1 2/3 cups (13 1/4 oz./375 g) butter at room temperature
1 3/4 cups (5 1/3 oz./150 g) flour

+ for the *détrempe*:

1/2 cup (4 oz./110 g) butter
2/3 cup (5 1/3 oz./150 g) mineral water
1/2 teaspoon white vinegar
1 tablespoon (1/2 oz./15 g) *fleur de sel*, preferably Guérande
4 cups (12 1/3 oz./350 g) flour
Confectioners' sugar

Dark Chocolate Chips:

1 1/4 teaspoons (6 g) *Fleur de sel*, preferably Guérande
10 1/2 oz. (300 g) Araguani 72% dark chocolate (Valrhona)

Pastry Cream:

1 3/4 tablespoons (1/3 oz./9.5 g) flour
1/4 cup (1 oz./34 g) flan powder or corn starch
1 1/3 cups (11 3/4 oz./335 g) whole milk
3 1/3 tablespoons (1 1/3 oz./40 g) superfine sugar (divided)
1/3 cup (2 3/4 oz./80 g) egg yolks
2 1/3 tablespoons (1 oz./33 g) butter

Pure Origin Peru Chocolate Pastry Ganache:

5 2/3 oz. (160 g) Pure Origin Peru chocolate
3/4 oz. (20 g) pure cocoa paste (Valrhona)
2/3 cup (5 oz./140 g) whole milk

Pure Origin Peru chocolate Pastry Cream

600 g pastry cream (prepared with the ingredients above)
300 g Pure Origin Peru chocolate pastry ganache (prepared with the ingredients above)

Infiniment Chocolat Pure Origin Peru Cream:

17 2/3 oz. (500 g) Pure Origin Peru chocolate pastry cream (see recipe above)
7 tablespoons (3 1/2 oz./100 g) liquid cream

Finishing:

Cellophane paper

Preparation Time:

About 45 mins. (1 day in advance);
45 mins. (the same day).

Chilling Time:

3 x 1 h. (1 day in advance);
2 h. + 1 h. (the same day).

Cooking Time:

A few minutes (1 day in advance);
about 1 h. (the same day).

Preparation:

One day in advance, prepare the puff pastry:

In the bowl of a mixer or a processor fitted with a plastic blade, mix 1 2/3 cup (13 1/4 oz./375 g) softened butter to a creamy texture. Add the flour and mix until it forms a ball. Turn the dough onto a sheet of cooking parchment and form into a flat rectangle about 3/4 in. (2 cm) thick. Wrap in plastic film. Let rest in the refrigerator for one hour. For the *détrempe*, melt 1/2 cup (4 oz./110 g) butter slowly over low heat. Let cool. Combine the mineral water, vinegar and *Fleur de sel* in a mixing bowl. Add the flour and the cooled melted butter. Combine, mixing as little as possible. Form the dough into a flat square of about 3/4 in. (2 cm) thick. Wrap in plastic film, let rest in the refrigerator for one hour.

Dust the butter–flour rectangle with a little flour, roll out lengthwise into a 1/3 in. thick sheet about twice as long as the *détrempe*. Place the *détrempe* in the center of the first sheet of dough. Fold the ends of the dough over the *détrempe* square to enclose it completely as within an envelope. Using a rolling pin, tap the surface of the dough lightly, then roll out, rolling from the center toward the ends, to form a rectangle three times longer than the width. Fold the bottom quarter of the dough up toward the center, then fold the top quarter down toward the center so that the edges of the two flaps meet. Fold the dough in half and place in the refrigerator to chill for one hour. When chilled, place the dough square on a lightly floured work surface, with the folded edge to your left, and repeat the same rolling and folding procedure. Flatten the dough square lightly, cover and refrigerate overnight.

Prepare the chocolate slivers: Crush the *Fleur de sel* with a rolling pin. Sift through a fine sieve. Chop the chocolate with a serrated knife and place it in a bowl over a bain-marie of simmering water, stirring gently with a wooden spoon until the temperature of the chocolate reaches 130°F (55°C). Remove the bowl immediately from the bain-marie and place it in a bowl of cold water with four or five ice cubes. Stir the chocolate from time to time, scraping it from the sides of the bowl toward the center as it begins to set. Once the chocolate has cooled to 80°F (27°C), return the bowl to the bain-marie, monitoring the temperature carefully with a thermometer until the chocolate warms to between 88°F and 90°F (31°C–32°C). Stir in the sifted *Fleur de sel*. Place a large sheet of rhodoid plastic* on a work surface. Pour the chocolate onto the plastic and using a spatula, spread into a thin, even layer. Cover the chocolate with a second sheet of rhodoid and top with light weights to keep the sheet of chocolate flat. Refrigerate until the following day.

The following day, weigh out 1 1/3 lb. (660 g) of the puff pastry for the mille-feuille. (Refrigerate or freeze the remaining dough for another use.) Place the square of puff pastry on a lightly floured work surface with the folded edge to your left. Roll out, as before, into a long rectangle. Fold up the bottom third of the dough rectangle over the center, then fold the top third over the first third. Refrigerate to rest for thirty minutes. Cut the dough square into three equal parts. On a floured work surface, roll each piece of dough out to a rectangle of 8 1/2 x 10 in. (22 cm x 26 cm), about 1/16 in. thick. Lift the dough from time to time with your hands, sliding it on the work surface to allow it to retract. Trim the edges of the three rectangles evenly, so they are all the same size. Prick the surface of each with a fork and refrigerate to rest for two hours.

Line two pastry sheets with cooking parchment and brush lightly with water. Place the rectangles of puff pastry on the baking sheets. Preheat the oven on convection setting to 355°F (180°C/Gas Mark 6). Sprinkle the puff pastry rectangles evenly with sifted sugar. Place in the oven and bake for about ten minutes. Remove from the oven and place a pastry rack on top of the puff pastry on each pastry sheet, pressing down lightly, to prevent the pastry from rising too much. Return the pastry sheets topped with their racks to the oven to bake for an additional thirty minutes.

Remove the pastry sheets from the oven. Remove the racks, cover each sheet of puff pastry with cooking parchment and carefully invert each with the aid of a pastry sheet onto the work surface. Slide the inverted dough onto pastry sheets again, removing the cooking parchment. Sprinkle with sifted confectioners' sugar. Return the pastry to the oven preheated on convection setting to 450°F (230°C/Gas Mark 7–8) and let caramelize for five to seven minutes, watching carefully. Remove from the oven and let the pastry rectangles cool, shiny, caramelized side up.

Prepare the pastry cream: Sift the flour with the flan powder. Combine the milk and one tablespoon (15 g) of the sugar in a saucepan, and bring to a boil. Whisk the remaining sugar with the egg yolks in a bowl. Add the sifted flour and flan powder. Pour the warm milk over the egg–flour mixture, whisking briskly. Pour the mixture back into the saucepan, bring to a boil and cook, stirring constantly, for five minutes. Remove from the heat and let cool. When the pastry cream reaches 122°F (50°C), stir in the butter. Press a sheet of plastic film onto the surface of the cream.

Prepare the Pure Origin Peru chocolate pastry ganache: Chop the chocolate and cocoa paste with a serrated knife, and place in a bowl. Bring the milk to a boil in a saucepan and pour, one-third at a time, over the chocolate, stirring from the center out in small, then progressively larger concentric circles. Mix with a hand blender until smooth. Place the bowl in a bain-marie of simmering water. Once the temperature has reached 130°F (55°C), add the pastry cream, mixing until smooth. Let cool to 77°F–85°F (25°C–30°C).

Prepare the Infiniment Chocolat Pure Origin Peru cream: Once the chocolate ganache has cooled to 77°F–85°F (25°C–30°C), place 17 2/3 oz. (500 g) in a bowl. Place the cream in a bowl and whip to soft peaks with a whisk. Fold the whipped cream delicately into the chocolate ganache. Spoon into a pastry bag fitted with a basket-weave tip.

Assemble the Infiniment Chocolat mille-feuille: Break half of the dark chocolate–*Fleur de sel* sheet into uneven fragments. Place the first rectangle of puff pastry on a work surface, caramelized side up. Pipe the chocolate cream in closely spaced waves onto the sheet of puff pastry. Sprinkle with fragments of dark chocolate. Place the second rectangle of puff pastry on top, caramelized side up, and pipe with waves of chocolate cream, as for the first layer. Sprinkle with chocolate slivers. Top with the third rectangle of puff pastry, caramelized side up. Let rest, refrigerated, for one hour before serving.

* Transparent plastic celluloid used in pastry and confectionery.

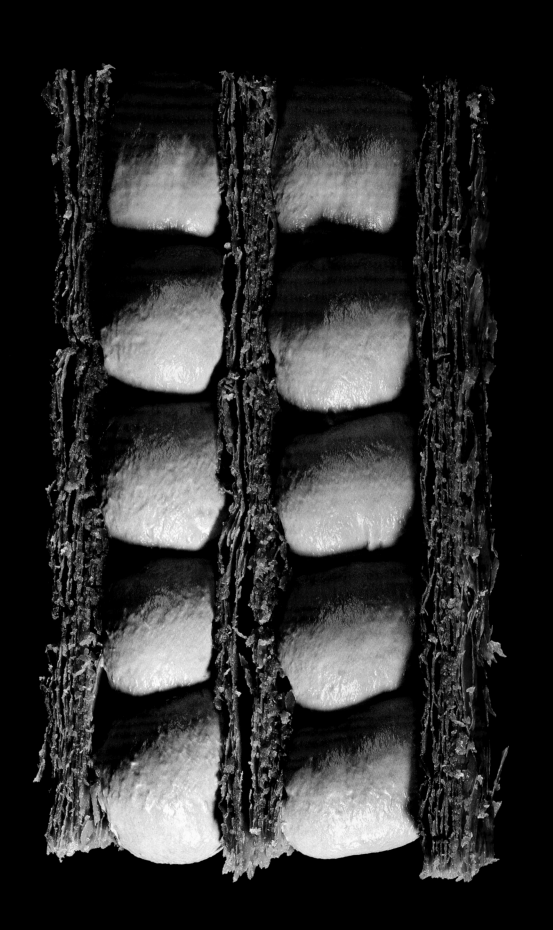

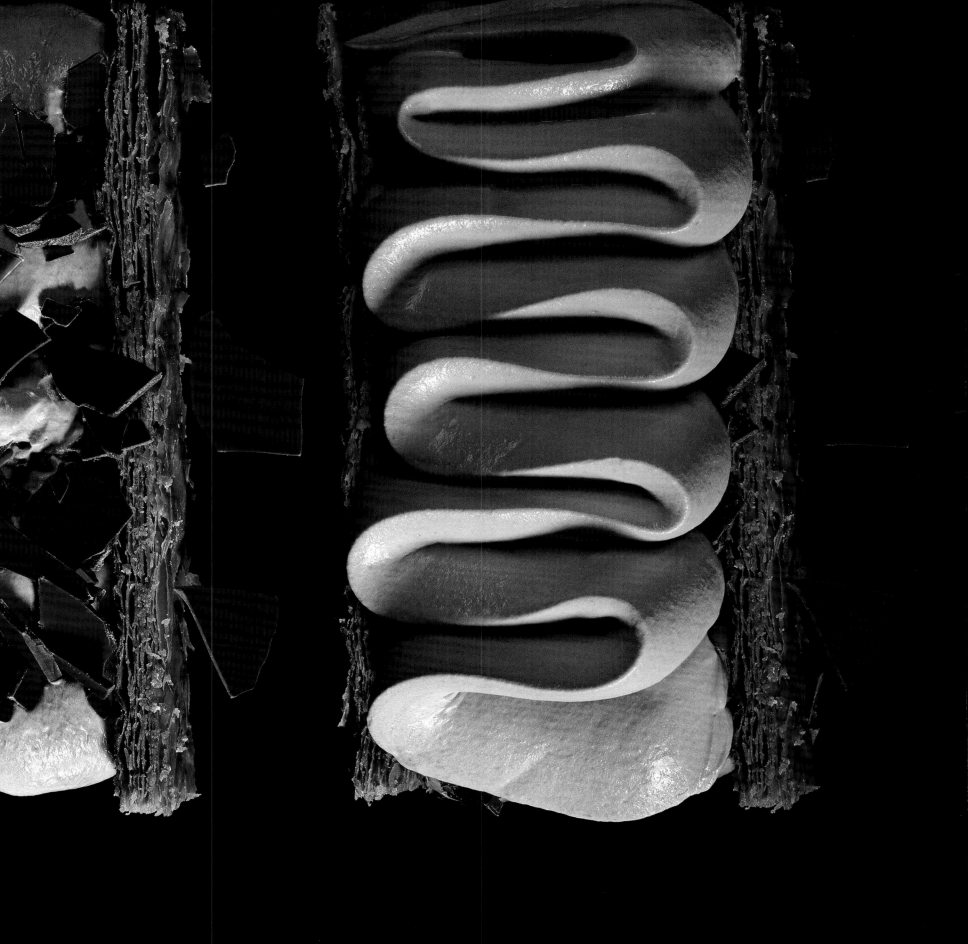

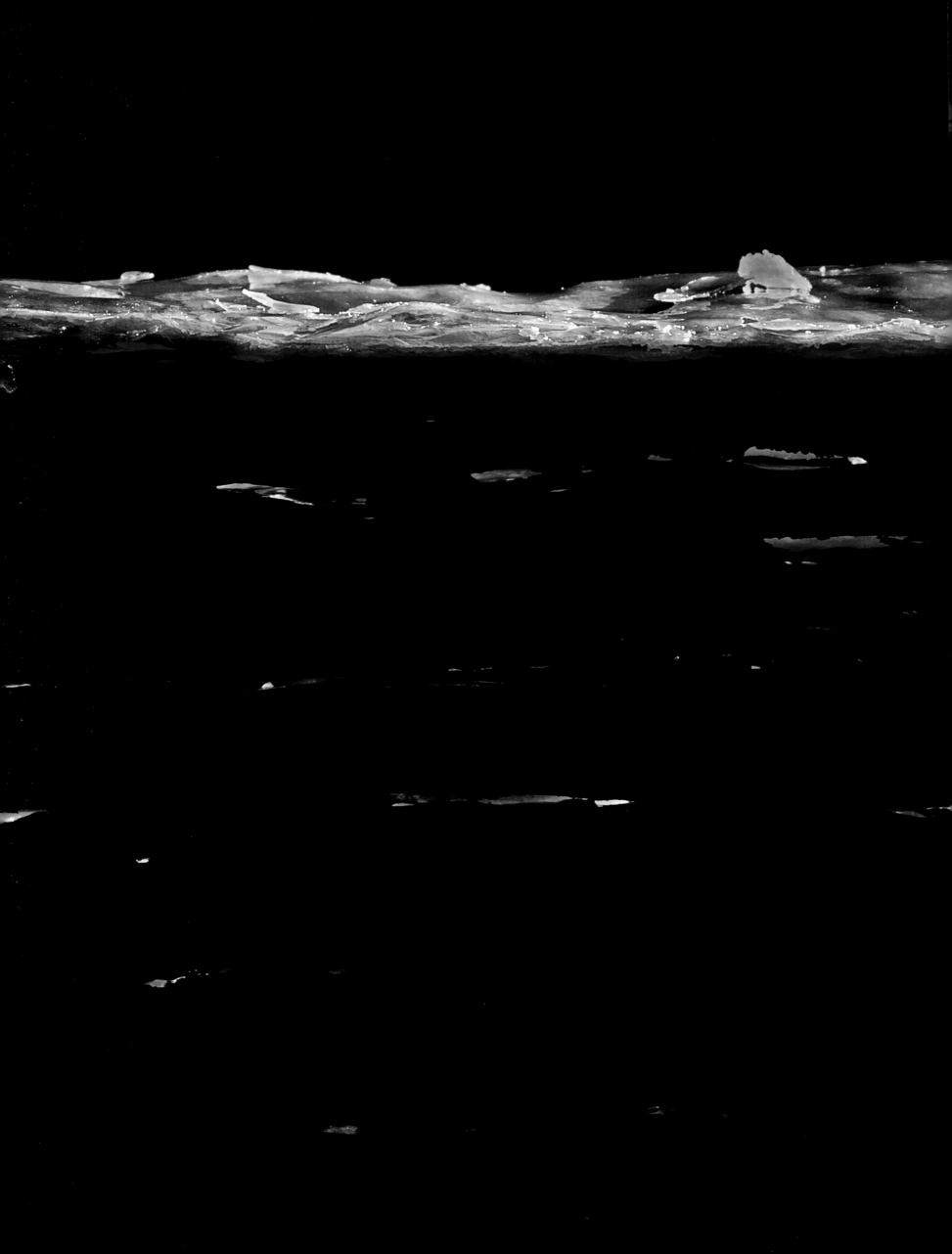

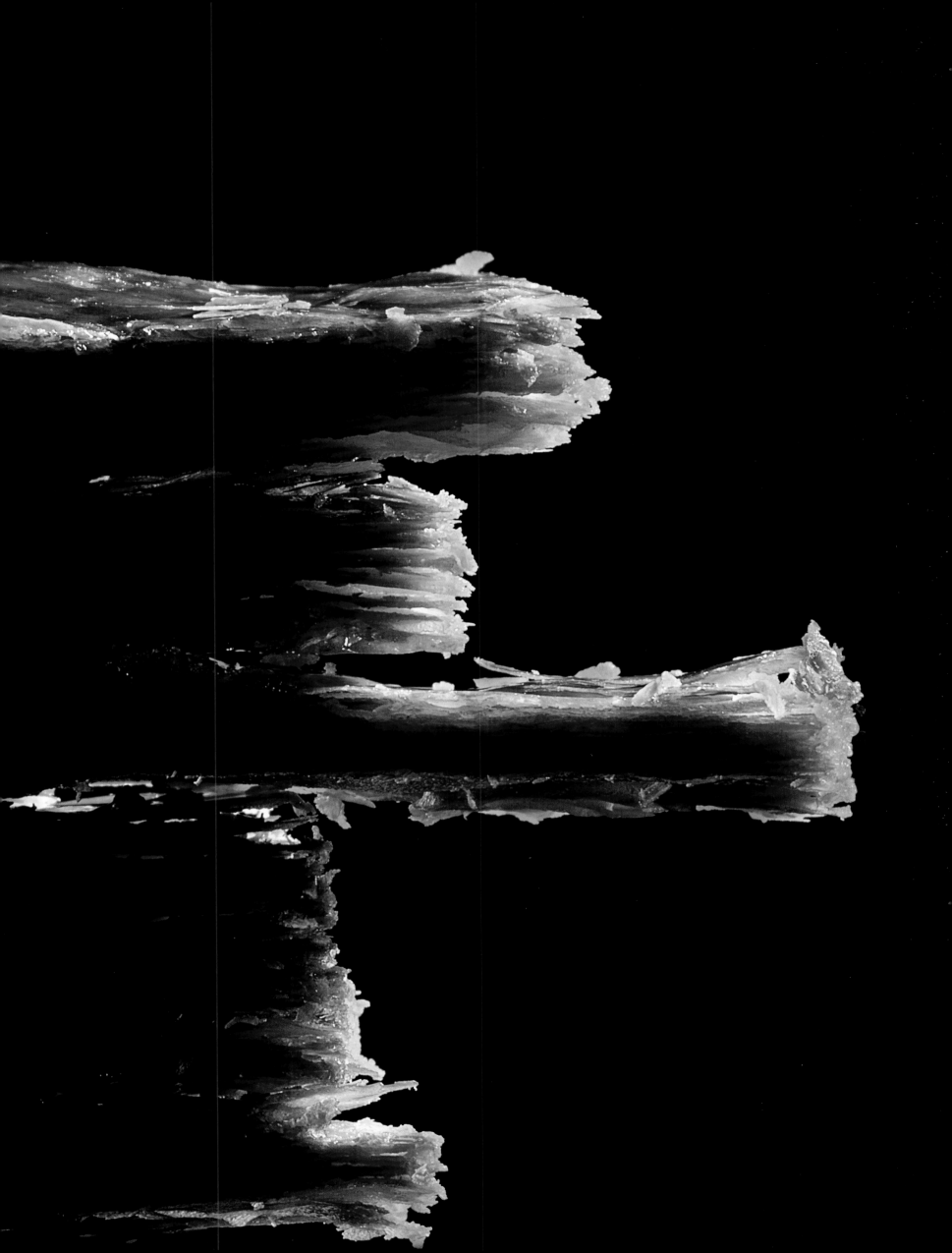

Tablette Chocolat au Lait et Gingembre

Milk Chocolate and Ginger Bar

Makes 3 chocolate bars

Ingredients:

1 oz. (25 g) candied ginger
11 3/4 oz. (335 g) milk chocolate,
45% cocoa
1/2 oz. (15 g) cocoa butter (Valrhona)
1/16 teaspoon (0.35 g) ginger
flavoring
1/8 teaspoon (0.7 g) ginger powder
1/32 teaspoon (0.16 g) cardamom
powder

Finishing:

Cellophane paper

———

Preparation Time:

30 mins. (1 day in advance);
8 mins. (the same day).

Cooking Time:

A few minutes.

Setting Time:

24 h.

Preparation:

One day in advance, rinse and dry three chocolate-bar molds measuring 3 x 6 in. (7.5 cm x 15.5 cm). Store in a room at about 72°F (22°C). Rinse the candied ginger to remove as much sugar as possible. Dry. Chop into small pieces.

———

Temper the chocolate: Chop the chocolate and the cocoa butter with a serrated knife, and place in a bowl over a bain-marie of simmering water, stirring gently with a wooden spoon until the temperature of the chocolate reaches 130°F (55°C). Remove the bowl immediately from the bain-marie and place it in a bowl of cold water with four or five ice cubes. Stir the chocolate from time to time, scraping it from the sides of the bowl as it begins to set. Once the chocolate has cooled to 80°F (27°C), return the bowl to the bain-marie, monitoring the temperature carefully with a thermometer until the chocolate warms to between 88°F and 90°F (31°C–32°C). Stir in the ginger flavoring, ginger and cardamom powders, and the candied ginger pieces.

———

Warm the chocolate-bar molds to about 72°F (22°C). Pour the preparation evenly into the chocolate-bar molds and tap them lightly on a work surface covered with a kitchen towel to remove any air bubbles. Smooth the surface of the chocolate with a spatula and clean the edges of the molds to remove any chocolate that may have dripped over the sides. Let the chocolate bars set overnight in a room at about 65°F (18°C).

———

The following day, remove the chocolate from the molds and wrap in cellophane paper. Store in a dry place at about 60°F (16°C) or in an airtight container in the refrigerator. Remove from the refrigerator two hours before tasting.

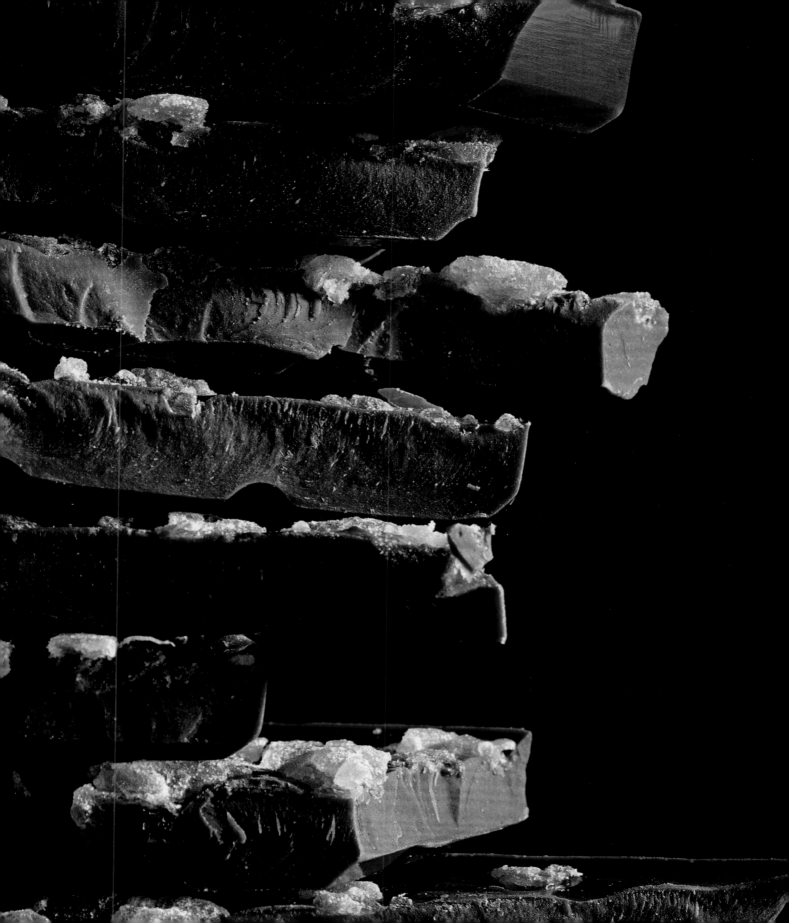

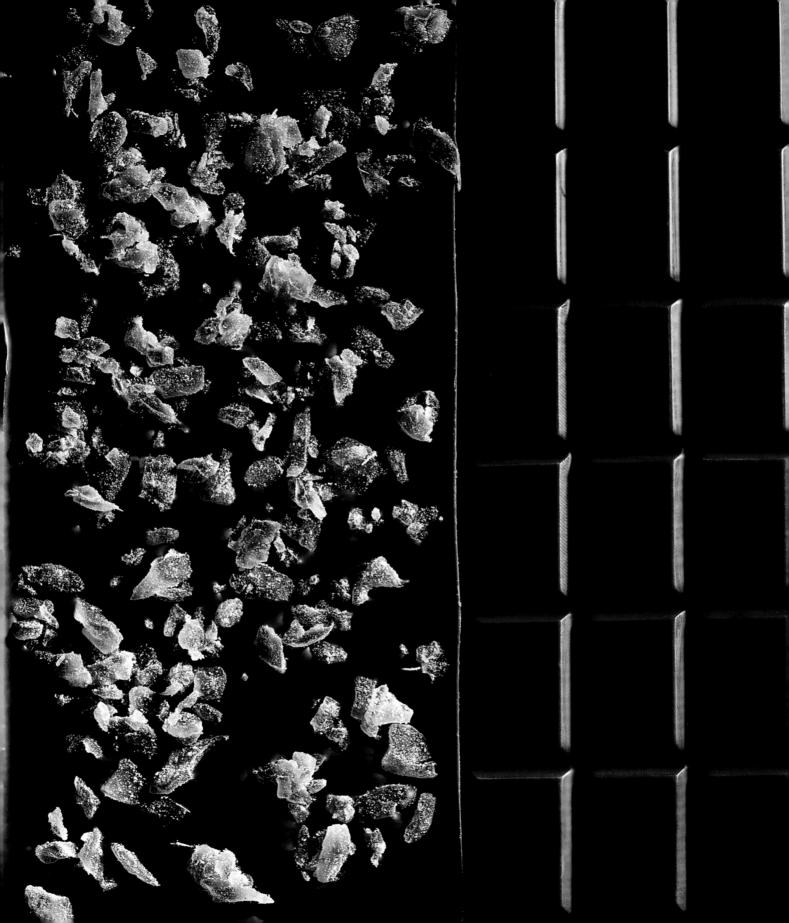

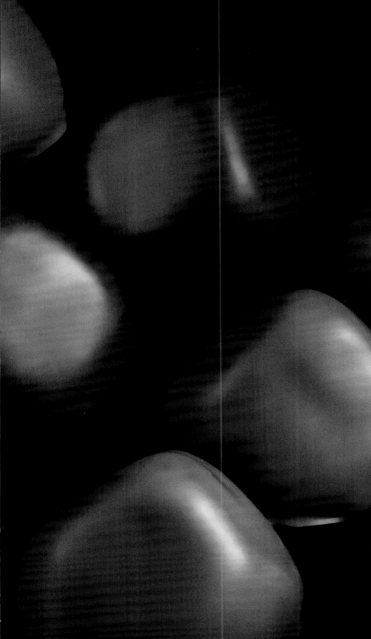

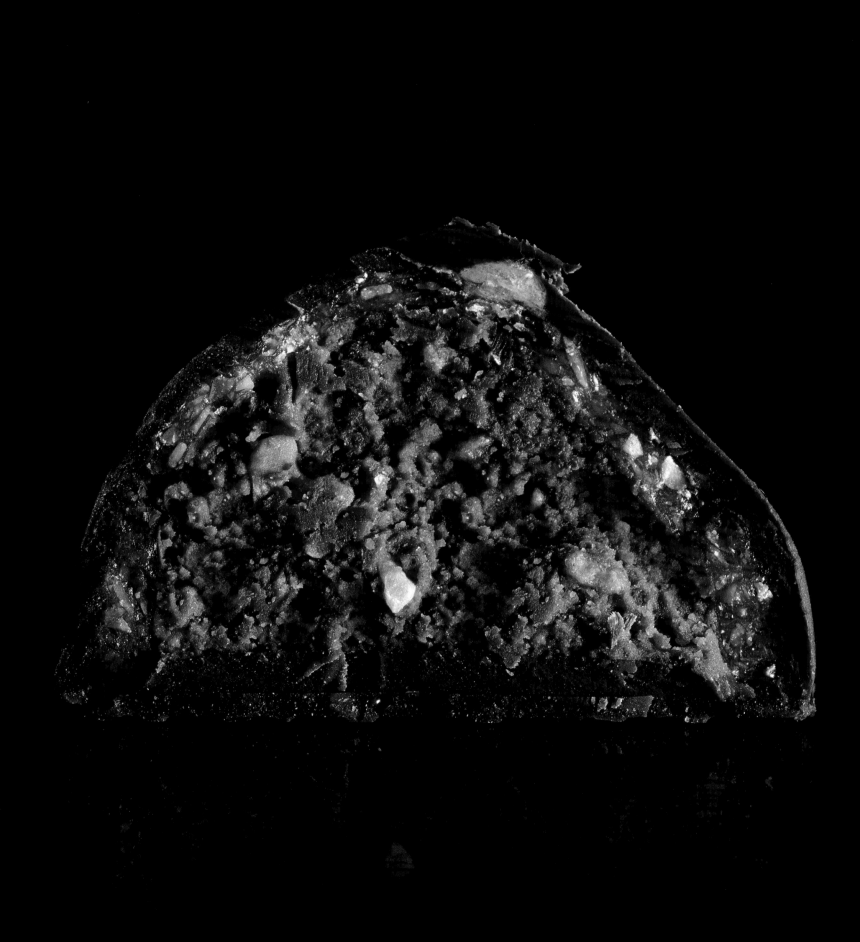

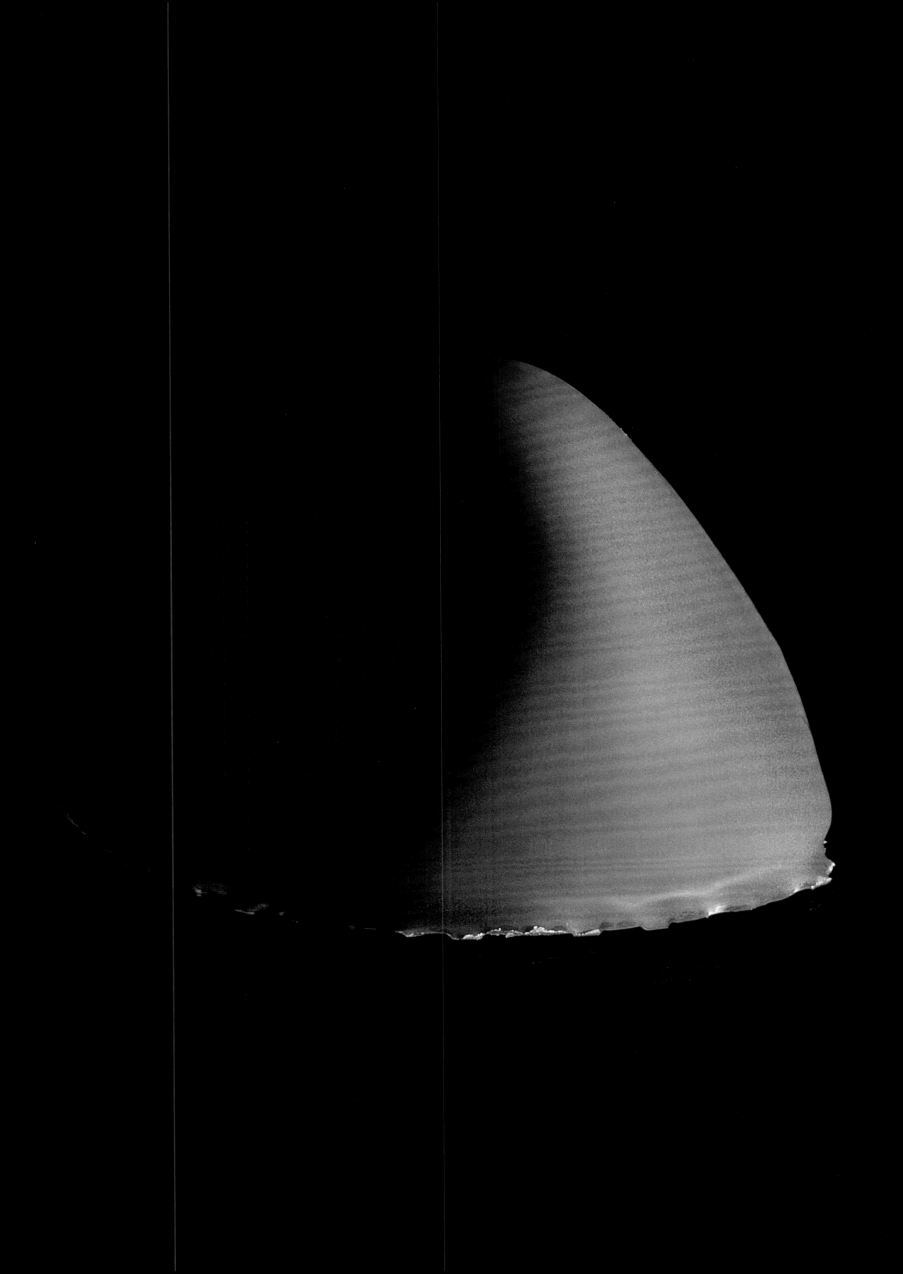

mys
teri
ous

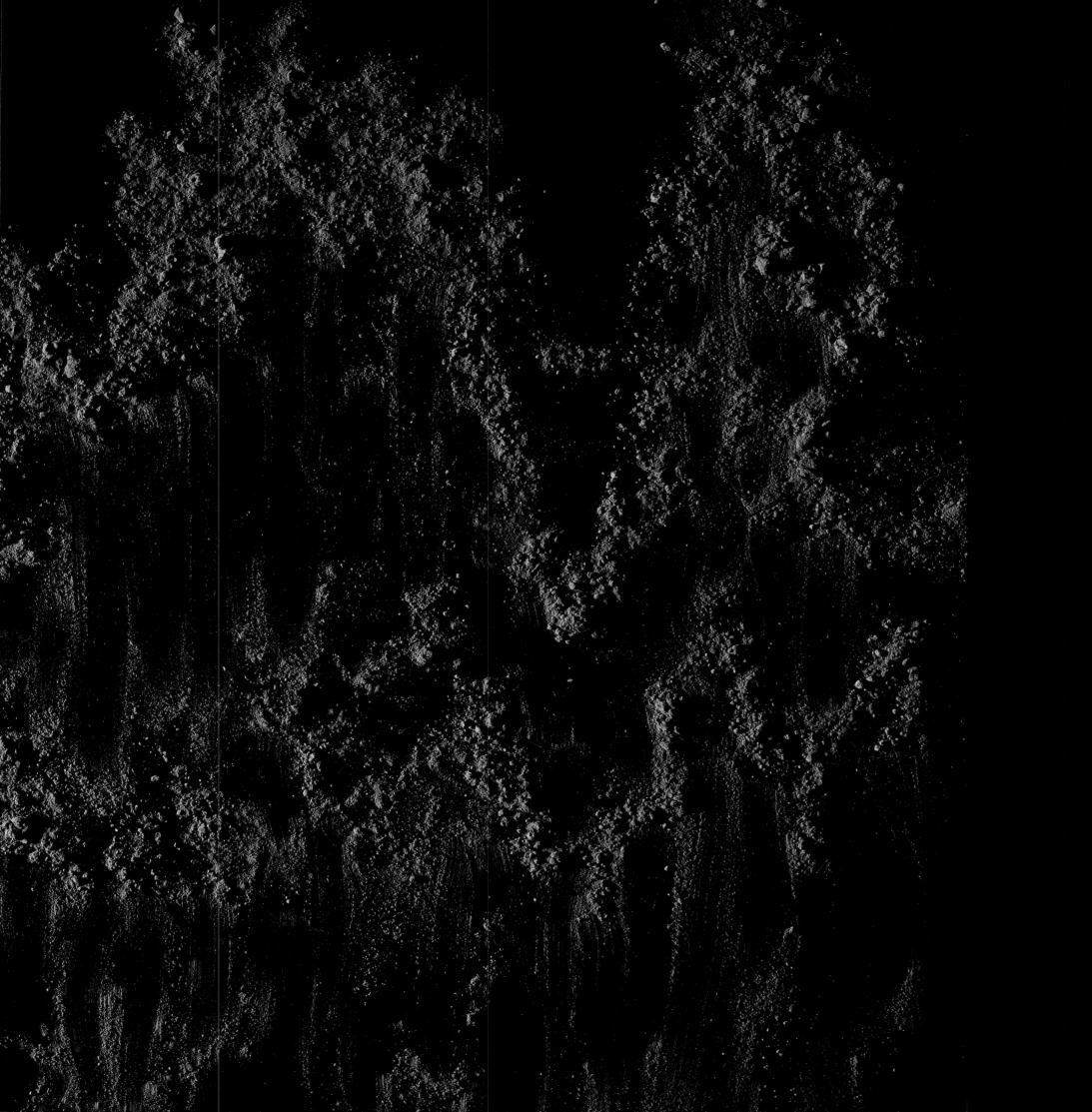

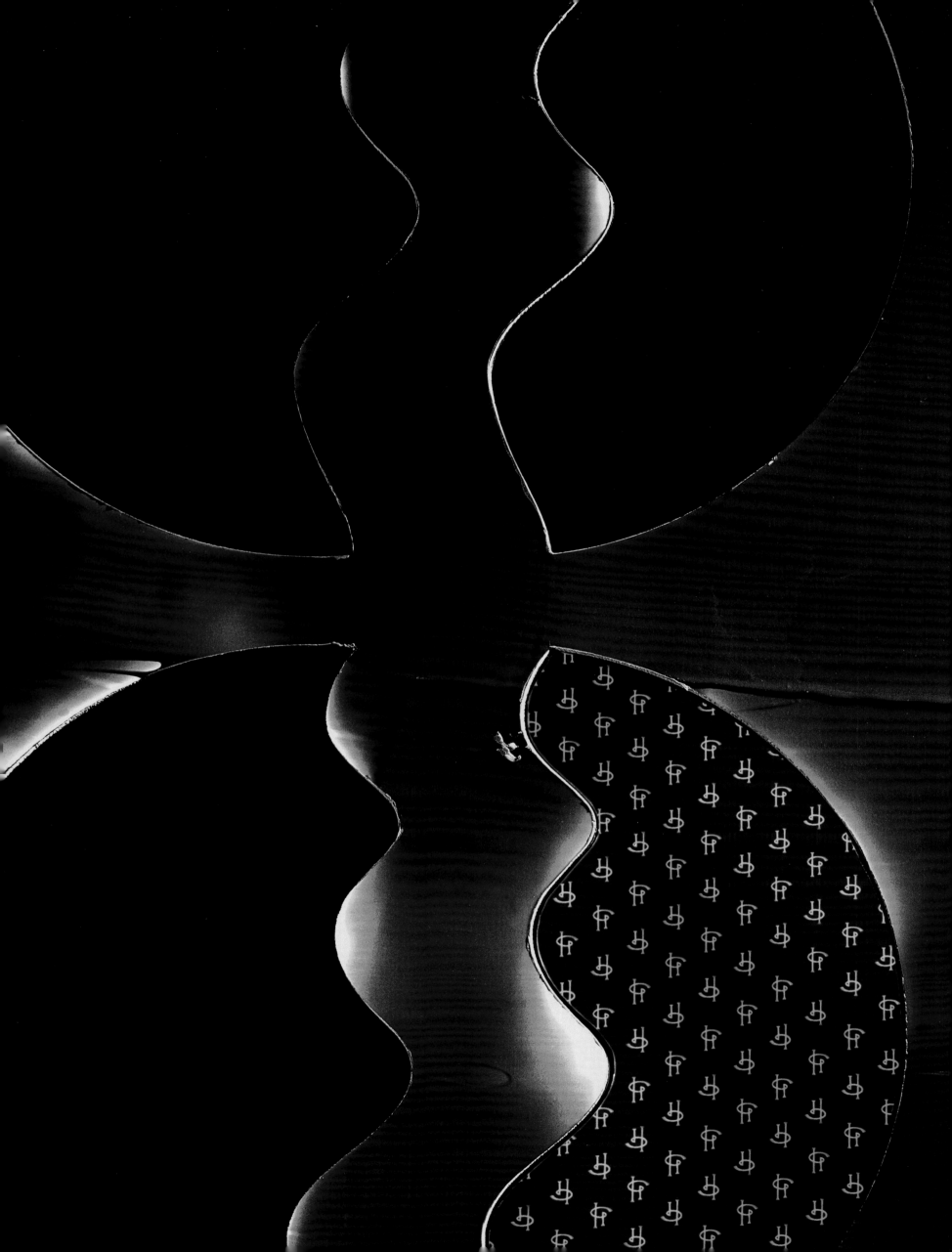

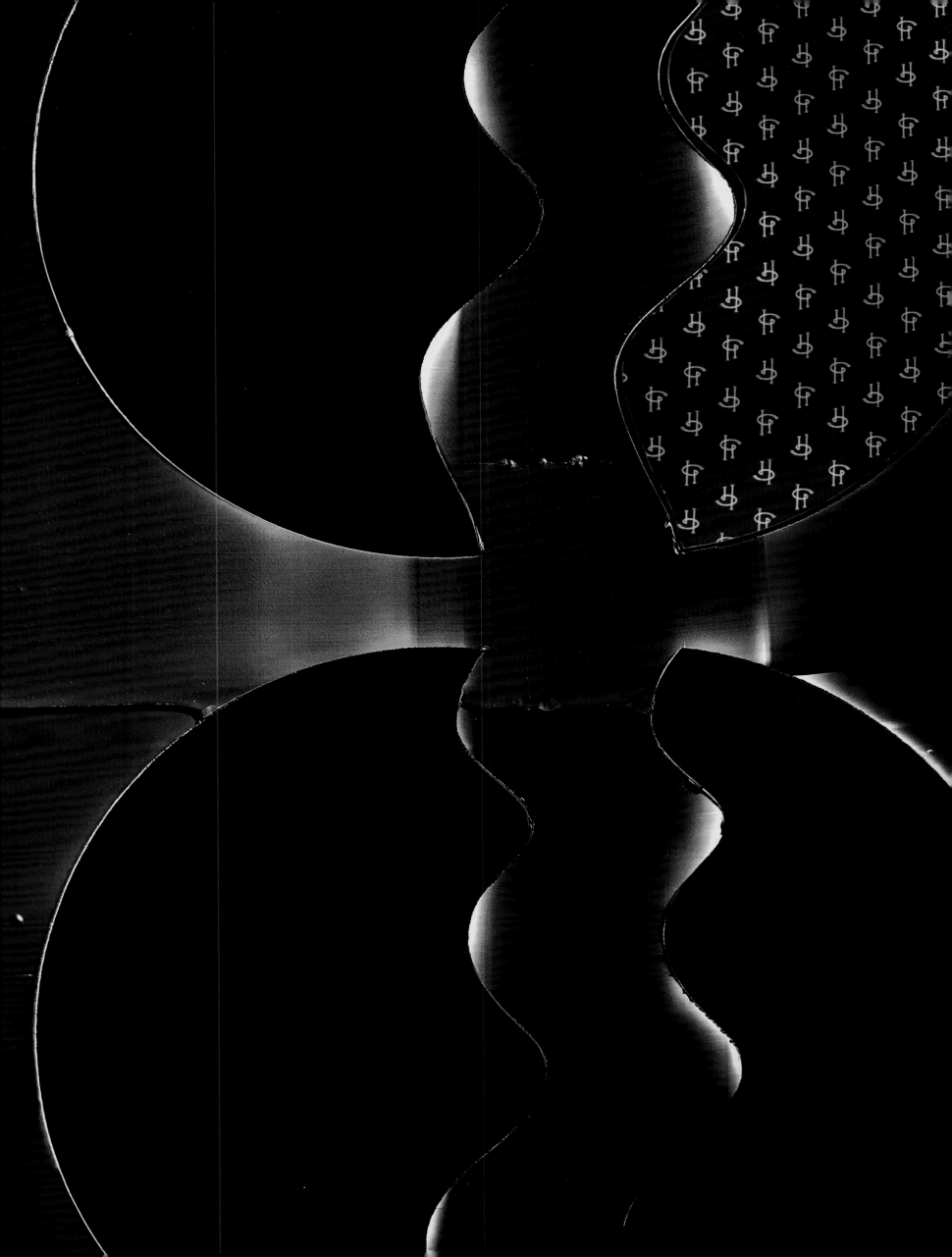

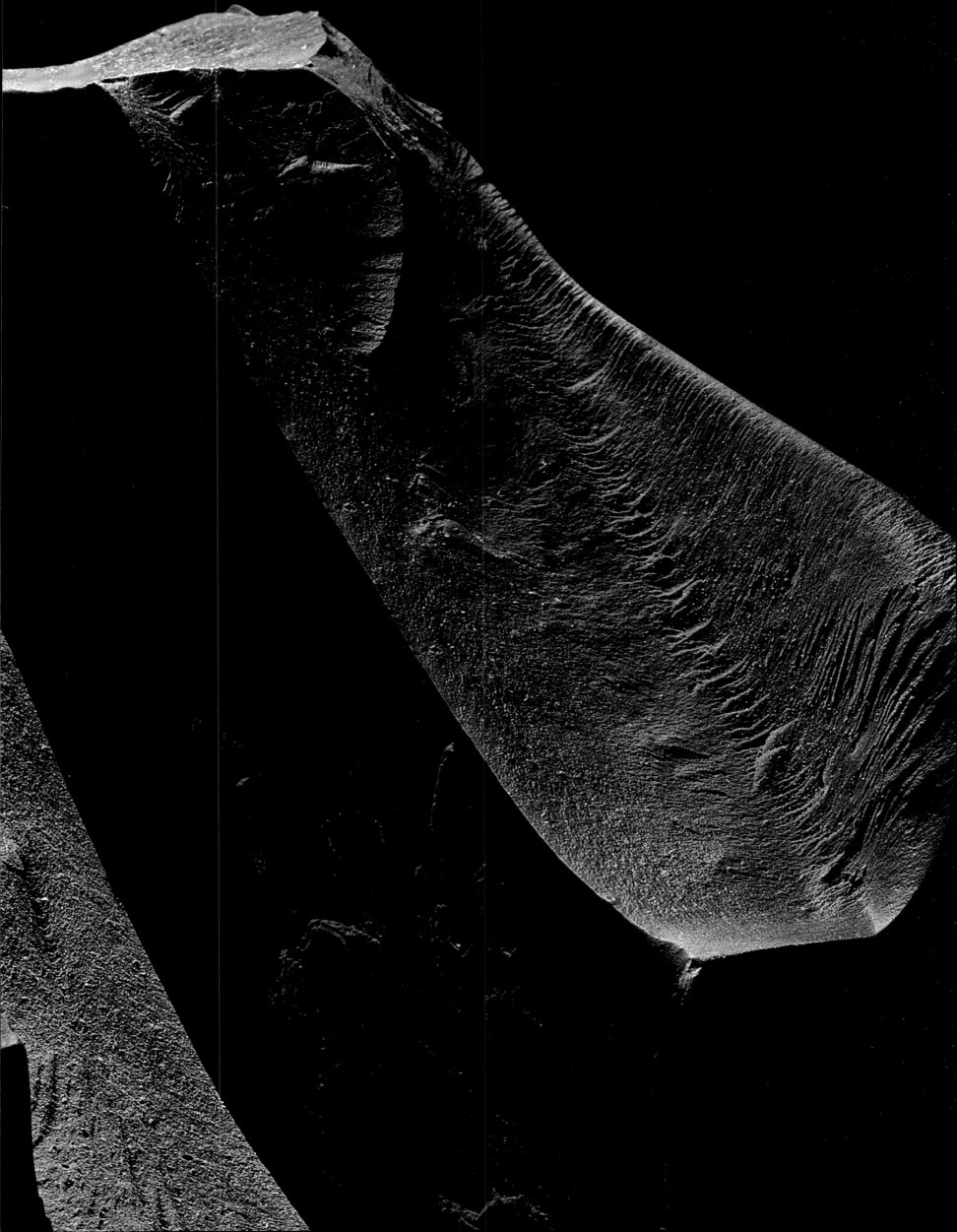

"I like to combine chocolate with other ingredients and I also like to use it by itself, with all its specificities, as long as it is outstanding cocoa."

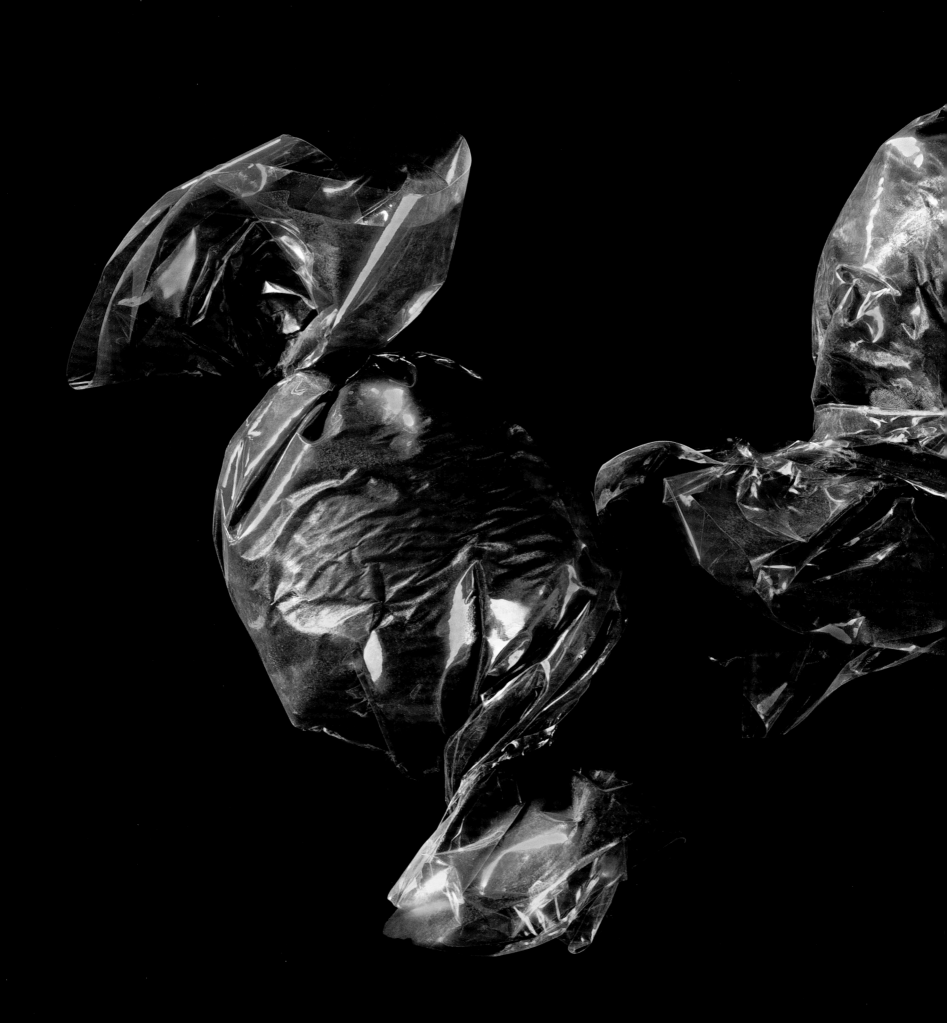

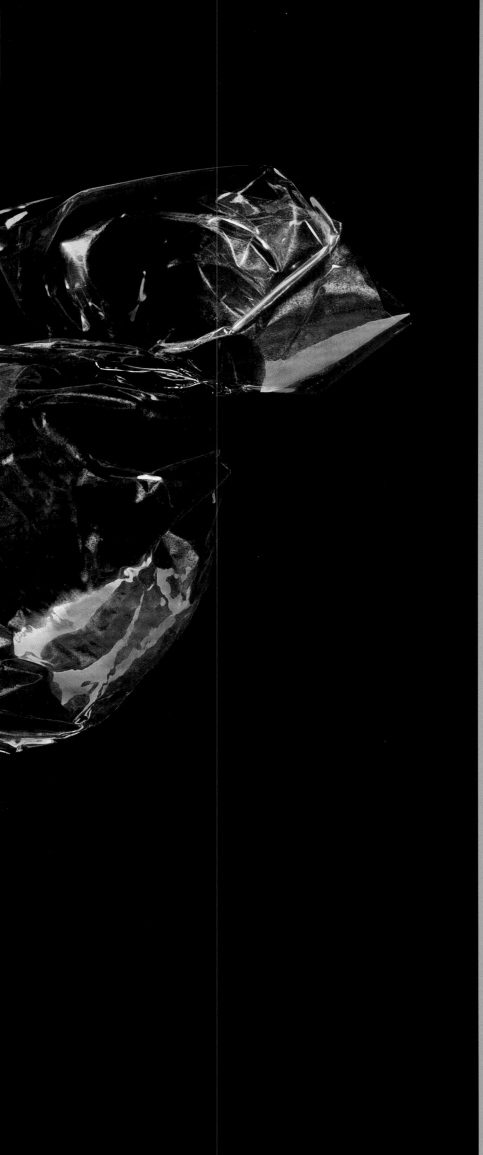

"Whatever
architecture
of taste
I have in
mind, my
only goal
is to create
something
very good,
something
that stirs
the emotions."

Truffes au Chocolat au Lait et Thé Vert Matcha

Milk Chocolate and Matcha Green Tea Truffles

Makes about 70 truffles

Ingredients:

Roasted Pistachios:

7 oz. (200 g) whole pistachios, skinned

Milk Chocolate and Matcha Green Tea Ganache:

6 1/2 tablespoons (3 1/3 oz./95 g) butter
21 1/2 oz. (610 g) milk chocolate, 45% cocoa
4 3/4 tablespoons (1 oz./30 g) matcha green tea powder
2 1/2 cups (21 oz./600 g) liquid cream

Finishing:

Pistachio powder

Preparation Time:

45 mins.

Cooking Time:

About 18 mins.

Preparation:

Prepare the roasted pistachios: Preheat the oven to 340°F (170°C/Gas Mark 5–6). Spread the pistachios out on a baking sheet lined with cooking parchment. Place it in the preheated oven to toast the pistachios for about fifteen minutes, stirring and turning every five minutes. Remove and set aside to cool.

Prepare the milk chocolate and matcha green tea ganache:
Cut the butter into pieces. Chop the chocolate with a serrated knife and place in a bowl with the matcha green tea powder. Bring the cream to a boil. Pour it, one third at a time, over the chocolate and matcha tea powder, stirring from the center out in small, then progressively larger concentric circles. Once the temperature of the chocolate has reached 95°F–105°F (35°C–40°C), incorporate, little by little, the pieces of butter, whisking until the ganache is smooth. Line the bottom and sides of a small baking dish with plastic film. Pour the ganache into the dish in a layer of about 1/3 in. (1 cm) thick. Cover with plastic film, pressing the film directly onto the surface of the chocolate. Refrigerate until the ganache is set.

Sprinkle the pistachio powder in a bowl. Remove the plastic film from the ganache and turn it out onto a cutting board. Cut into cubes of 1/3 in. (1 cm). Press a roasted pistachio into the center of each cube, then roll into a ball between the palms of your hands. Place the balls, one by one, in the bowl with the pistachio powder and roll to coat with the powder. Place the truffles in a sifter to remove any excess pistachio powder. Store in an airtight container.

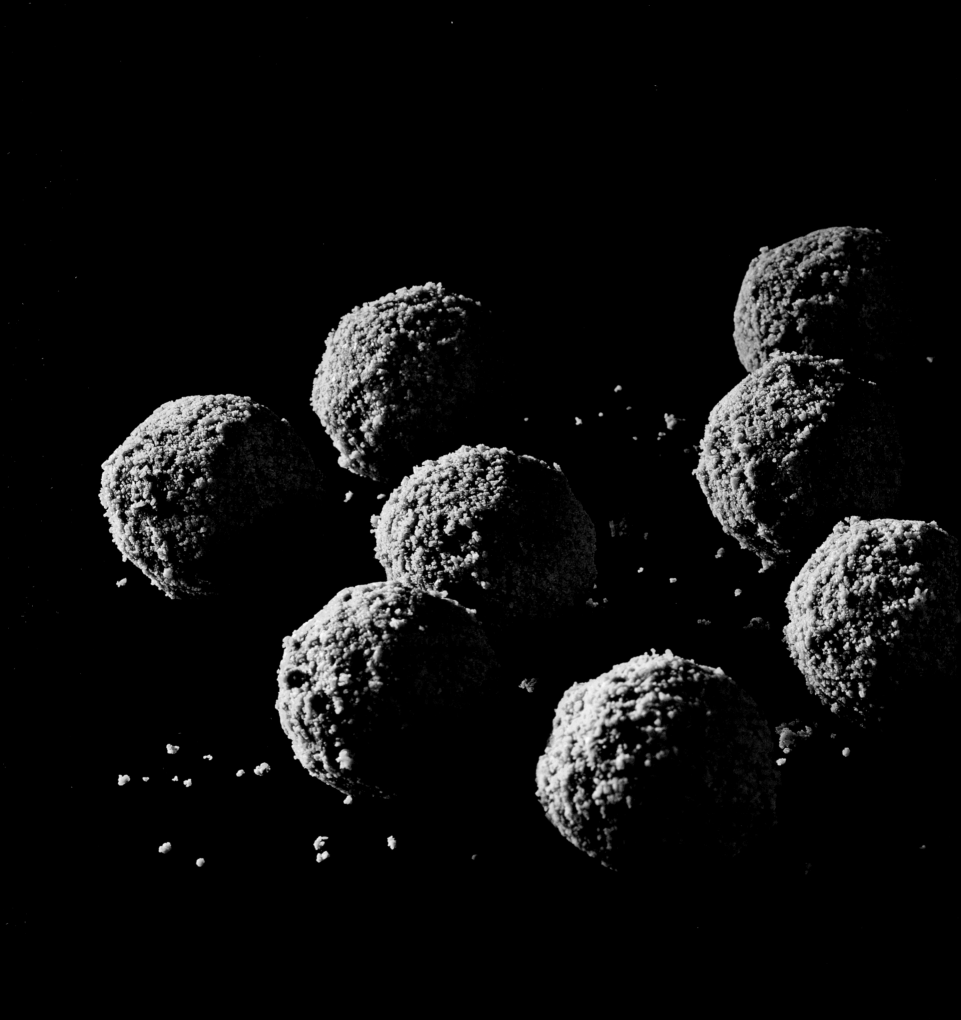

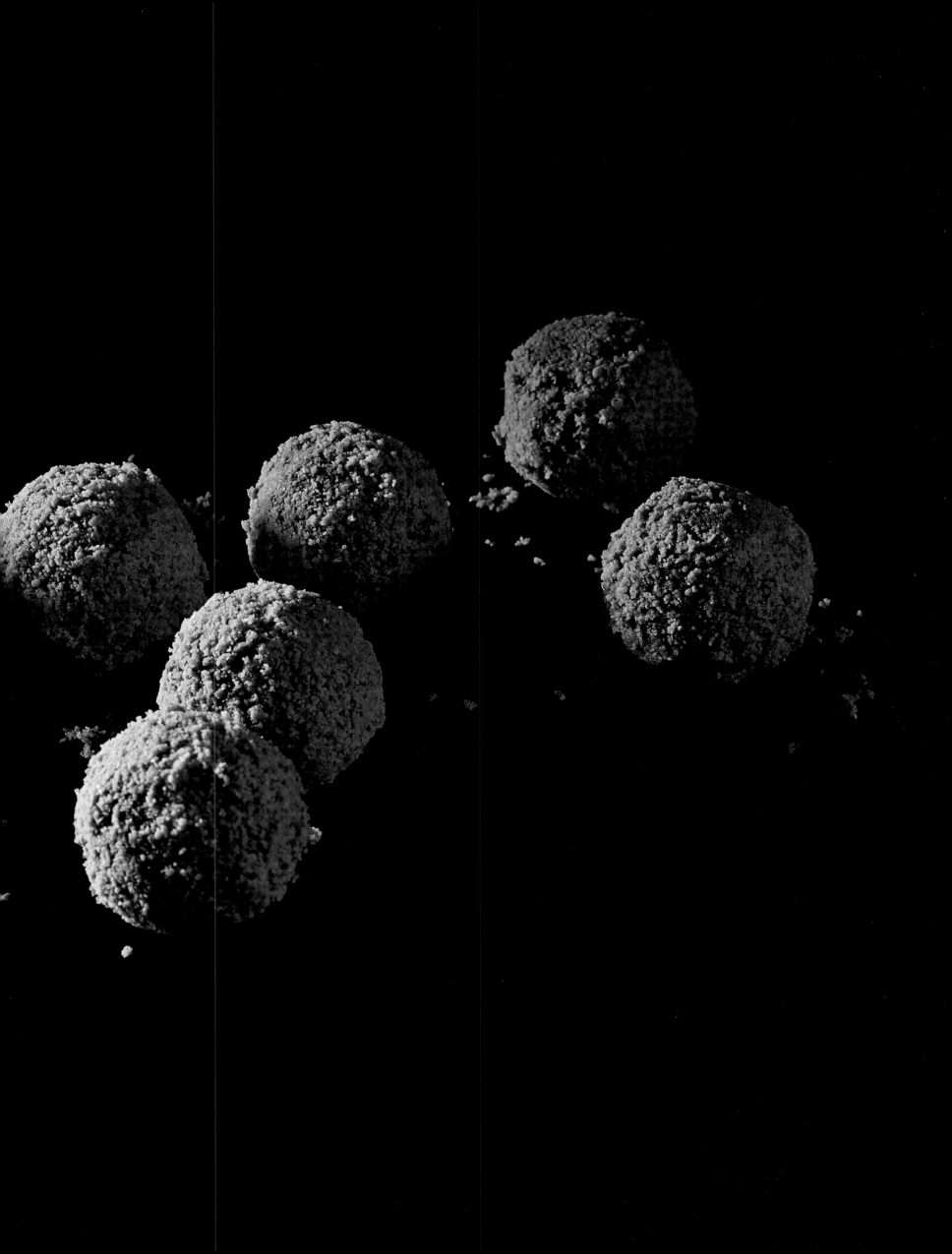

Cake Pain d'Épices Azur

Azur Gingerbread Cake

Makes 2 cakes, each about 6 x 4 in.
(16 cm x 10 cm)

Ingredients:

Homemade Orange Marmalade:

1 2/3 lb. (750 g) organic (untreated)
oranges
1 organic (untreated) lemon
2 1/2 cups (1 lb./500 g) granulated
sugar
2/3 cup (5 1/3 oz./150 g) mineral
water
1 pinch green cardamom powder
1/3 teaspoon (1.5 g) fresh peeled
ginger

Gingerbread Cake Batter:

3/4 cup (8 3/4 oz./250 g) homemade
orange marmalade (see recipe
above), or store-bought artisanal
marmalade
6 1/2 tablespoons (1 3/4 oz./50 g)
wheat flour
1/3 cup (1 1/4 oz./35 g) potato starch
1 1/4 cups (5 1/3 oz./150 g) rye flour
1 1/3 tablespoons (2/3 oz./17 g)
baking soda
7 tablespoons (3 1/2 oz./100 g)
butter
3 1/4 tablespoons (1 oz./30 g) light
brown sugar
1/4 cup (2 3/4 oz./80 g) corn syrup
3/4 cup (8 3/4 oz./250 g) multiflower
honey
3/4 teaspoon (3 g) *Fleur de sel*,
preferably Guérande
1/2 cup + 1 tablespoon
(4 1/2 oz./130 g) eggs
2 1/3 tablespoons (2/3 oz./18 g)
gingerbread spices
4 1/4 oz. (120 g) artisanal Kôchi yuzu
puree

Chocolate and Yuzu Ganache:

5 1/3 oz. (150 g) Manjari 64% dark
chocolate (Valrhona)
1/4 cup (2 oz./55 g) butter
2 1/3 tablespoons (1 1/4 oz./35 g)
yuzu juice
2/3 cup (5 1/4 oz./150 g) liquid cream

Chocolate Ganache Icing:

2 2/3 oz. (75 g) Extra Noir 53%
chocolate (Valrhona)
1/3 cup (2 2/3 oz./75 g) liquid cream
2 1/4 teaspoons (5 g) cocoa powder

Dark Chocolate Glaze:

2 3/4 oz. (80 g) Araguani 72% dark
chocolate (Valrhona)
7 oz. (200 g) dark chocolate glaze
(Valrhona)
1 1/2 tablespoons (2/3 oz./20 g)
grape seed oil

Finishing:

Golden sprinkles

Preparation Time:

15 mins. (2 days in advance);
30 mins. (1 day in advance);
30 mins. (the same day).

Cooking Time:

About 1 h. (2 days in advance);
about 25 mins. (1 day in advance);
a few minutes (the same day).

Chilling Time:

2 h.

Preparation:

**Two days in advance, prepare the orange
marmalade:** Rinse the oranges and lemon in water.
Place them in a large, heavy saucepan with enough
water to cover. Bring to a boil and cook for
thirty minutes. Drain the fruit in a colander, then refresh
under a stream of cold water. Cut into thick rounds,
discarding the ends and seeds, then dice in small
pieces, collecting any juices that run off. Place the diced
fruit in the colander over a bowl, pouring the juices back
over the fruit, and let drain twenty minutes.
Combine the sugar and mineral water in a saucepan,
and cook, monitoring the temperature with a
thermometer, to 239°F (115°C). Add the juices drained
from the fruit. Bring back to a boil and cook to
234°F (112°C). Add the diced fruit and a generous pinch
of cardamom. Using a Microplane or fine grater, grate
the ginger and add to the fruit. Bring to a boil and cook
to 223°F (106°C). Turn into a bowl and set aside at
room temperature overnight.

**The following day, prepare the gingerbread cake
batter:** Weigh out 3/4 cup (250 g) of orange marmalade.
Sift the wheat flour, potato starch, rye flour and baking
soda together. In the bowl of a mixer fitted with a plastic
blade, combine the butter, brown sugar, corn syrup,
honey, the cup of orange marmalade and *Fleur de sel*,
and mix on high speed for five minutes. Add the eggs
and mix for ten minutes. Add the sifted dry ingredients
and the spices, and mix to a smooth dough.

Chop the yuzu puree coarsely. Preheat the oven to
355°F (180°C/Gas Mark 6). Line the bottom and sides
of an oven baking pan of about 19 1/2 x 12 in.
(50 cm x 30 cm) with cooking parchment. Pour the
batter into the pan, spreading it out evenly and
smoothing the surface with an elbow spatula. Place the
pan in the oven and cook for eighteen minutes. Remove
from the oven and let cool briefly, before spreading the
yuzu puree uniformly over four-fifths of the surface of the
gingerbread cake, leaving a vertical band of cake
without the puree. (The last unglazed band will be the
top of the cake.) Let cool completely, then cut the
gingerbread cake vertically into five bands of the same
dimension (four glazed with yuzu puree, one unglazed).

Prepare the chocolate and yuzu ganache: Chop the chocolate with a serrated knife and place it in a bowl over a bain-marie of simmering water to melt. Cut the butter into pieces. Heat the yuzu juice to 115°F–125°F (45°C–50°C). Bring the cream to a boil in a separate saucepan. Pour the cream and the yuzu juice, one-third at a time, over the chocolate, stirring from the center out in small, then progressively larger concentric circles. Once the temperature of the mixture has reached 140°F (60°C), incorporate the butter pieces, little by little. Mix until the ganache is smooth. Pour into a shallow dish and cover with a sheet of plastic film, pressed directly onto the surface of the ganache. Refrigerate until the ganache has a creamy texture.

Place a frame of at least 2 1/3 to 3 in. (7 to 8 cm) high, and the length and width of the gingerbread cake bands on a pastry sheet lined with a silicone sheet. Place the first band of cake glazed with the yuzu puree in the bottom of the frame. Spread the band of gingerbread cake with a first layer of about 3 1/2 oz. of chocolate yuzu ganache. Position the second glazed band of cake on top of the first, spread with a layer of chocolate yuzu ganache and continue in the same manner with the two remaining yuzu-glazed gingerbread cake bands. Invert the fifth gingerbread cake band (unglazed) on top of the pile, cooked side up. Refrigerate for thirty minutes until set. Place a sheet of silicon paper or cooking parchment on the cake. Top with light weights placed along the length of the cake to help the layers stick together. Refrigerate overnight.

The day of serving, prepare the chocolate ganache icing: Chop the chocolate with a serrated knife and place it in a bowl over a bain-marie of simmering water. Bring the cream and the cocoa powder to a boil. Pour the cocoa cream, one-third at a time, over the chocolate, stirring from the center out in small, then progressively larger concentric circles. Mix with a hand blender. Set aside to cool at room temperature.

Prepare the dark chocolate glaze: Chop the chocolate with a serrated knife and place it in a bain-marie over simmering water with the dark chocolate glaze to melt to 113°F (45°C). Add the grape seed oil and stir to combine well.

Remove the silicon or cooking parchment from the cake. Turn the frame over and spread the cake with dark chocolate glaze. Refrigerate until the chocolate glaze sets. Remove the frame, running the blade of a small knife dipped in warm water between the cake and the frame. Cut into two cakes of identical size.

Heat the chocolate icing to 115°F–125°F (45°C–50°C). Insert a knife in the center of the first gingerbread cake and dip in the icing. Remove and drain on a pastry rack placed over a rimmed baking sheet. Dip the second cake in the icing in the same manner. When the cakes have drained, place them in the refrigerator to set.

Heat the dark chocolate glaze to 95°F–105°F (35°C–40°C). Insert a knife in the first cake and dip in the chocolate glaze. Remove from the glaze, invert the cake onto a pastry rack placed over a rimmed baking sheet and let drain. Proceed in the same manner for the second cake. Scatter the top of each cake with golden sprinkles. Allow to set a room temperature, then refrigerate for at least two hours. Remove from the refrigerator two hours before serving.

Chocolat show Aztec

Aztec Chocolat Show

Makes 10 glasses, 2 3/4 in. (7 cm)
high by 1 3/4 in. (4.5 cm) diameter
and 3 oz. (85g) capacity

Ingredients:

**Orange Marmalade
(3 1/3 lb./1.5 kg):**

1 2/3 lb. (750 g) oranges, untreated
2 lemons, untreated
2 1/2 cups (1 lb./500 g) granulated
sugar
2/3 cup (5 1/3 oz./150 g) mineral
water
1 pinch green cardamom powder
1/3 teaspoon (1.5 g) fresh ginger

Araguani Chocolate Cream:

5 2/3 oz. (160 g) Araguani 72% dark
chocolate (Valrhona)
1/2 cup (4 1/2 oz./125 g) whole milk
1/2 cup (4 1/2 oz./125 g) liquid cream
2 oz. (60 g) egg yolks
1/4 cup (1 3/4 oz./50 g) superfine
sugar

**Araguani Chocolate Whipped
Cream:**

1 1/3 oz. (40 g) Araguani 72% dark
chocolate (Valrhona)
3/4 cup + 2 1/2 teaspoons
(7 oz./200 g) liquid cream
2 1/2 teaspoons (1/3 oz./10 g)
superfine sugar

Balsamic Vinegar Reduction:

1/4 cup (2 oz./60 g) Modena
balsamic vinegar

**Orange Compote with Balsamic
Vinegar:**

1 teaspoon (5 g) powdered gelatin, or
2 1/2 gelatin sheets (2 g each)
2 tablespoons (1 oz./32 g) balsamic
vinegar reduction (see recipe above)
1/2 cup (4 1/2 oz./120 g) homemade
orange marmalade (see recipe
above), or store-bought artisanal
marmalade

Preparation Time:

45 mins. (1 day in advance);
20 mins. (the same day).

Cooking Time:

About 40 mins. (1 day in advance);
about 10 mins. (the same day).

Preparation:

**A day in advance, prepare the orange marmalade, the
chocolate cream and the chocolate whipped cream:**
For the orange marmalade, rinse the oranges and
lemons. Place them in a large pan, add enough water
to cover, bring to a boil and cook for thirty minutes. Drain
the fruit in a colander and rinse under cold water. Cut
the oranges and lemons into thick rounds, discarding
the ends and the seeds. Chop into small pieces,
collecting the juices, and return the fruit to the colander
set over a bowl. Pour the juices over and let drain for
twenty minutes. Combine the mineral water and sugar in
a saucepan, and cook to 240°F (115°C). Add the citrus
juices from the bowl. Bring back to a boil and cook to
235°F (112°C). Add the orange and lemon pieces, and
a generous pinch of cardamom. Grate the peeled fresh
ginger with a Microplane and add to the fruit. Bring back
to a boil and let cook to 225°F (106°C). Pour into a
shallow dish and let cool at room temperature overnight.

For the Araguani chocolate cream: Chop the
chocolate with a serrated knife and place it in a bowl.
Bring the milk and cream to a boil in a saucepan. Whisk
the egg yolks and sugar together in a bowl. Pour the
milk–cream mixture over the egg yolk–sugar mixture,
whisking. Pour the mixture back into the saucepan and
heat, whisking, until it reaches 185°F (85°C). Pour the
mixture, one-third at a time, over the chocolate, stirring
from the center out in small, then progressively larger
concentric circles. Mix with a hand blender. Cover with a
sheet of plastic film, pressed directly onto the surface of
the cream, and refrigerate overnight.

For Araguani the chocolate whipped cream: Chop
the chocolate with a serrated knife and place it in a bowl
over a bain-marie of simmering water. Combine the
cream and sugar in a saucepan, and bring to a boil.
Pour the cream, one-third at a time, over the chocolate,
stirring from the center out in small, then progressively
larger concentric circles. Cover with a sheet of plastic
film, pressed directly onto the surface of the cream,
and refrigerate overnight.

**The following day, prepare the balsamic vinegar
reduction:** Pour the vinegar into a small saucepan and
reduce by about half to obtain 1 oz. (32 g), a little more
than two tablespoons. Keep warm over a bain-marie.

Prepare the orange compote: Sprinkle the powdered gelatin in a few tablespoons warm water to soften. If using sheet gelatin, place in a bowl of cold water to soften fifteen minutes, then squeeze between the palms of your hands to drain. Add the gelatin to the warm vinegar reduction. Stir the vinegar reduction into the 1/2 cup (4 1/2 oz./120 g) orange marmalade, combine well and set aside to set at room temperature.

Divide the chocolate cream among the glasses. Refrigerate until the cream sets. Just before serving, prepare the chocolate whipped cream and spoon it into a pastry bag fitted with a F8 star tip.

Pipe onto the chocolate cream in the glasses and garnish with the orange–vinegar compote.

Chocolat show à la Menthe Fraîche

Fresh Mint Chocolat Show

Makes 10 glasses, 2 3/4 in. (7 cm)
high by 1 3/4 in. (4.5 cm) diameter
and 3 oz. 85g capacity

Ingredients:

Caraibe Chocolate Cream:

4 1/2 oz. (130 g) Caraibe 66% dark
chocolate (Valrhona)
6 1/2 tablespoons (3 1/2 oz./100 g)
whole milk
6 1/2 tablespoons (3 1/2 oz./100 g)
liquid cream
1 3/4 oz. (50 g) egg yolks
3 tablespoons + 1 teaspoon
(1 1/2 oz./40 g) superfine sugar

Fresh Mint Granita:

1 oz. (25 g) fresh mint leaves
1 2/3 cups (14 oz./400 g) mineral
water
6 tablespoons + 2 teaspoons
(2 3/4 oz./80 g) superfine sugar

Finishing:

5 fresh mint leaves

Preparation Time:

15 mins. (1 day in advance);
15 mins. (the same day).

Cooking Time:

About 15 mins. (1 day in advance);
a few minutes (the same day).

Infusing Time:

20 mins.

Preparation:

A day in advance, prepare the Caraibe chocolate cream: Chop the chocolate with a serrated knife and place it in a bowl. Combine the milk and cream in a saucepan, and bring to a boil. Whisk the egg yolks and sugar together in a bowl. Pour the milk–cream mixture over the egg yolk–sugar mixture, whisking, then pour back into the saucepan. Continue whisking over low heat until the mixture reaches 185°F (85°C). Pour the mixture, one-third at a time, over the chocolate, stirring from the center out in small, then progressively larger concentric circles. Mix with a hand blender. Cover with plastic film, pressing the film directly onto the surface of the cream. Refrigerate overnight.

The following day, prepare the fresh mint granita: Rinse and carefully dry the mint leaves. Chop the mint as finely as possible. Combine the mineral water and sugar in a saucepan, and bring to a boil. Add the chopped mint. Remove from the heat and set aside to infuse for twenty minutes. Strain, reserving the mint leaves and the sugar syrup. Place the mint leaves in the bowl of a food processor and process, adding the syrup little by little. Pour into a stainless steel recipient and place in the freezer. Remove from the freezer every five minutes as it begins to freeze, pulling the tines of a fork through the mixture to form coarse ice crystals.

Divide the chocolate cream among the serving glasses. Refrigerate until the cream sets. Just before serving with the other two Chocolat Shows, Aztec and Inca, slice the fresh mint leaves finely. Spoon the mint granita onto the cream in each glass. Decorate with the mint leaves.

Chocolat show Inca

Inca Chocolat Show

Makes 10 glasses, 2 3/4 in. (7 cm)
high by 1 3/4 in. (4.5 cm) diameter
and 3 oz. (85g) capacity, preferably
heat-resistant

Ingredients:

Hot Chocolate Ganache:

5 1/4 oz. (150 g) Araguani 72% dark
chocolate (Valrhona)
7 tablespoons (3 1/2 oz./100 g)
butter
1 1/2 oz. (40 g) egg yolks
1 3/4 oz. (50 g) whole eggs
3 tablespoons + 1 teaspoon
(1 1/2 oz./40 g) superfine sugar

Avocado and Banana Compote:

1 teaspoon (2 g) powdered gelatin, or
1 sheet (2 g) gelatin
2 1/2 oz. (70 g) ripe avocado flesh
1 tablespoon (15 g) fresh lemon juice
1/8 teaspoon (0.2 g) lime zest
1/4 cup (2 oz./60 g) liquid cream
2 oz. (55 g) banana puree
2/3 cup (4 1/2 oz./130 g) superfine
sugar
1 tablespoon (15 g) fresh orange juice
2 drops Tabasco
1/8 teaspoon (0.2 g) ground white
pepper

Avocado and Banana Cubes:

1 ripe avocado
1 banana
Lemon juice

Preparation Time:

30 mins.

Cooking Time:

About 15 mins.

Preparation:

Prepare the hot chocolate ganache: Chop the chocolate with a serrated knife and place it in a bowl over a bain-marie of simmering water to melt. Melt the butter in a saucepan. Whisk the eggs, egg yolks and sugar together in a bowl. Stir in the melted chocolate and butter. Divide the mixture equally among the serving glasses and refrigerate.

Prepare the avocado and banana compote: Sprinkle the powdered gelatin into a tablespoon of warm water to soften. (If using sheet gelatin, place the sheet in a bowl of cold water to soften fifteen minutes, then remove from the water and squeeze between the palms of your hands to drain.) Cut a ripe avocado in half. Remove the pit and scoop out 2 1/2 oz. (70 g) of the flesh. Drizzle the avocado flesh immediately with the lemon juice. Grate the lime zest with a Microplane. Whip the cream to soft peaks. In a Thermomix or a food processor, combine the avocado, banana puree, sugar, orange juice, lime zest, Tabasco and white pepper, and mix. Turn one-third of the avocado–banana mixture into a bowl and add the softened gelatin powder, stirring briskly. (If using sheet gelatin, melt the gelatin sheet, soften and squeezed out as indicated above, in a bowl over a bain-marie before adding it to the avocado–banana mixture.) Add the remaining avocado mixture to the bowl. Fold the whipped cream delicately into the mixture with a rubber spatula, folding gently with a lifting motion from the bottom to the surface. Spoon into a pastry bag without a tip and refrigerate.

Shortly before serving, prepare the avocado and banana cubes: Peel the avocado and banana, and cut their flesh into 1/4-in. (5 mm) cubes. Place in a bowl and toss immediately with a little lemon juice. Remove glasses of chocolate ganache from the refrigerator and place on a baking sheet at room temperature to warm slightly. Preheat the oven on convection setting to 355°F (180°C/Gas Mark 6). Place the glasses of chocolate ganache in the oven and cook for eight minutes. Remove from the oven and let cool for two minutes. Pipe the avocado–banana compote onto the top of each serving, and sprinkle with the avocado and banana cubes. Serve immediately with the other two Chocolat Shows, fresh mint and Aztec.

Cocktail Whisky Chocolat

Chocolate Whisky Cocktail

Makes 10 cocktails

Ingredients:

Cold Chocolate:

3 oz. (85 g) Extra Amer 67% dark
chocolate (Valrhona)
2 cups (16 1/2 oz./470 g) mineral
water
2 1/2 tablespoons (1 1/4 oz./35 g)
superfine sugar
2 tablespoons + 2 1/2 teaspoons
(3/4 oz./20 g) cocoa powder
(Valrhona)

Chocolate Whisky Cocktail:

21 oz. (600 g) cold chocolate
1 1/4 cups (10 1/2 oz./300 g) cocoa
liqueur
1 1/4 cups (10 1/2 oz./300 g) pure
malt whisky
1 1/4 cups (10 1/2 oz./300 g) Baileys

Finishing:

3 1/2 oz. (100 g) chocolate sprinkles
(Valrhona)
1/16 oz. (2 g) edible gold powder
3 tablespoons cane sugar syrup
Crushed ice

––––

Preparation Times:

10 mins.

Cooking Time:

3 mins.

Preparation:

Prepare the cold chocolate: Chop the chocolate with a serrated knife and place it in a bowl. Combine the mineral water and sugar in a saucepan, and bring to a boil. Whisk in the cocoa powder and cook, stirring, until the mixture coats the back of a spoon. Pour the mixture, one-third at a time, over the chocolate, stirring from the center out in small, then progressively larger concentric circles. Mix with a hand blender and store in the refrigerator in an airtight container until chilled.

––––

Add the cocoa liqueur, whisky and Baileys to the cold chocolate, and return to the refrigerator in the airtight container until just before serving.
Combine the chocolate sprinkles and the gold powder, stirring with a wooden spoon. Store in a separate airtight container in the refrigerator until just before serving.

––––

Just before serving, pour the cane sugar syrup into a shallow dish. Pour the chocolate sprinkles–gold powder mixture into a second shallow dish. Dip the rim of each cocktail glass quickly in the sugar syrup, then in the chocolate sprinkles–gold powder mixture.
Place the crushed ice in a cocktail shaker, add the chocolate mixture, shake vigorously. Filter the mixture through the strainer of the shaker and pour into the cocktail glasses. Serve immediately.

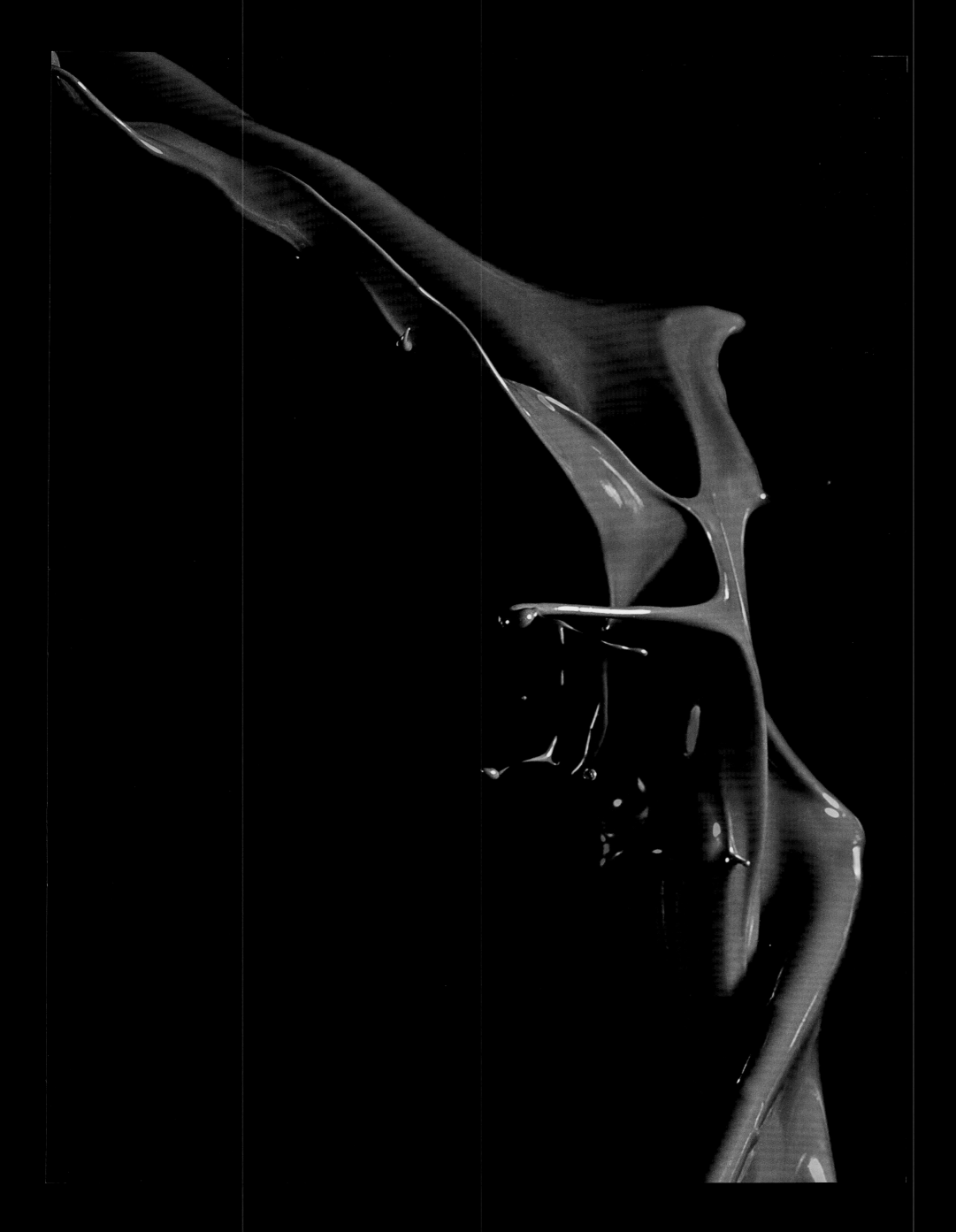

Macaron Jardin Zen

Jardin Zen Macaron

Makes about 72 macarons
(or about 144 shells)

Ingredients:

Chocolate Macaron Shells:

1/2 cup (4 oz./110 g), or about
4 "liquefied" egg whites, divided (see
note)
1 3/4 cups (5 1/3 oz./150 g) ground
almonds
3/4 cup + 2 1/2 tablespoons
(5 1/3 oz./150 g) confectioners' sugar
2 oz. (60 g) pure cocoa paste
(Valrhona)
6 drops (0.25 g) carmine red liquid
food coloring
3 1/2 tablespoons (1 3/4 oz./50 g)
mineral water
3/4 cup (5 1/3 oz./150 g) superfine
sugar

Plain Macaron Shells:

1/2 cup (4 oz./110 g), or about
4 "liquefied" egg whites, divided (see
note)
1 3/4 cups (5 1/3 oz./150 g) ground
almonds
1 cup + 2 1/2 tablespoons
(5 1/3 oz./150 g) confectioners' sugar
3 1/2 tablespoons (1 3/4 oz./50 g)
mineral water
3/4 cup (5 1/3 oz./150 g) superfine
sugar

Sweet Shortcrust Pastry:

2 cups (8 3/4 oz./250 g) flour
3/4 cup (3 1/3 oz./95 g)
confectioners' sugar
2/3 cup (5 1/3 oz./150 g) butter at
room temperature
1/3 cup (1 oz./30 g) ground almonds
2 pinches *Fleur de sel*, preferably
Guérande
1/4 teaspoon vanilla powder,
or 1/4 fresh vanilla bean, split and
scraped
1 egg

Baked and Buttered Sweet
Shortcrust Pastry:

3 1/2 oz. (100 g) Sweet Shortcrust
pastry
2 3/4 tablespoons (1 1/2 oz./40 g)
softened butter

Jardin Zen Ganache:

6 tablespoons (3 oz./85 g) butter
10 1/2 oz. (300 g) Paineiras 64%
dark chocolate (Valrhona)
1 1/4 cups (10 1/2 oz./300 g) liquid
cream
5 1/3 oz. (150 g) white miso paste

Preparation Time:

2 mins. (5 days in advance);
1 h. 45 mins. (the same day).

Cooking Time:

20 mins. + 16 mins. + 12 mins.

Chilling Time:

4 h. + 2 x 2 h. + 20 mins. + 24 h.

Resting Time:

30 mins.

Preparation:

Five days in advance, place the egg whites for the two different macaron shells in a bowl, cover the bowl tightly with plastic film, pierce a few holes in the film and refrigerate to liquefy.

—

One day in advance, prepare the Sweet Shortcrust pastry: Sift the flour and confectioners' sugar separately. Cut the butter into pieces and place it in the bowl of a mixer fitted with the plastic blade. Mix until the butter is creamy. Add, in the following order, the sifted confectioners' sugar, the ground almonds, *Fleur de sel*, vanilla, egg and sifted flour, and mix just until the dough forms a ball. Do not overmix, since overworking will make the dough lose its delicate, flaky texture. Remove the dough, form into a ball and flatten gently. Wrap in plastic film and refrigerate for at least four hours.

—

Preheat the oven on convection setting to 340°F (170°C/Gas Mark 5–6).
Weigh 3 1/2 oz. (100 g) of the chilled Sweet Shortcrust pastry. (Reserve or freeze the remaining pastry dough for another use.) On a floured work surface, roll the dough out into a very thin sheet, about 1/16 in. (2 mm). Brush off excess flour and roll the sheet of dough around a rolling pin to transfer to a baking sheet lined with cooking parchment. Place in the oven and cook for twenty minutes, until the dough is golden brown. Remove from the oven and let cool.

—

For the baked and buttered Sweet Shortcrust pastry: Break the dough into pieces, place it in the bowl of a mixer fitted with a plastic blade and mix to a powder. Add the softened butter and mix until the butter is incorporated with the Sweet Shortcrust pastry powder. Turn the buttered pastry onto a floured work surface and roll out to 1/2 in. (1.5 cm) thick. Place on a baking sheet lined with cooking parchment and refrigerate for twenty minutes. Place in the oven, preheated on convection setting to 340°F (170°C/Gas Mark 5–6), and bake for sixteen minutes. Remove from the oven and let cool, then cut into 1/2-in. (1.5 cm) cubes.

—

Prepare the chocolate macaron shells: Sift the ground almonds and confectioners' sugar together. Chop the cocoa paste and place it in a bowl over a bain-marie of simmering water to melt at 122°F (50°C). Combine 1/4 cup (55 g) of liquefied egg whites with the food coloring. Pour onto the sifted almond powder–sugar mixture without mixing.

—

Combine the sugar and water in a saucepan, and bring to a boil, monitoring the temperature with a thermometer. Meanwhile place the remaining 1/4 cup (55 g) of liquefied egg whites in the bowl of a mixer fitted with a wire whisk. Once the sugar syrup has reached 239°F (115°C), begin beating the egg whites on high speed. Once the syrup has reached 244°F (118°C), reduce the mixer speed to medium and begin pouring the syrup in a steady stream into the egg whites. Continue beating until the mixture cools to 122°F (50°C). Using a spatula, fold the meringue mixture into the almond–sugar–egg white mixture. Add the melted cocoa paste, folding gently until the mixture loses a little volume. Spoon the batter into a pastry bag fitted with a No. 11 (1/2-in. diameter) plain tip. Line a baking sheet with cooking parchment and pipe out rounds of batter about 1 1/2 in. (3.5 cm) in diameter, spaced about 3/4 in. apart. Tap the baking sheet gently on a work surface covered with a kitchen towel to smooth the surface. Set aside at room temperature for at least thirty minutes to allow a "skin" to form.

Prepare the plain macaron shells: Sift the ground almonds and confectioners' sugar together. Pour 1/4 cup (55 g) of the egg whites onto the sifted almond powder–sugar mixture without mixing.

Combine the sugar and water in a saucepan, and bring to a boil, monitoring the temperature with a thermometer. Meanwhile place the remaining 1/4 cup (55 g) of liquefied egg whites in the bowl of a mixer fitted with a wire whisk. Once the sugar syrup has reached 239°F (115°C), begin beating the egg whites on high speed. Once the syrup has reached 244°F (118°C), reduce the mixer speed to medium and begin pouring the syrup in a steady stream into the egg whites. Continue beating until the mixture cools to 122°F (50°C). Using a spatula, fold the meringue mixture into the almond–sugar–egg white mixture, turning gently until the mixture loses a little volume. Spoon the batter into a pastry bag fitted with a No. 11 (1/2-in. diameter) plain tip. Line a baking sheet with cooking parchment and pipe out rounds of batter about 1 1/2 in. in diameter, spaced about 3/4 in. apart. Tap the baking sheet gently on a work surface covered with a kitchen towel to smooth the surface. Set aside at room temperature for at least thirty minutes to allow a "skin" to form.

Preheat the oven on convection setting to 355°F (180°C/Gas Mark 6). Place the baking sheets of chocolate and plain macaron shells in the oven, and bake for twelve minutes, opening and closing the oven door quickly twice during the baking to release steam. Remove from the oven and slide the macaron shells onto the work surface.

Prepare the Jardin Zen ganache: Cut the butter into

pieces. Chop the chocolate with a serrated knife and place it in a bowl. Bring the cream to a boil in a small saucepan. Pour the cream, one-third at a time, over the chocolate, stirring from the center out in small, then progressively larger concentric circles. Add the white miso paste and stir. Once the temperature of the chocolate has reached 95°F–104°F (35°C–40°C), incorporate the butter, little by little, mixing after each addition. Pour into a shallow dish. Press a sheet of plastic film directly onto the surface of the ganache. Refrigerate until the texture is creamy. Spoon the ganache into a pastry bag fitted with a No. 11 plain tip. Turn the plain macaron shells, flat side up, on a sheet of cooking parchment. Fill each generously with the Jardin Zen ganache. Place a cube of the buttered Sweet Shortcrust pastry in the center of each, pressing down lightly. Pipe with a dot of the ganache. Cover the filled plain macarons with the chocolate macaron shells. Refrigerate for twenty-four hours. Remove the macarons from the refrigerator two hours before serving.

Note: "Liquefied" egg whites are egg whites that have been allowed to rest for several days to lose their elasticity. Simply place the egg whites in a bowl, cover with plastic film, pierce a few holes in the film and refrigerate for five to seven days.

sen
sual

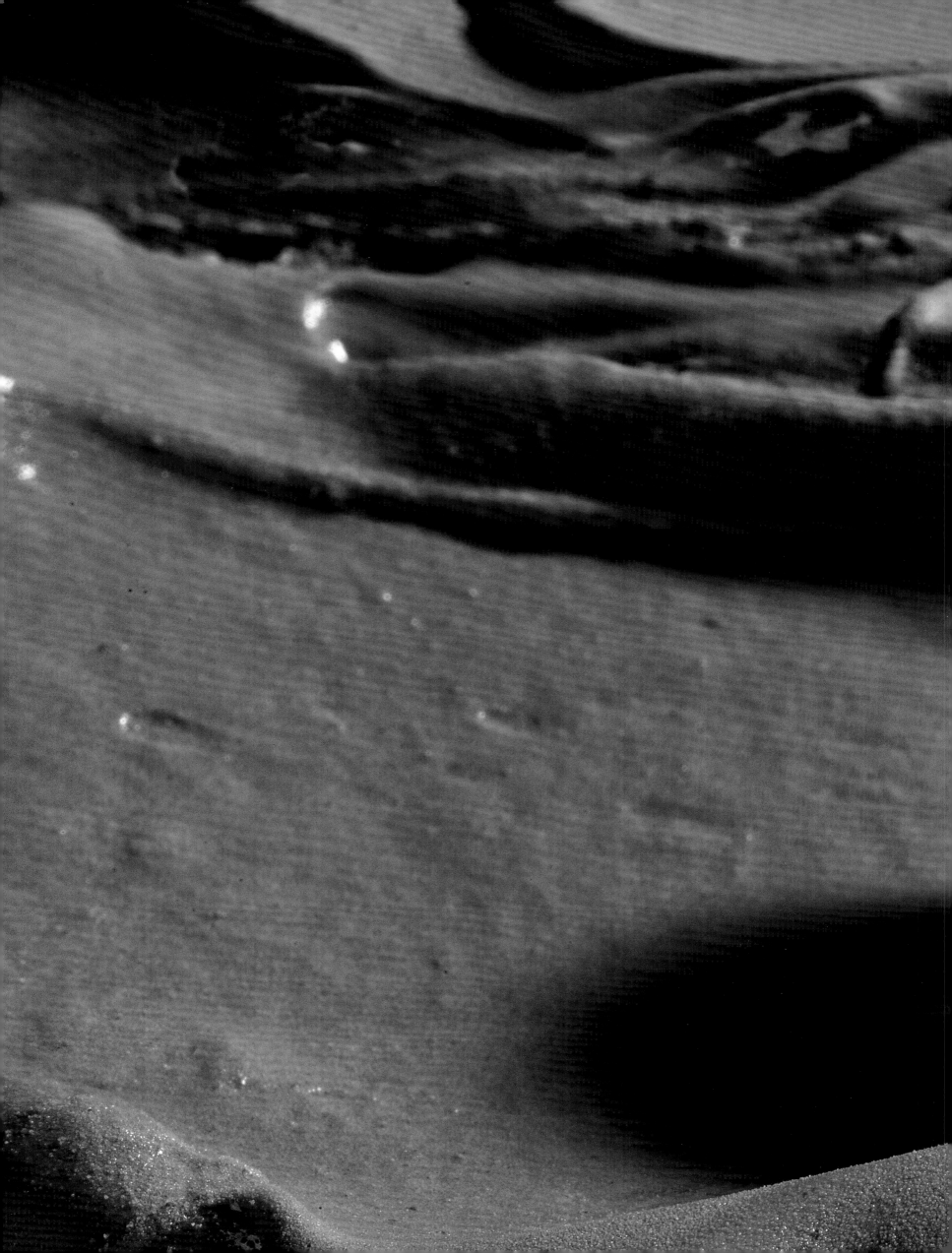

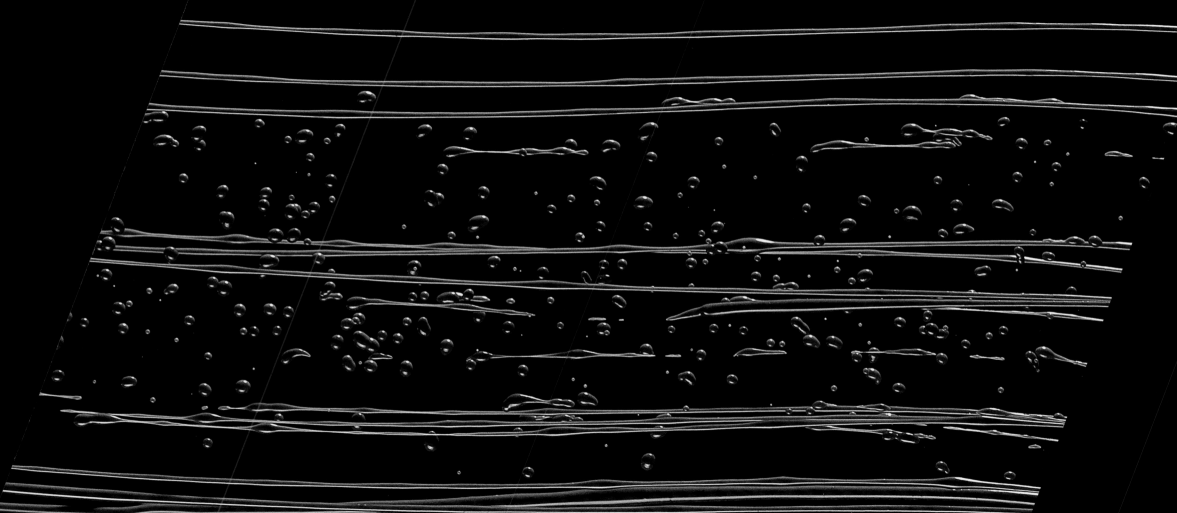

Baba Infiniment Chocolat

Infiniment Chocolat Baba

Serves 8

Ingredients:

Baba Dough:

2/3 oz. (18 g) fresh baker's yeast
(about 1 heaping tablespoon)
1/3 cup (3 oz./85 g) whole eggs
3/4 cup + 2 tablespoons (4 oz./110 g)
flour
2 1/2 tablespoons (1 oz./30 g)
superfine sugar
4 1/2 tablespoons (2 1/3 oz./65 g)
butter + butter for the mold
1/3 teaspoon (2 g) *Fleur de sel*,
preferably Guérande

Aged Dark Rum Imbibing Syrup:

1/2 tablespoon (1/6 oz./5 g) fresh
lemon zest
1 tablespoon (1/2 oz./12 g) fresh
orange zest
2 cups (17 2/3 oz./500 g) mineral
water
1 1/3 cup (8 3/4 oz./250 g) superfine
sugar
1 vanilla bean, preferably Madagascar
2 tablespoons (1 oz./25 g) pineapple
puree
1/4 cup (1 3/4 oz./50 g) aged
"agricultural" rum

Dark Chocolate Whipped Cream:

2 2/3 oz. (75 g) Guanaja 70% dark
chocolate (Valrhona)
1 1/2 cups (12 1/3 oz./350 g)
liquid cream
1 tablespoon + 3/4 teaspoon (15 g)
superfine sugar

Crunchy Dark Chocolate Cubes:

5 (3/4 oz./20 g) Gavottes Crepe
Dentelle cookies
1 oz. (30 g) Guanaja 70% dark
chocolate (Valrhona)
2 teaspoons (1/3 oz./10 g) butter
2 3/4 oz. (80 g) pure Italian hazelnut
paste (Valrhona)
2 tablespoons (3/4 oz./20 g) cocoa
nibs (Valrhona)

Chocolate Ganache:

5 1/4 oz. (150 g) Extra Noir 53% dark
chocolate (Valrhona)
2/3 cup (5 1/4 oz./150 g) liquid cream
1 1/2 tablespoons (1/3 oz./10 g)
sifted cocoa powder (Valrhona)

Dark Chocolate Glaze:

5 2/3 oz. (160 g) Araguani 72% dark
chocolate (Valrhona)
14 oz. (400 g) dark chocolate glaze
(Valrhona)
3 tablespoons (1 1/3 oz./40 g) grape
seed oil

Chocolate Sauce:

1 oz. (25 g) Guanaja 70% dark
chocolate (Valrhona)
1/4 cup (1 3/4 oz./50 g) mineral water
1 1/2 tablespoon (1/2 oz./15 g)
superfine sugar
3 1/2 tablespoons (3/4 oz./25 g)
heavy cream

Chocolate Icing:

3 1/2 oz. (100 g) Guanaja 70% dark
chocolate (Valrhona)
1/3 cup (2 3/4 oz./80 g) liquid cream
1 tablespoon + 1 teaspoon
(3/4 oz./20 g) butter
3 1/2 oz. (100 g) chocolate sauce
(see recipe above)

Finishing:

Aged "agricultural" rum
Gold leaf

————

Preparation Time:

25 mins. (2 days in advance);
15 mins. (1 day in advance);
40 mins. (the same day).
Rising Time for the dough:
about 2 h.

Cooking Time:

About 20 mins. (2 days in advance);
about 5 mins. (1 day in advance);
about 15 mins. (the same day).
Infusing time for the rum syrup:
overnight

Chilling Time:

2 h. + 2 h.

Preparation:

Two days in advance, prepare the baba dough:
In the bowl of a stand mixer fitted with a hook
attachment, combine the yeast crumbled into small
pieces and three-quarter of the eggs. Add the sifted
flour and sugar. Mix on first speed until the dough is well
mixed and smooth. Mix on second speed for
five minutes. Add the remaining eggs and continue
mixing until the dough pulls away from the sides of the
bowl. Cut the butter into small pieces and add to the
mixer, little by little, along with the *Fleur de sel*. Continue
mixing until the dough pulls away from the sides of the
bowl. Brush a 7-in. (18 cm) diameter savarin mold* with
butter. With your hands, carefully form the dough into
a ring with a hole in the center (like a doughnut) about
the size of the savarin mold and fit the dough evenly into
the mold. Tap the bottom of the mold lightly on the
work surface to eliminate any air bubbles.
Cover the mold with a kitchen towel and set aside
to rise in a warm area 83°F to 86°F (28°C to 30°C) for
about two hours, until the dough rises up to the edge
of the mold. Preheat the oven on convection setting
to 340°F (170°C/Gas Mark 5–6).
Place the baba in the oven and cook for about twenty
minutes. Remove the baba from the mold and set aside
to dry at room temperature for two days. The baba
should be very dry to absorb a maximum of syrup.

————

**One day in advance, prepare the rum syrup and the
dark chocolate whipped cream:** Using a vegetable
peeler, peel pieces of lemon and orange zest. In a small
saucepan, combine the lemon and orange zest with the
mineral water and sugar. Split the vanilla bean in half
lengthwise, scrape out the seeds, and add the seeds
and bean pod to the saucepan. Bring to a boil. Remove
from the heat. Add the pineapple puree and rum. Cover
and set aside to infuse overnight.
For the chocolate whipped cream, chop the chocolate
using a serrated knife, place it in a bowl over a bain-marie
of simmering water to melt. Meanwhile, bring the cream
and sugar to a boil in a saucepan. Pour the cream,
one-third at a time, over the melted chocolate, stirring
from the center out in small, then progressively larger
concentric circles. Press a piece of plastic film directly
onto the surface of the chocolate cream and refrigerate
overnight.

————

The same day, prepare the dark chocolate cubes:
Break the Gavottes cookies into crumbs. Chop the
chocolate using a serrated knife. Place it in a bowl with
the butter over a bain-marie of simmering water to melt.
Add the hazelnut paste, chocolate nibs and crushed
Gavottes cookies. Pour the mixture onto a sheet of
rhodoid** plastic and form into a neat square about

3/8 in. (1 cm) thick. Smooth the top with a spatula, refrigerate until firm. Cut into 3/8 in. (1 cm) cubes. Refrigerate until using.

___

Prepare a disk of dark chocolate whipped cream: Whip the chilled chocolate cream. Spoon into a pastry bag fitted with a plain No. 12 tip. Plunge a pastry ring, 5 1/2 in. in diameter by 1/2 in. high (14 cm x 1.5 cm), into hot water. Drain and dry the ring. Place the warm (not too hot) ring on a baking sheet and pipe the whipped chocolate cream into the ring. Smooth the surface with a spatula. Remove the pastry ring and place the cream in the freezer. Store the remaining chocolate whipped cream in the pastry bag in the refrigerator.

___

Prepare the chocolate ganache: Chop the chocolate using a serrated knife, place it in a bowl. Combine the cream and the cocoa powder in a saucepan, and bring to a boil. Pour the cream, one-third at a time, over the chocolate, stirring from the center out in small, then progressively larger concentric circles. Let cool.

Prepare the chocolate glaze: Chop the chocolate using a serrated knife, combine with the dark chocolate glaze in a bowl over a bain-marie of simmering water and melt to 113°F (45°C). Add the grape seed oil. Stir to mix well.

Prepare the chocolate sauce: Chop the chocolate using a serrated knife, combine in a saucepan with the mineral water, sugar and cream, and bring slowly to a boil. Cook gently until the chocolate coats the back of a spoon.

Prepare the chocolate icing: Chop the chocolate with a serrated knife and place it in a bowl. Bring the cream to a boil and pour it, one-third at a time, over the chocolate, stirring from the center out in small, then progressively larger concentric circles.
Mix with a hand blender until smooth. Let cool to 140°F (60°C), then incorporate the butter and 1/2 cup (100 g) of the chocolate sauce.

Assembling and finishing: Strain the imbibing syrup into a saucepan large enough to contain the baba. Heat to 122°F (50°C). Place the baba in the saucepan to soak for three minutes, spooning the syrup regularly over it. Turn the baba over in the syrup and let soak for another three minutes, spooning with the syrup. Remove the baba with a skimmer and place it on a rack over a rimmed baking sheet. Drizzle generously with the aged rum. Let drain and chill for two hours in the refrigerator.

___

In a bain-marie or microwave oven, heat, separately, the chocolate ganache, dark chocolate glaze and the chocolate icing.

___

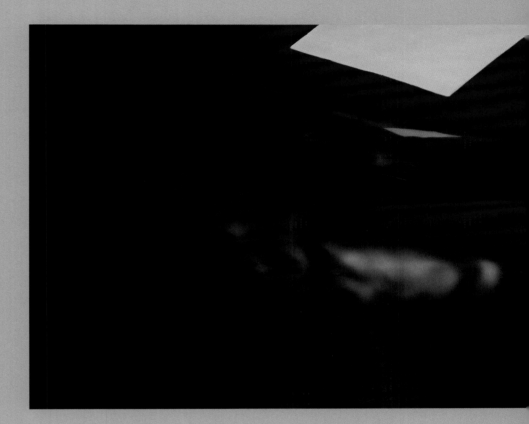

Pour the chocolate ganache over the baba on the rack set over the baking sheet. Let the ganache set for several minutes, then pour the dark chocolate glaze evenly over the baba. Let drain, then transfer the baba to a serving plate.

___

Place the frozen disk of dark chocolate whipped cream on a rack. Coat it with the chocolate icing. Let set.

___

Pipe the remaining, unfrozen dark chocolate whipped cream into the center of the baba, filling it about half full. Arrange the crisp chocolate cubes on top. Cover them with more chocolate whipped cream up to a little below the crown of the baba. Place the disk of frozen chocolate whipped cream on top and decorate with gold leaf. Refrigerate the baba for two hours before serving.

___

* A savarin mold is a ring shaped mold with a hole in the center.
** Transparent plastic celluloid used in pastry and confectionery.

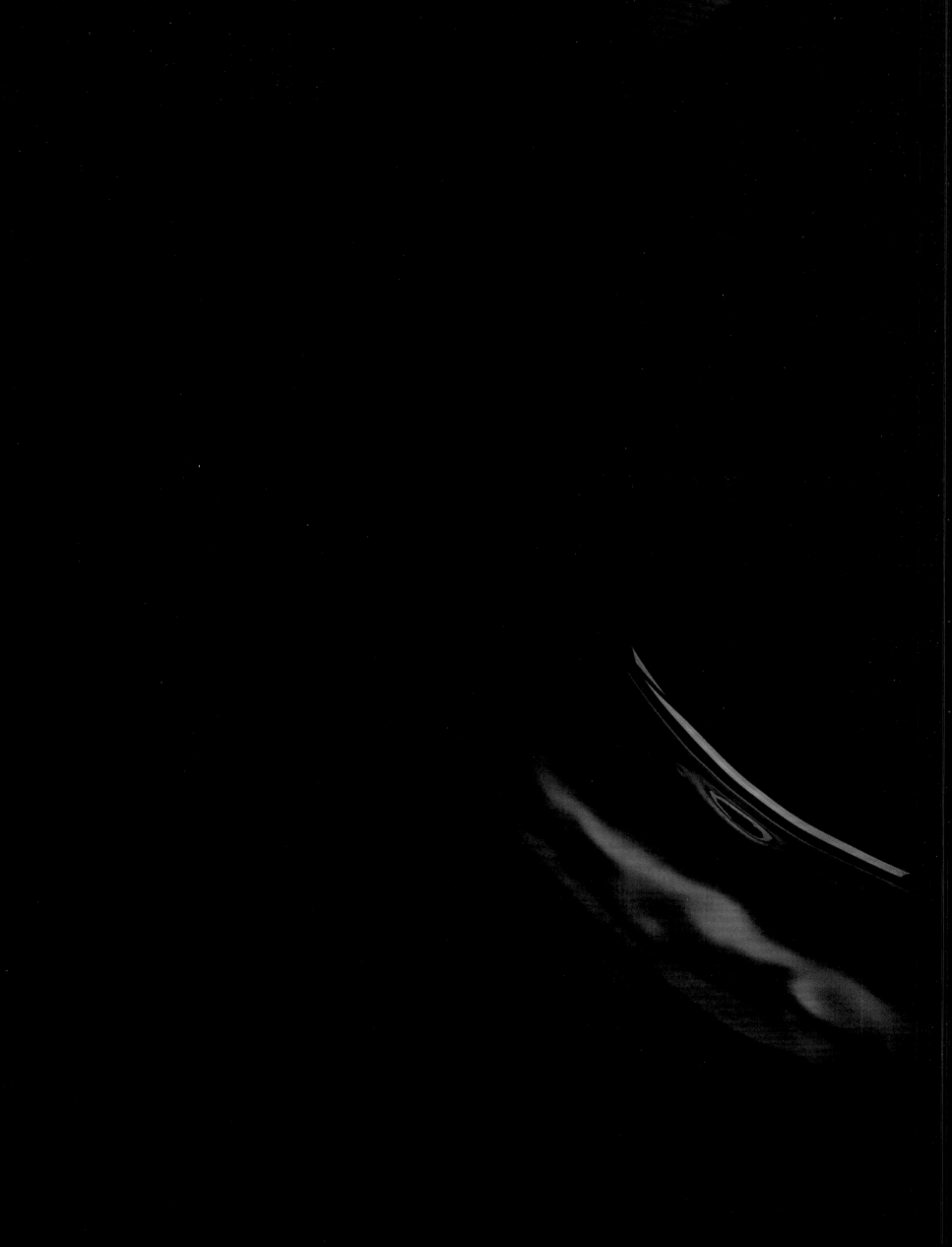

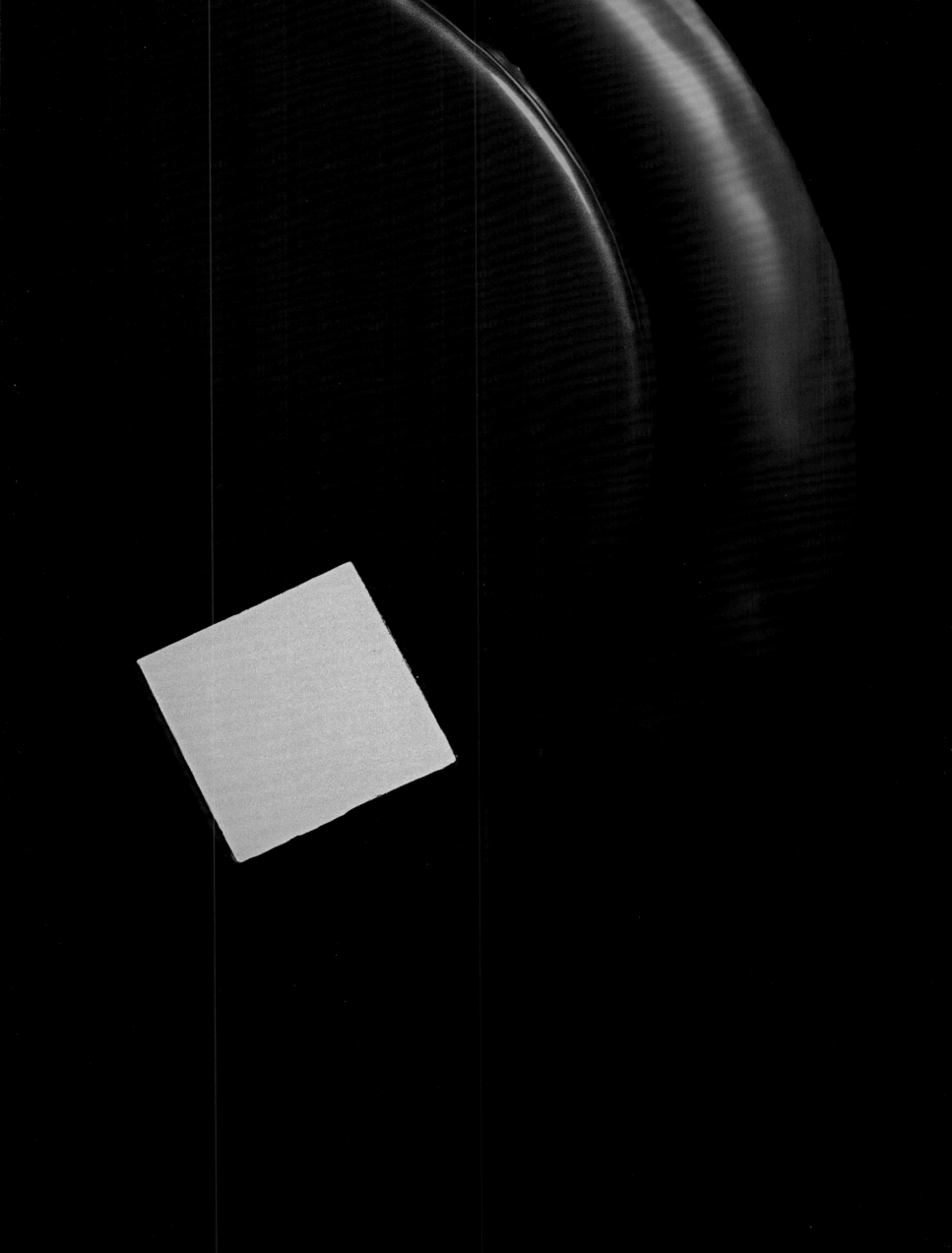

Chou Mogador
Mogador Puffs

Makes 10 puffs

Ingredients:

Milk Chocolate and Passion Fruit Whipped Cream:

About 20 passion fruit for
3/4 cup + 1 tablespoon (7 oz./200 g)
fresh passion fruit juice
8 3/4 oz. (250 g) Jivara 40% milk
chocolate (Valrhona) or milk
chocolate, 40% cocoa
1 2/3 cups (14 oz./400 g) liquid
cream

Dried Passion Fruit Seeds:

20 passion fruit
Water

Caramelized Vanilla Syrup:

3 teaspoons (1/3 oz./10 g) allspice
berries
2 Madagascar vanilla beans
1 1/2 cups (10 1/2 oz./300 g)
superfine sugar
14 thin slices fresh ginger
2 cups (17 2/3 oz./500 g) mineral
water
1 cup (10 1/2 oz./ (300 g) fresh
banana puree
2 3/4 tablespoons (1 1/2 oz./40 g)
aged "agricultural" rum
1/3 cup (2 3/4 oz./80 g) lemon juice

Caramelized Pineapple:

2 pineapples, ripe but firm (preferably
shipped by air, not boat)

Passion Fruit Crumble Mixture:

1/3 cup (1 1/2 oz./40 g) flour
3/4 oz. (20 g) dried passion fruit
seeds (obtained from the 20 passion
fruit above)
2 3/4 tablespoons (1 1/2 oz./40 g)
butter at room temperature
3 1/3 tablespoons (1 1/2 oz./40 g)
superfine sugar
3 drops yellow food coloring

Choux Pastry Dough:

7 tablespoons + 2 teaspoons
(3 3/4 oz./110 g) butter
1/2 cup (4 1/3 oz./125 g) mineral
water
1/2 cup (4 1/3 oz./125 g) whole milk
1 1/4 teaspoonS (5 g) superfine sugar
1 teaspoon (5 g) Fleur de sel,
preferably Guérande
1 cup + 2 tablespoons (5 oz./140 g)
flour
1 cup (8 3/4 oz./250 g) eggs (about
4 large eggs)

Milk Chocolate and Passion Fruit Cream:

6 oz. (175 g) Jivara 40% milk
chocolate (Valrhona) or milk
chocolate, 40% cocoa
4 1/2 tablespoons (2 2/3 oz./75 g)
egg yolks
1/3 cup (2 oz./60 g) superfine sugar
7 tablespoons (3 1/2 oz./100 g) fresh

passion fruit juice (obtained from the
fruit used to make the dried seeds)
1/4 cup (2 oz./55 g) whole milk
2/3 cup (5 1/2 oz./155 g) liquid cream

Mogador Chocolate Shortbread dough:

1 oz. (30 g) Jivara 40% milk
chocolate (Valrhona) or milk
chocolate, 40% cocoa
1/3 oz. (8 g) "crispy" passion fruit
(Sosa) or other freeze-dried passion
fruit
5 1/2 tablespoons (1 1/4 oz./35 g)
flour
2 1/2 teaspoons (6 g) cocoa powder
(Valrhona)
1/4 teaspoon (1 g) baking soda
2 tablespoons (1 oz./30 g) butter
2 tablespoons (3/4 oz./24 g) light
brown sugar
2 1/2 teaspoons (1/3 oz./10 g)
superfine sugar
1/4 teaspoon (1 g) Fleur de sel,
preferably Guérande
1/12 teaspoon (0.4 g) natural vanilla
extract without alcohol

Finishing:

Cocoa powder

Preparation Time:

45 mins. (1 day in advance);
1 h. (the same day).

Cooking Time:

About 4 h. (1 day in advance);
about 50 mins. (the same day).

Chilling Time:

2 h. + 30 mins. + 1 h.

Preparation:

A day in advance, prepare the milk chocolate and passion fruit whipped cream:
Cut the passion fruit in half. Scrape out the pulp and strain through a sieve to obtain 3/4 cup plus 1 1/2 tablespoons (7 oz./200 g) juice.
Chop the chocolate with a serrated knife and place it in a bowl over a bain-marie of simmering water to melt to 115°F (45°C). Bring the cream to a boil in saucepan and pour it, one-third at a time, over the chocolate, stirring from the center out in small, then progressively larger concentric circles. Add the passion fruit juice. Mix with a hand blender. Press a sheet of plastic film directly onto the surface of the cream and refrigerate overnight.

Also a day in advance, prepare the dried passion fruit seeds: Place a flat fine-mesh drum sieve over a bowl. Cut each passion fruit in half, and rub the cut side of the fruit against the mesh of the sieve to separate the seeds and juice. Collect the seeds, and set aside 3 1/2 oz. (100 g) of the juice for the milk chocolate and passion fruit cream. Bring water to a boil in a saucepan, add the passion fruit seeds and boil for three minutes. Drain the water from the seeds and repeat this blanching operation two or three times, until there is no pulp remaining on the seeds.
Preheat the oven on convection setting to 120°F (50°C/Gas Mark 1–2). Spread the passion fruit seeds out on a pastry sheet lined with cooking parchment. Place in the oven and let dry for three hours, or a little longer if necessary. Remove from the oven and let cool. Store in a well-sealed container overnight.

A day in advance, prepare the vanilla syrup and the caramelized pineapple: Place the allspice berries in a bowl or a mortar and crush with a pestle. Split the vanilla beans in half lengthwise, then in half again. Place the sugar in a saucepan and caramelize until it turns a deep amber color. Add the vanilla beans, ginger slices and the crushed allspice. Five seconds later, pour the mineral water onto the caramel. Bring to a boil, then add the banana puree, rum and lemon juice. Mix and remove from the heat.
Preheat the oven on convection setting to 445°F (230°C/Gas Mark 7–8). Slice off the two ends of the pineapple. Remove the skin with a serrated knife and use the tip of a paring knife to remove the "eyes." Cut the pineapple in quarters and remove the pithy center. Place the pineapple pieces in a baking dish deep enough for them to be completely submerged in the caramelized vanilla syrup. Pour in the caramelized syrup and place the baking dish in the oven for forty minutes, basting and turning the pineapple pieces on all sides every

ten minutes. Remove from the oven and let cool at room temperature, then refrigerate overnight.

The following day, prepare the passion fruit crumble mixture: Combine the flour and dried passion fruit seeds. Cut the butter into pieces and place it in the bowl of a mixer fitted with a plastic blade. Beat until the butter is creamy. Mix in the sugar and yellow coloring. Add the flour–passion fruit seed mixture and beat very rapidly just until the dough is well mixed. Turn the dough out onto a sheet of cooking parchment and roll out to a thickness of about 1/4 in. (1 cm). Press a sheet of plastic film directly onto the surface of the dough and refrigerate for two hours. Once chilled, roll the dough out on a lightly floured work surface to a thickness of between 1/8 and 1/16 in. Using a 2 1/2-in. (6 cm) diameter round cookie cutter, cut ten rounds of dough. Place on a baking sheet lined with cooking parchment and refrigerate for thirty minutes.

Prepare the choux pastry: Cut the butter into pieces. Combine the water, milk, sugar, *Fleur de sel* and butter pieces in a saucepan, and bring to a boil. Add the flour all at once, stirring briskly with a spatula until the mixture is smooth. Continue stirring for two to three minutes until the dough dries enough to pull away from the sides of the pan. Turn the mixture into a bowl and add the eggs, little by little, stirring briskly after each addition until well incorporated. The dough is ready when it forms a smooth ribbon.
Preheat the oven on convection setting to 410°F (210°C/Gas Mark 7). Spoon the dough into a pastry bag fitted with a No. 12 plain pastry tip. Line a pastry sheet with cooking parchment, and pipe out ten puffs of about 2 1/2 in. (6 cm) diameter, leaving about 2 in. between each. Place a round of the passion fruit crumble on top of each puff. Place the pastry sheet in the preheated oven and turn off the heat immediately for ten minutes. After ten minutes, turn the oven back on to 340°F (170°C/Gas Mark 5–6) and cook for an additional ten minutes. After ten minutes, open the oven door very slightly (place a spoon in the door to keep it ajar if necessary) and cook for an additional ten minutes. Remove from the oven and transfer the puffs to a pastry rack to cool.

Prepare the milk chocolate and passion fruit cream: Chop the chocolate with a serrated knife and place it in a bowl. Whisk the egg yolks and sugar together in a bowl. Heat the passion fruit juice to 120°F (50°C) and set aside. Bring the milk and cream to a boil in a saucepan, and pour, whisking, over the egg yolk–sugar mixture. Whisk in the warm passion fruit juice. Pour the mixture back into the saucepan and heat, whisking constantly, to 185°F (85°C). Pour this mixture, one-third

at a time, over the chocolate, stirring from the center out in small, then progressively larger concentric circles. Mix with a hand blender. Press a sheet of plastic film directly on the surface of the mixture and refrigerate.

Prepare the roasted pineapple cubes: Drain the pieces of pineapple for one hour. Cut into 1/3-in. (7 mm) cubes.

Prepare the Mogador chocolate shortbread dough: Chop the chocolate with a serrated knife. Crush the largest pieces of "crispy" passion fruit with a fork. Sift the flour, cocoa powder and baking soda together. Place the butter in the bowl of a mixer fitted with a paddle. Mix to soften the butter, then add the brown sugar, superfine sugar, *Fleur de sel* and vanilla, and combine. Incorporate the flour–cocoa–baking soda mixture, mixing very rapidly until the ingredients are just combined, without overworking. Turn the dough out onto a sheet of cooking parchment and roll out to a thickness of 1/3 in. (7 mm). Slide the dough onto a baking sheet and refrigerate for one hour. When chilled, cut the shortbread dough into 1/3-in. (7 mm) cubes and arrange on a baking sheet lined with cooking parchment, leaving about 1/2 in. (1.5 cm) between each. Preheat the oven on convection setting to 330°F (165°C/Gas Mark 5–6). Place in the oven and bake for ten minutes.

Assemble the Mogador puffs: Whip the cream prepared the previous day to light peaks. Spoon into a pastry bag fitted with a F8 star tip. Remove the chocolate and passion fruit cream from the refrigerator. Mix to a smooth texture and pour into a separate pastry bag fitted with a No. 10 plain tip.
Using a serrated knife, slice horizontally through the top one-third of each puff. Sprinkle the puff tops with a mist of cocoa powder and set aside. Fill the base of each puff with the chocolate–passion fruit cream. Add about 3/4 oz. (20 g) of roasted, caramelized pineapple cubes and five cubes of Mogador chocolate shortbread dough. Pipe a wave of chocolate whipped cream on each puff. Place two chocolate shortbread cubes in the center and three more cubes around each. Finish by piping a dot of chocolate whipped cream on top and place a top on each puff, pressing lightly. Refrigerate the puffs until serving.

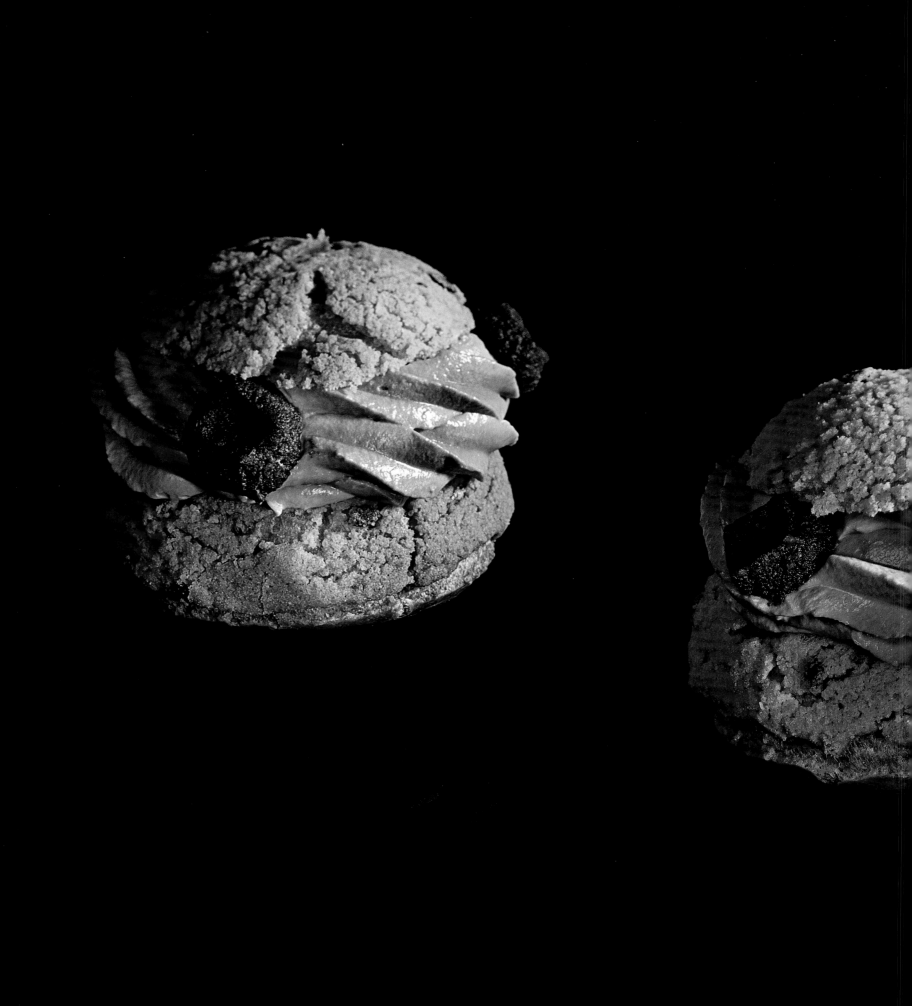

Galette Azur

Azur Galette

Serves 6 to 8

Ingredients:

Inverted Puff Pastry:

1 2/3 cupS (13 1/4 oz./375 g) butter
at room temperature
1 1/4 cup (5 1/3 oz./150 g) flour

+ for the *détrempe*:

1/2 cup (4 oz./110 g) butter
2/3 cup (5 1/3 oz./150 g) mineral water
1/2 teaspoon white vinegar
1 tablespoon (1/2 oz./15 g)
Fleur de sel, preferably Guérande
2 3/4 cups (12 1/3 oz./350 g) flour

Yuzu Pastry Cream:

1 1/3 tablespoons (1/3 oz./10 g) flour
1/4 cup (2 oz./60 g) whole milk
2 1/2 tablespoons (1 1/2 oz./40 g)
yuzu juice
1 1/2 tablespoons (1 oz./25 g)
egg yolk
1 tablespoon (1/2 oz./12 g)
superfine sugar
2 teaspoons (1/3 oz./10 g) butter

Yuzu Almond Cream:

1/2 cup (4 1/3 oz./125 g) butter at
room temperature
1 cup (4 1/3 oz./125 g) confectioners'
sugar
1 1/2 cups (4 1/3 oz./125 g) ground
almonds
1/3 cup (2 2/3 oz./75 g) whole eggs
2 1/2 tablespoons (1/2 oz./15 g)
flan powder or corn starch
5 1/3 oz. (150 g) Yuzu pastry cream
(see recipe above)
2 1/2 teaspoons (12 g) white rum

Chocolate and Yuzu Ganache:

5 1/3 oz. (150 g) Manjari 64%
chocolate (Valrhona)
5 oz. (140 g) Extra Amer 67% dark
chocolate (Valrhona)
1/3 cup (3 1/2 oz./100 g) egg yolks
1/4 cup (1 3/4 oz./50 g) superfine
sugar
2 3/4 tablespoons (1 1/2 oz./40 g)
liquid cream
1/4 cup (2 oz./60 g) yuzu juice
3 1/2 tablespoons (1 3/4 oz./50 g)
butter
1 3/4 oz. (50 g) candied yuzu rind

Egg Wash:

1 3/4 tablespoons (3/4 oz./25 g) egg
3/4 tablespoon (1/2 oz./12 g) egg yolk
1/2 teaspoon (2 g) superfine sugar
1 pinch (0.3 g) salt

Sugar Syrup:

1/4 cup (1 3/4 oz./50 g) superfine
sugar
3 tablespoons (45 g) mineral water

Finishing:

1 porcelain token
2/3 oz. (20 g) candied yuzu peel

Preparation Time:

15 mins. (1 day in advance);
45 mins. (the same day).

Chilling Time:

3 x 1 h. (1 day in advance);
about 4 h. 20 mins. (the same day).

Cooking Time:

About 1 h. 15 mins.

Preparation:

A day in advance, prepare the puff pastry: In the bowl
of a mixer or processor fitted with a plastic blade, mix
the 1 2/3 cups softened butter to a creamy texture.
Add the flour and mix until it forms a ball. Turn the
dough onto a sheet of cooking parchment and form into
a flat rectangle about 3/4 in. (2 cm) thick. Wrap in plastic
film. Let rest in the refrigerator for one hour. For the
détrempe, melt 1/2 cup (4 oz.) butter slowly over low
heat. Let cool. Combine the mineral water, vinegar
and salt in a mixing bowl. Add the flour and the cooled
melted butter. Combine, mixing as little as possible.
Form the dough into a flat square of about 3/4 in. (2 cm)
thick. Wrap in plastic film, let rest in the refrigerator for
one hour.
Dust the butter–flour rectangle with a little flour, roll out
lengthwise into a 1/3 in. thick sheet about twice as long
as the *détrempe*. Place the *détrempe* in the center
of the first sheet of dough. Fold the ends of the dough
over the *détrempe* square to enclose it completely
as within an envelope. Using a rolling pin, tap the
surface of the dough lightly, then roll out, rolling from
the center toward the ends, to form a rectangle three
times longer than the width. Fold the bottom quarter
of the dough up toward the center, then fold the top
quarter down toward the center so that the edges of the
two flaps meet. Fold the dough in half and place in the
refrigerator to chill for one hour. Once chilled, place
the dough square on a lightly floured work surface,
with the folded edge to your left, and repeat the same
rolling and folding procedure. Flatten the dough square
lightly, cover and refrigerate overnight.

The next day, weigh out 1 3/4 lb. (800 g) of the puff
pastry for the galette. (Reserve or freeze the remaining
dough for another use.) Place the square of puff pastry
on a lightly floured work surface with the folded edge to
your left. Roll out, as before, into a long rectangle. Fold
up the bottom third of the dough, then fold the top third
over the first third. Refrigerate to rest for thirty minutes.
Cut the dough square into two equal pieces. Roll out the
first piece of dough to a thickness of a little less than
1/8 in. (2 mm), lifting the dough sheet from time to time
with your hands to allow it to retract. Prepare an 11-in.
(28 cm) round of cardboard. Place the cardboard in
center of the dough and cut delicately around the edges
with the tip of a small knife. Place the dough round on
the cardboard. Proceed in the same manner for the
second piece of dough. Place the dough rounds on
two separate baking sheets and refrigerate for one hour.

Prepare the yuzu pastry cream: Sift the flour. In
separate saucepans, bring the milk to a boil and heat
the yuzu juice. Whisk the egg yolks with the sugar in

a bowl. Add the flour and mix. Pour the hot milk over the egg yolk–sugar–flour mixture, whisking constantly. Add the hot yuzu juice and pour the mixture back into the saucepan. Bring to a boil and cook for five minutes, stirring constantly. Remove from the heat. When the pastry cream cools to about 125°C (50°C), add the butter, stirring until melted.

Prepare the yuzu almond cream: In the bowl of a mixer fitted with a paddle attachment, beat the butter for several seconds, then add the confectioners' sugar, ground almonds, eggs and flan powder. Add 5 1/3 oz. (150 g) of the yuzu pastry cream and the rum. Mix on slow speed. Refrigerate until using.

Prepare the chocolate and yuzu ganache: Chop the chocolates with a serrated knife and place them in a bowl over a bain-marie of simmering water to melt. Whisk the egg yolks and sugar in a bowl. In separate saucepans, bring the cream and the yuzu juice to a boil. Pour the cream, one-third at a time, over the chocolate, stirring from the center out in small, then progressively larger concentric circles. Stir in the warm yuzu juice. Once the mixture has reached 125°F (50°C), add the butter, then incorporate the egg yolk–sugar mixture. Mix with a hand blender. Place a 10-in. pastry ring on a baking sheet lined with cooking parchment. Pour the chocolate yuzu ganache evenly into the pastry ring. Chop the candied yuzu rind coarsely and sprinkle evenly over the surface of the ganache. Insert the porcelain token in the ganache, pressing lightly. Refrigerate until just before serving.

To assemble the galette: Spoon the yuzu almond cream into a pastry bag without a tip. Turn the first round of puff pastry onto a baking sheet. Brush a little water in a ring of about 3/4 in. wide around the rim of the pastry round, taking care not to let the water drip over the edges. Pipe a spiral of the yuzu almond cream on the pastry round. Position the second round of puff pastry on top of the first, lining up the edges. Press gently but firmly around the edges to seal the two rounds of pastry together. Refrigerate for thirty minutes. Once chilled, decorate the rim of the galette using the back of the blade of a small knife, holding the dough gently between your finger and the knife, to make a knife mark about every 1/4 in. of the rim, while turning the galette.

Prepare the egg wash: Combine the egg, egg yolk, sugar and salt in a bowl, and mix with a hand blender. Brush uniformly over the surface of the galette, taking care not to let the egg wash drip over the edges. Refrigerate for twenty minutes, then brush with a second layer of egg wash. Using the back of the blade of a small knife, mark the top of the galette with parallel arc-shaped lines, spaced about 3/4 in. apart, starting in the center of the galette and moving out toward the edges. Prick the top of the galette in several places with the point of a knife. Refrigerate for two hours. Preheat the oven on convection setting to 445°F (230°C/Gas Mark 7–8). Brush a sheet of cooking parchment lightly with water and place on a baking sheet. Transfer the galette to the parchment lined with baking sheet, place in the oven and reduce the temperature immediately to 355°F (180°C/Gas Mark 6). Bake for about forty minutes.

Prepare the sugar syrup: Bring the water and sugar to a boil in a saucepan. Let cool. When the galette comes out of the oven, brush it with the sugar syrup. Decorate with the candied yuzu rind. Return the galette to the oven for two minutes to dry the sugar syrup. Remove the galette from the oven and transfer to a rack to cool. Once cooled, slice the galette in half horizontally, carefully removing and setting aside the top layer of puff pastry. Remove the pastry ring from the chilled chocolate yuzu ganache and place the chocolate disk in the center of the galette, on top of the almond cream. Place the top layer of puff pastry on top. Preheat the oven on convection setting to 355°F (180°C/Gas Mark 6). Place the galette in the oven to warm for ten minutes. Remove from the oven and let cool for ten to fifteen minutes before serving.

Soufflé Chocolat Aztec

Aztec Chocolate Soufflé

Makes 6 individual soufflés

Ingredients:

Homemade Orange Marmalade:

1 2/3 lb. (750 g) organic (untreated)
oranges
1 organic (untreated) lemon
2 2/3 cups (17 2/3 oz./500 g)
granulated sugar
2/3 cup (5 1/3 oz./150 g) mineral
water
1 pinch green cardamom powder
1 small knob, roughly 1/3 teaspoon
(1.5 g) fresh ginger

Balsamic Vinegar Reduction:

6 1/2 tablespoons (3 1/2 oz./100 g)
Modena balsamic vinegar

**Orange and Balsamic Vinegar
Sorbet:**

1 2/3 tablespoons (3/4 oz./25 g)
mineral water
1 1/2 tablespoonS (2/3 oz./18 g)
superfine sugar
1 cup (8 3/4 oz./250 g) fresh-
squeezed orange juice
4 1/2 oz. (125 g) homemade orange
marmalade (see recipe above)
4 tablespoons (2 1/2 oz./70 g)
reduced balsamic vinegar (see recipe
above)

Chocolate Soufflé:

Softened butter and granulated sugar
to line the 6 soufflé molds
7 oz. (200 g) Araguani 67% dark
chocolate (Valrhona)
5 1/3 oz. (150 g) pure cocoa paste
(Valrhona)
2 3/4 cups (21 oz./600 g) egg whites
1 1/4 cups (8 1/2 oz./240 g) superfine
sugar
6 tablespoons (4 1/2 oz./120g)
homemade orange marmalade (see
recipe above)

—

Preparation Time:

15 mins. (1 day in advance);
35 mins. (the same day).

Cooking Time:

About 1 h. (1 day in advance);
about 30 mins. (the same day).

Preparation:

A day in advance, prepare the orange marmalade:
Rinse the oranges and lemon in water. Place them
in a large, heavy saucepan with enough water to cover.
Bring to a boil and cook for thirty minutes. Drain the fruit
in a colander. Refresh the oranges and lemon under
a stream of cold water. Cut into thick rounds, discarding
the ends and seeds, then dice in small pieces,
collecting any juices that run off. Place the diced fruit
in the colander over a bowl, pouring the juices back over
the fruit and let drain twenty minutes.
Combine the sugar and mineral water in a saucepan,
and cook, monitoring the temperature with a
thermometer, to 239°F (115°C). Add the juices drained
from the fruit. Bring back to a boil and cook until the
juices reach 234°F (112°C). Add the diced fruit and
a generous pinch of cardamom. Using a Microplane
or fine grater, grate the ginger and add it to the fruit.
Bring to a boil and cook to 223°F (106°C). Pour into
a bowl and set aside at room temperature overnight.

**The following day, prepare the balsamic vinegar
reduction:** Pour the vinegar into a small saucepan
and cook until reduced by about one-third of its volume,
to obtain about 1/3 cup (70 g). Set aside to cool.

Prepare the orange and balsamic vinegar sorbet:
Combine the water and sugar, and bring to a boil.
Let cool. Add the freshly squeezed orange juice,
1/2 cup (4 1/2 oz./125 g) of the orange marmalade
and the balsamic vinegar reduction. Blend with a hand
mixer, then process in an ice cream or sorbet machine
according to the manufacturer's instructions.

Prepare the chocolate soufflés: Brush the bottom
and sides of the soufflé molds with butter. Sprinkle with
sugar. Invert the molds and tap lightly to remove any
excess sugar. Refrigerate.
Chop the chocolate and the cocoa paste with a serrated
knife, and place them in a bain-marie over simmering
water to melt to 113°F (45°C). Combine the egg whites
and the sugar in the bowl, and place them over
a bain-marie to heat until the egg white–sugar mixture
reaches 113°F (45°C). Beat the egg whites in a stand
mixer until smooth, firm and shiny, and until cooled
to 77°F (25°C). Add the melted chocolate. Beat at slow
speed for a few seconds, then remove the bowl from
the mixer and use a spatula to delicately fold in the
chocolate. Spoon the preparation into a pastry bag
without a tip.

Preheat the oven on convection setting to
355°F (180°C/Gas Mark 6). Place a baking sheet in
the oven to heat. Meanwhile, fill the bottom of each
soufflé mold with 1 to 1 1/2 tablespoons (20 g to 25 g)
of the marmalade. Divide the chocolate soufflé mixture
among the soufflé molds. Smooth the top of each
soufflé and run your finger around the inner rim
of each mold to remove about 1/4 in. (0.5 cm) of the
batter. Transfer the soufflé molds to the hot baking
sheet and place them in the oven to cook for ten to
twelve minutes.
Serve the soufflés hot, right out of the oven,
accompanied by the orange and balsamic vinegar
sorbet.

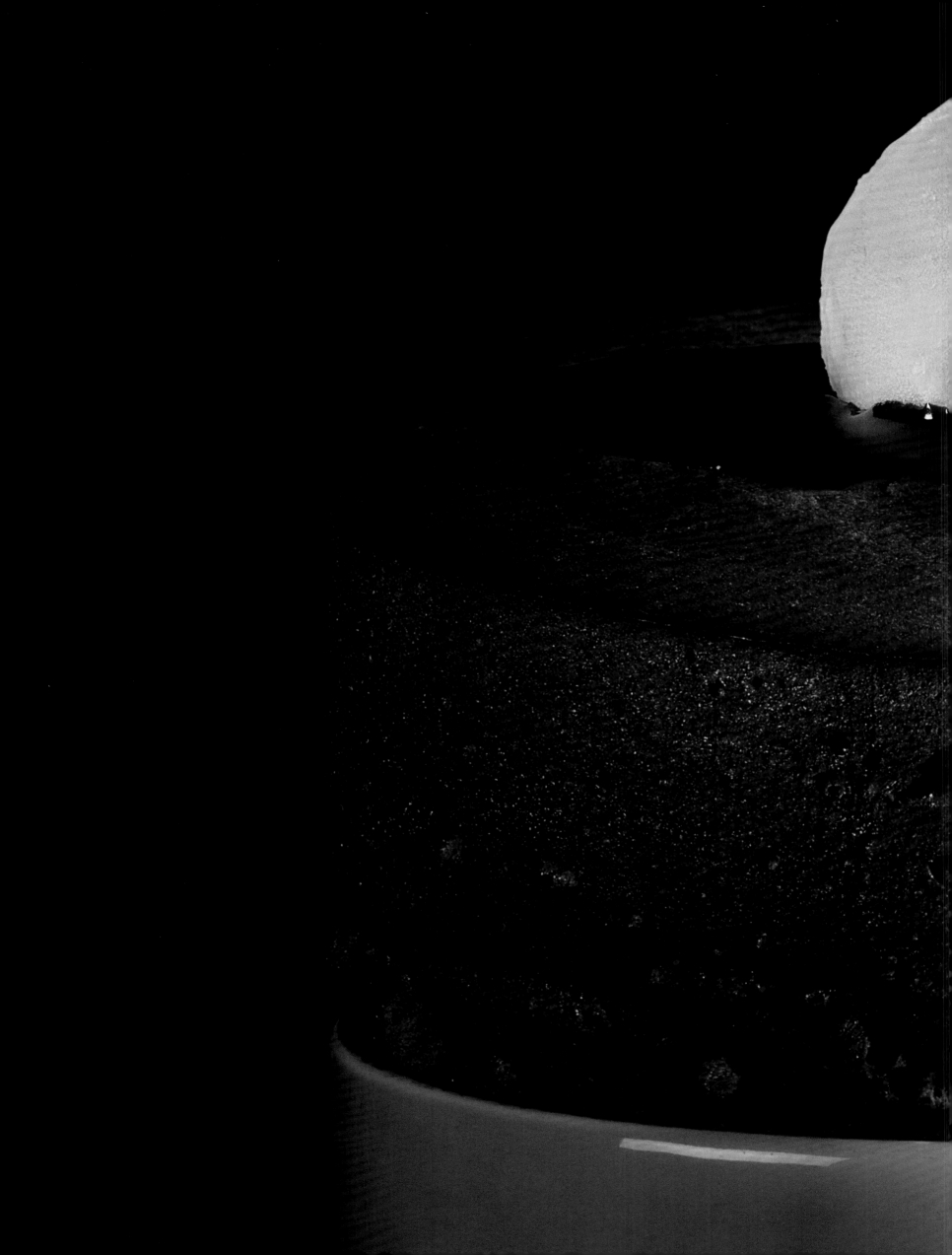

Tarte Mogador

Mogador Tart

Serves 6 to 8

Ingredients:

Caramelized Vanilla Syrup:

1 Madagascar vanilla bean
3/4 cup (5 1/4 oz./150 g) superfine
sugar
7 thin slices fresh ginger
1/2 tablespoon (5 g) allspice berries,
crushed
1 cup (8 3/4 oz./250 g) mineral water
1/2 cup (5 1/4 oz./150 g) fresh
banana puree
1 tablespoon + 1 teaspoon
(3/4 oz./20 g) aged "agricultural" rum
2 tablespoons + 2 teaspoons
(1 1/3 oz./40 g) lemon juice

Caramelized Pineapple:

1 pineapple, ripe but firm (preferably
one shipped by air, not boat)

Shortcrust Pastry:

1 cup (4 1/2 oz./125 g) flour
6 tablespoons (1 3/4 oz./50 g)
confectioners' sugar
5 tablespoons + 1/2 teaspoon
(2 2/3 oz./75 g) butter
2 3/4 tablespoons (15 g) ground
almonds
1/8 teaspoon (0.5 g) *Fleur de sel*,
preferably Guérande
1/8 teaspoon (0.5 g) vanilla powder
2 tablespoons (1 oz./30 g) whole egg

Flourless Chocolate Biscuit:

3 oz. (90 g) Extra Amer 67% dark
chocolate (Valrhona)
1/4 cup (1 1/4 oz./35 g)
confectioners' sugar
2 teaspoons (5 g) cocoa powder
(Valrhona)
5 tablespoons + 1/2 teaspoon
(2 2/3 oz./75 g) butter
2 tablespoons + 1 teaspoon
(1 1/3 oz./40 g) egg yolks
2 tablespoons (1 oz./30 g) whole egg
2/3 cup (5 1/4 oz./150 g) egg whites
1/4 cup (1 3/4 oz./50 g) superfine
sugar

Chocolate Macaron Batter:

2/3 cup (4 1/2 oz./130 g), or about 6
"liquefied" egg whites, divided (see
note)
1 cup + 2 1/2 tablespoons
(5 1/4 oz./150 g) confectioners' sugar
1 3/4 cups (5 1/4 oz./150 g) ground
almonds
2 oz. (60 g) pure cocoa paste
(Valrhona)
5 drops (0.2 g) carmine red food
coloring
2 1/2 tablespoons (1 1/4 oz./35 g)
mineral water
3/4 cup (5 1/4 oz./150 g) superfine
sugar

**Milk Chocolate and Passion
Fruit Ganache:**

3 tablespoons (1 1/2 oz./45 g) butter
at room temperature
8 2/3 oz. (245 g) Jivara 40% milk
chocolate (Valrhona) or
milk chocolate, 40% cocoa
About 10 passion fruit for 1/2 cup
(4 oz./115 g) passion fruit juice
1/3 oz. (10 g) candied ginger

Exotic Glaze:

2 1/2 teaspoons (10 g) pectin NH
1/2 cup (3 1/2 oz./100 g) superfine
sugar
5 fresh mint leaves
1 cup (8 3/4 oz./250 g) mineral water
Zest of 1/4 orange, untreated
Zest of 1/4 lemon, untreated
Pods of 2 used vanilla beans
2 teaspoons (10 g) lemon juice

Preparation Time:

2 mins. (5 days in advance;
35 mins. (1 day in advance);
2 h. 45 mins. (the same day).

Cooking Time:

50 mins. (1 day in advance);
about 1 h. (the same day).

Chilling Time:

4 h.

Resting Time:

30 mins.

Infusing Time:

30 mins.

Preparation:

Five days in advance, place the egg whites for the
chocolate macaron batter in a bowl, cover the bowl
tightly with plastic film, pierce a few holes in the film
and refrigerate to liquefy.

**A day in advance, prepare the caramelized vanilla
syrup and caramelized pineapple:** Split the vanilla
bean in half lengthwise, then in half again. Place the
sugar in a saucepan to melt and caramelize to a deep
amber color. Add the vanilla bean, ginger slices and the
crushed allspice. Five seconds later, add the mineral
water to the caramel. Bring to a boil, then add the
banana puree, rum and lemon juice. Mix and remove
from the heat.
Preheat the oven on convection setting to 445°F
(230°C/Gas Mark 7–8). Slice off the two ends of the
pineapple. Remove the skin, using a serrated knife,
and use the tip of a paring knife to remove the "eyes."
Cut the pineapple in quarters and remove the pithy core.
Place the pineapple pieces in a baking dish deep
enough for them to be completely submerged in the
caramelized vanilla syrup. Add the caramelized syrup
and place in the oven for forty minutes, basting and
turning the pineapple every ten minutes. Remove from
the oven and let cool at room temperature, then
refrigerate overnight.

The following day, prepare the shortcrust pastry:
Sift the flour and confectioners' sugar separately.
Cut the butter into cubes and place it in the bowl of
a mixer fitted with a plastic blade. Mix until the butter
is creamy. Add, in the following order, the sifted
confectioners' sugar, ground almonds, *Fleur de sel*,
vanilla, egg and sifted flour. Mix until the dough forms
a ball. Stop mixing immediately; the dough will lose
its flaky texture if overmixed. Wrap the dough in plastic
film, flatten lightly and refrigerate for at least four hours.

Prepare the flourless chocolate biscuit: Preheat
the oven on convection setting to 340°F (170°C/Gas
Mark 5–6). Chop the chocolate with a serrated knife and
place it in a bowl over a bain-marie of simmering water
to melt to 105°F (40°C). Sift the confectioners' sugar with
the cocoa powder. In the bowl of a mixer fitted with
a paddle, mix the butter to a creamy texture. Add the
sifted sugar–cocoa powder mixture and mix until just
combined, then add the melted chocolate gradually, one-
third at a time, taking care not to melt the butter. In
a bowl, whisk together the egg yolks with the whole egg.
In a second bowl, whisk the egg whites and superfine
sugar, beating to light peaks. Incorporate the eggs with
the chocolate mixture. Fold the whipped egg whites
delicately into the mixture, using a spatula to turn and lift

the mixture from the bottom up. Pour the mixture into a pastry bag fitted with a No. 9 plain tip. On a pastry sheet lined with cooking parchment, pipe the batter out in a 7 1/2-in. (19 cm) spiral. Place in the oven and bake for about twenty minutes. The biscuit should appear dry. Let cool on a pastry rack. (With the remaining dough, make small rectangular cookies for tea time.)

Prepare the chocolate macaron batter: Sift the confectioners' sugar and ground almonds together. Chop the cocoa paste with a serrated knife and place it in a bowl over a bain-marie of simmering water to melt to 122°F (50°C). Combine 1/3 cup (65 g) of liquefied egg whites with the carmine red food coloring. Pour onto the sifted almond powder–sugar mixture without mixing. Combine the water and sugar in a saucepan, and bring to a boil, monitoring the temperature with a thermometer. Meanwhile place the remaining 1/3 cup (65 g) of liquefied egg whites in the bowl of a mixer fitted with a wire whisk. Once the sugar syrup has reached 239°F (115°C), begin beating the egg whites on high speed. Once the syrup has reached 244°F (118°C), reduce the mixer speed to medium and begin pouring the syrup in a steady stream into the stiffly beaten egg whites. Continue beating until the mixture cools to 122°F (50°C). Using a spatula, fold the meringue mixture into the almond–sugar–egg white mixture. Add the melted cocoa paste, folding until the mixture loses a little volume. Spoon the batter into a pastry bag fitted with a No. 11 plain tip (1/2 in. diameter). Line baking sheets with cooking parchment and pipe out rounds of batter about 1 1/2 in. (3.5 cm) in diameter, spaced about 3/4 in. (2 cm) apart. Tap the baking sheets gently on a work surface covered with a kitchen towel to smooth the surface. Set aside at room temperature for at least thirty minutes to allow a "skin" to form. Preheat the oven on convection setting to 355°F (180°C/Gas Mark 6). Place the baking sheets in the oven and cook for twelve minutes, opening and closing the oven door quickly twice during the baking to release steam. Remove from the oven and slide the macaron shells on the cooking parchment onto the work surface.

Prepare the milk chocolate and passion fruit ganache: Cut the butter into cubes. Chop the chocolate with a serrated knife. Cut the passion fruit in half, scrape out the pulp and strain to collect 1/2 cup (115 g) juice. Place the chopped chocolate in a bowl over a bain-marie of simmering water and heat until about half melted. Bring the passion fruit juice to a boil and pour over the chocolate, stirring from the center out in small, then progressively larger concentric circles. Once the mixture has cooled to 140°F (60°C), incorporate the butter cubes, little by little. Mix until smooth. Pour the ganache into a shallow baking dish. Cover with a sheet

of plastic film, pressed directly onto the surface of the ganache. Refrigerate until the mixture has a creamy texture.

Prepare the exotic glaze: Combine the pectin and sugar in a bowl. Chop the mint leaves. In a saucepan, combine the mineral water, orange and lemon zests, and vanilla bean pods, and heat to 113°F (45°C). Stir in the pectin–sugar mixture. Bring to a boil and cook for three minutes. Remove from the heat, add the lemon juice and mint leaves. Set aside to infuse at room temperature for thirty minutes. Strain and refrigerate.

Drain the pieces of pineapple for one hour. Slice each piece of pineapple into matchstick pieces of a scant 1/4 in. (5 mm) thick.

Prepare the tart: Preheat the oven on convection setting to 340°F (170°C/Gas Mark 5–6). On a floured work surface, roll the shortcrust pastry out into a round of about 9 to 9 1/4 in. diameter. Place a tart ring of about 8 1/4 in. (21 cm) diameter by 3/4 in. (2 cm) high on a baking sheet lined with cooking parchment. Fit the dough round into the tart ring, trimming the rim evenly. Line the tart with a sheet of aluminum foil and fill with pie weights. Place in the oven and bake for about twenty-five minutes. Remove the aluminum foil and pie weights. The dough should be lightly and uniformly browned. If it seems a little pale, return the pie shell to the oven for several minutes. Let cool on a pastry rack before removing the tart ring.

Assembling and finishing: Cut the candied ginger into small cubes. Fill the tart shell about two-thirds full with the milk chocolate and passion fruit ganache. Sprinkle the candied ginger cubes generously over the ganache and cover with a second layer of milk chocolate and passion fruit ganache. Position the disk of flourless chocolate biscuit on top of the tart, pressing it lightly into the ganache until the ganache comes up a little around the edges and the biscuit is a little below the rim of the tart.

In a saucepan, heat the exotic glaze to 115°F (45°C). Arrange the sticks of pineapple in a dome on the chocolate biscuit. Brush with the warm glaze. Arrange the chocolate macaron shells in a crown around and between the pineapple dome. Store in the refrigerator and remove two hours before serving.

Note: "Liquefied" egg whites are egg whites that have been allowed to rest for several days to lose their elasticity. Simply place the egg whites in a bowl, cover with plastic film, pierce a few holes in the film, and refrigerate for five to seven days.

Macaron Mogador

Mogador Macaron

Makes about 72 macarons (or about 144 shells)

Ingredients:

Macaron Shell Batter:

1 cup (7 2/3 oz./220 g) or about 8 "liquefied" egg whites, divided (see note)
3 1/2 cups (10 1/2 oz./300 g) ground almonds
2 1/3 cups (10 1/2 oz./300 g) confectioners' sugar
5 teaspoons (5 g) lemon yellow food coloring
1/2 teaspoon (about 0.5 g) red food coloring
1 1/2 cups (10 1/2 oz./300 g) superfine sugar
1/3 cup (2 2/3 oz./75 g) mineral water

Passion Fruit and Milk Chocolate Ganache:

7 tablespoons (3 1/2 oz./100 g) butter at room temperature
19 1/2 oz. (550 g) Jivara 40% milk chocolate (Valrhona) or milk chocolate, 40% cocoa
10 passion fruit for about 1 cup (8 3/4 oz./250 g) passion fruit juice

Finishing:

Cocoa powder

Preparation Time:

2 mins. (5 days in advance);
1 h. (the same day).

Cooking Time:

About 25 mins.

Resting Time:

30 mins.

Chilling Time:

2 h. + 24 h.

Preparation:

Five days in advance, place the egg whites for the macaron shells in a bowl, cover the bowl tightly with plastic film, pierce a few holes in the film and refrigerate to liquefy.

One day in advance, prepare the batter for the macaron shells: Sift the ground almonds and the confectioners' sugar together in a bowl. Combine 1/2 cup (110 g) of liquefied egg whites with the food colorings. Pour onto the sifted almond powder-sugar mixture without mixing. Combine the sugar and water in a saucepan, and bring to a boil, monitoring the temperature with a thermometer. Meanwhile place the remaining 1/2 cup (110 g) of liquefied egg whites in the bowl of a stand mixer fitted with a wire whisk. Once the sugar syrup has reached 239°F (115°C), begin beating the egg whites on high speed. Once the syrup has reached 244°F (118°C), reduce the mixer speed to medium and begin pouring the syrup in a steady stream into the egg whites. Continue beating until the mixture cools to 122°F (50°C). Using a spatula, fold the meringue mixture into the almond–sugar–egg white mixture. Spoon the batter into a pastry bag fitted with a No. 11 (1/2 in. diameter) plain pastry tip. Line baking sheets with cooking parchment and pipe out rounds of batter about 1 1/2 in. (3.5 cm) in diameter, spaced about 3/4 in. apart. Tap the baking sheets gently on a work surface covered with a kitchen towel to smooth the surface. Set aside at room temperature for at least thirty minutes to allow a "skin" to form.
Preheat the oven on convection setting to 355°F (180°C/Gas Mark 6). Place the baking sheets in the oven and bake for twelve minutes, opening and closing the oven door quickly twice during the baking to release steam. Remove from the oven and slide the macaron shells onto the work surface.

Prepare the passion fruit and milk chocolate ganache: Cut the butter into cubes. Chop the chocolate using a serrated knife and place it in a bowl. Cut each passion fruit in half, scrape out the pulp and rub through a drum sieve set over a small saucepan to produce about a cup (8 3/4 oz./250 g) of juice. Bring the passion fruit juice to a boil in a saucepan. Place half of the chocolate in a bowl over a bain-marie of simmering water to melt. Pour the melted chocolate, one-third at a time, over the remaining chocolate, stirring from the center out in small, then progressively larger concentric circles. Once the mixture has reached 140°F (60°C), incorporate, little by little, the cubes of butter. Stir until the ganache is smooth. Pour into a shallow dish. Press a sheet of plastic film directly onto the surface of the chocolate cream and refrigerate until the texture is creamy.Spoon the ganache into a pastry bag fitted with a No. 11 plain pastry tip. Turn half of the macaron shells over, flat side up, on the work surface and pipe the ganache generously onto each shell. Cover each with a second macaron shell. Refrigerate for twenty-four hours.
The following day, remove the macarons from the refrigerator two hours before serving.

Note: "Liquefied" egg whites are egg whites that have been allowed to rest for several days to lose their elasticity. Simply place the egg whites in a bowl, cover with plastic film, pierce a few holes in the film, and refrigerate for five to seven days.

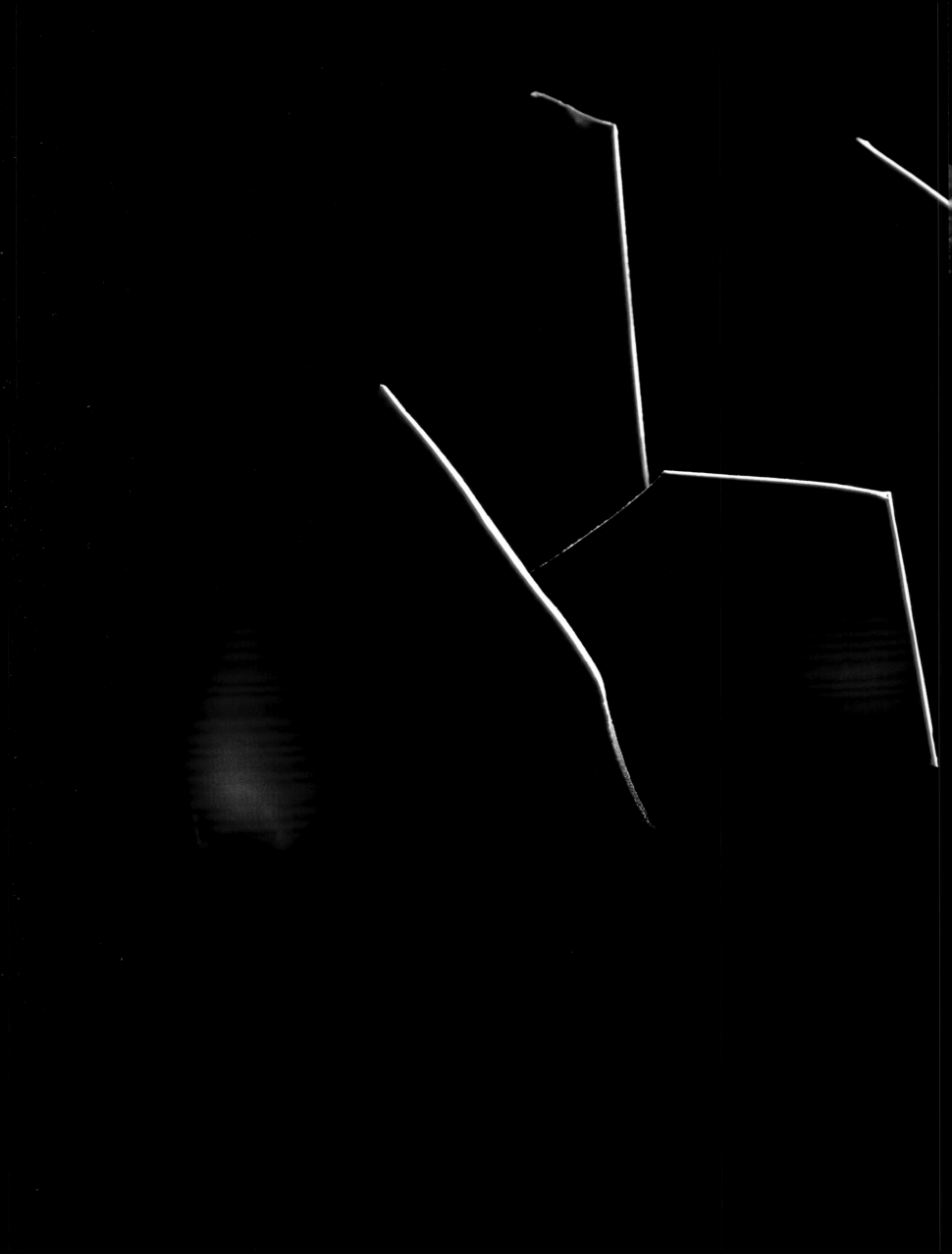

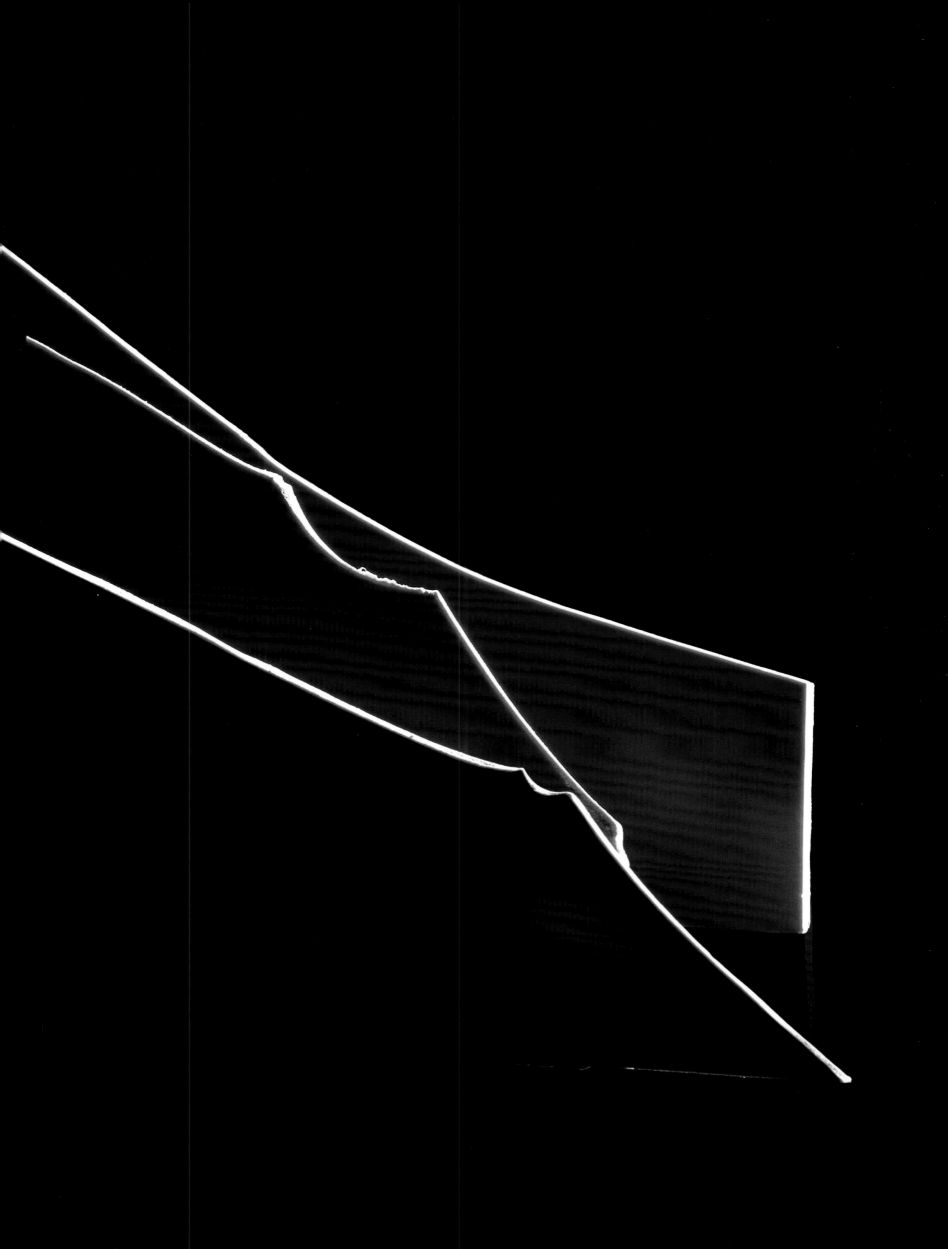

Formidable Mousse Minute au Chocolat

Wonderful Instant Chocolate Mousse

Serves 8

Ingredients:

Dark Chocolate with *fleur de sel* layer:

1 1/2 teaspoons (6 g) *Fleur de sel*, preferably Guérande
10 1/2 oz. (300 g) Araguani 72% dark chocolate (Valrhona)

Homemade Hazelnut Praline:

2 cups (11 1/3 oz./320 g) hazelnuts, divided
3 vanilla beans
14 1/4 tablespoons (6 oz./170 g) superfine sugar
1/4 cup (1 3/4 oz./50 g) mineral water

Infiniment Praliné Noisette Praline:

1/4 cup (1 3/4 oz./50 g) mineral water
7 oz. (200 g) homemade hazelnut praline (see recipe above)
3 1/2 oz. (100 g) pure hazelnut paste

Crunchy Hazelnut Praline Cubes:

2 oz. (60 g) milk chocolate
1 tablespoon + 2 teaspoons (3/4 oz./25 g) butter
4 1/4 oz. (120 g) Praliné Fruité (Valrhona)
4 1/4 oz. (120 g) pure hazelnut paste
4 oz. (115 g) golden sprinkles (Valrhona)

Cold Chocolate Soup:

3 1/2 oz. (100 g) Ampamakia 68% dark chocolate (Valrhona)
1 cup (8 3/4 oz./250 g) mineral water
2 1/2 teaspoons (1/3 oz./10 g) superfine sugar
1/12 teaspoon (0.5 g) *Fleur de sel*, preferably Guérande

Genova Bread:

Butter and flour for the mold
1/2 cup (2 oz./60 g) flour
1/2 teaspoon (2 g) baking powder
8 3/4 oz. (250 g) almond paste
3/4 cup (6 1/2 oz./185 g) whole eggs
1/2 tablespoon (8 g) Ricard, or other anise-flavored liqueur
5 tablespoons (2 2/3 oz./75 g) butter

Instant Chocolate Mousse:

7 oz. (200 g) Ampamakia 68% dark chocolate (Valrhona)
1 3/4 cups (14 oz./400 g) liquid cream
3/4 cup + 1 tablespoon (7 oz./200 g) whole milk

Preparation Time:

10 mins. (1 day in advance);
about 40 mins. (the same day).

Cooking Time:

A few minutes (1 day in advance);
about 50 mins. (the same day).

Preparation:

One day in advance, prepare the dark chocolate with *Fleur de sel:* Crush the *Fleur de sel* with a rolling pin. Sift through a fine sieve. Chop the chocolate with a serrated knife and place it in a bowl over a bain-marie of simmering water to melt, stirring gently with a wooden spoon until the temperature of the chocolate reaches 130°F (55°C). Remove the bowl immediately from the bain-marie and place it in a bowl of cold water with four or five ice cubes. Stir the chocolate from time to time, scraping it from the sides of the bowl as it begins to set. Once the chocolate has cooled to 80°F (27°C), return the bowl to the bain-marie to warm slightly, monitoring the temperature carefully with a thermometer until the chocolate warms to between 88°F and 90°F (31°C–32°C). Stir in the sifted *Fleur de sel*. Place a sheet of rhodoid plastic* on a work surface. Pour the chocolate onto the plastic and spread out into a thin, even layer with a spatula. Cover the chocolate with a second sheet of rhodoid and top with light weights to keep the chocolate flat. Refrigerate until the following day.

—

The following day, prepare the homemade hazelnut praline: Preheat the oven to 300°F (150°C/Gas Mark 3). Spread the hazelnuts on a baking sheet lined with cooking parchment and place in the oven to toast for fifteen minutes. Turn the hot hazelnuts into a drum sieve and rub against the sieve to remove the skins. Chop the hazelnuts finely. Place 1 1/2 cups of the chopped warm hazelnuts in a saucepan with the vanilla beans split in half lengthwise and scraped. (Reserve the remaining 1/2 cup hazelnuts for the hazelnut cubes.) In a second saucepan, combine the sugar and water, and cook to 250°F (121°C). Pour the sugar syrup over the hazelnuts and vanilla, and cook, stirring constantly, until well caramelized. Pour the mixture immediately onto a baking sheet and let cool. Coarsely chop the pieces, then grind in a food processor to obtain nearly a paste but with some pieces remaining.

—

Prepare the Infiniment Praliné Noisette praline: Heat the mineral water. Combine 7 oz. (200 g) of the homemade praline with the pure hazelnut paste in the bowl of a food processor fitted with a paddle attachment. Process to mix, then pour in the hot water and continue processing until smooth and well mixed.

—

Prepare the hazelnut praline cubes: Chop the chocolate with a serrated knife and place it in a bowl with the butter over a bain-marie. Combine the Praliné Fruité and hazelnut paste with the melted chocolate and butter. Stir in the golden sprinkles and the remaining 1/2 cup chopped, roasted hazelnuts reserved above. Pour the mixture into a shallow baking dish lined with plastic film and spread into an even 1/3 in. thick layer, smoothing the surface with a spatula. Refrigerate.

Prepare the cold chocolate soup: Chop the chocolate with a serrated knife and place it in a bowl. Combine the mineral water, sugar and *Fleur de sel* in a saucepan, and bring to a boil. Pour syrup, one-third at a time, over the chocolate, stirring from the center out in small, then progressively larger concentric circles. Refrigerate.

Prepare the Genova bread: Brush a round mold, about 7 in. (18 cm) diameter by 1 in. (2.5 cm) deep, with butter, dust with flour and invert to tap out excess flour. Sift the flour and baking powder together. Place the almond paste in the bowl of a mixer fitted with a paddle attachment, mix on slow speed, incorporating the eggs little by little. Remove the bowl and place it over a bain-marie of simmering water to heat to 130°F (55°C). Stir in the Ricard or anise liqueur, return the bowl to the mixer, replacing the paddle with the whisk attachment. Whisk until the texture is foamy, light and cooled. Preheat the oven on convection setting to 355°F (180°C/Gas Mark 6). Melt the butter. Remove the mixer bowl and fold the flour–baking powder mixture into the almond paste mixture, delicately lifting and turning the mixture with a rubber spatula, starting from the center and turning the bowl at the same time. Add the melted butter little by little, folding in the same manner. Pour 14 oz. (400 g) of the batter into the mold. Place in the oven to bake for thirty minutes. Insert the blade of a knife in the center of the cake to check doneness. If the blade comes out clean, the cake is ready. Unmold the cake onto a pastry rack lined with cooking parchment and let cool.

Prepare the instant chocolate mousse: Chop the chocolate with a serrated knife and place it in a bowl to melt over a bain-marie of simmering water. Bring the cream and milk to a boil in a saucepan, and pour, one-third at a time, over the chocolate, stirring from the center out in small, then progressively larger concentric circles. Mix using a hand blender and pour into a siphon. Keep at room temperature.

Just before serving, spread a spoonful of the Infiniment Praliné Noisette praline on a serving plate. With the siphon, pipe out a little of the chocolate mousse. Sprinkle with the crunchy hazelnut praline cubes. Top with more chocolate mousse and a few more hazelnut praline cubes. Serve the Genova bread separately, sliced and accompanied by a small bowl of the cold chocolate soup.

* Transparent plastic celluloid used in pastry and confectionery.

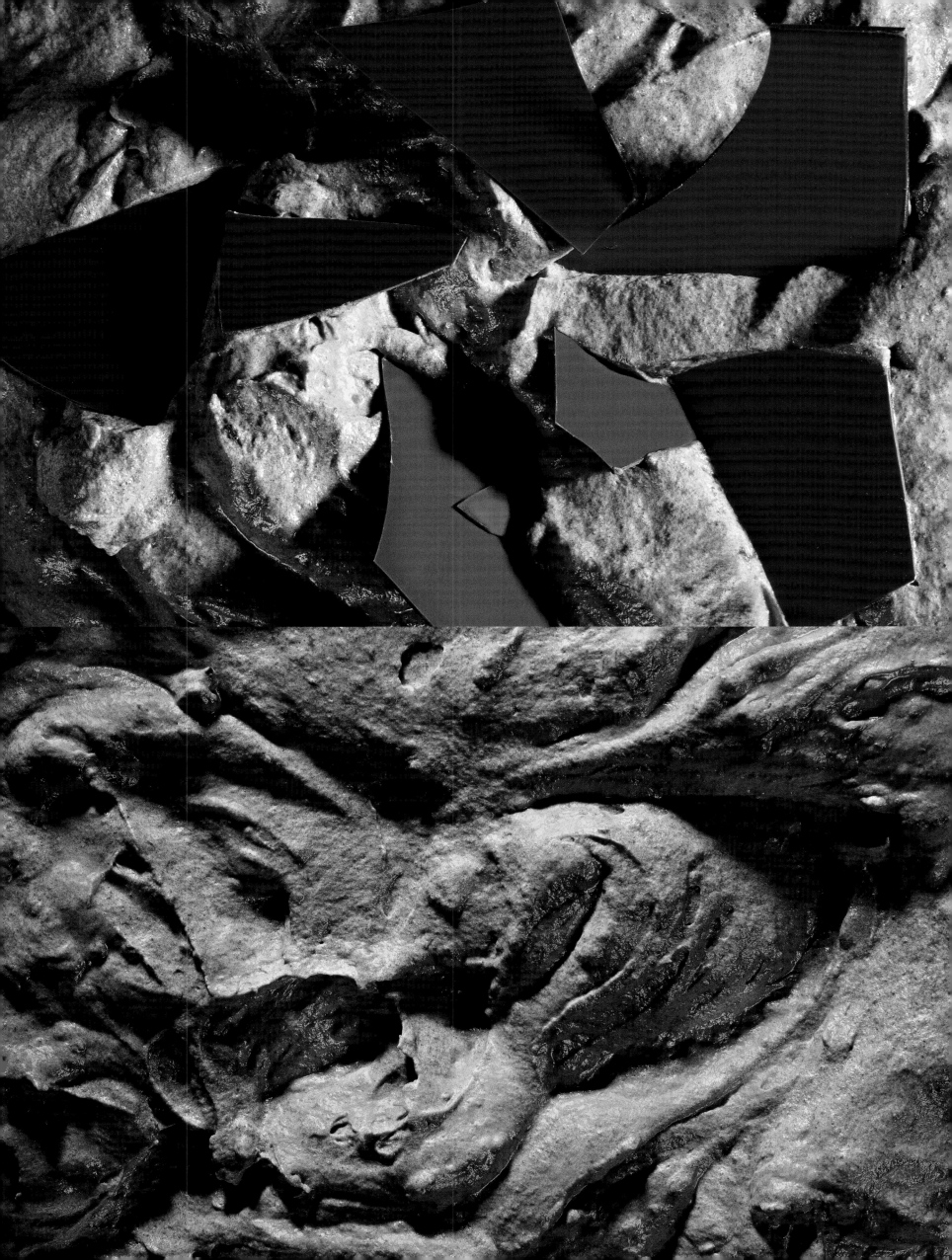

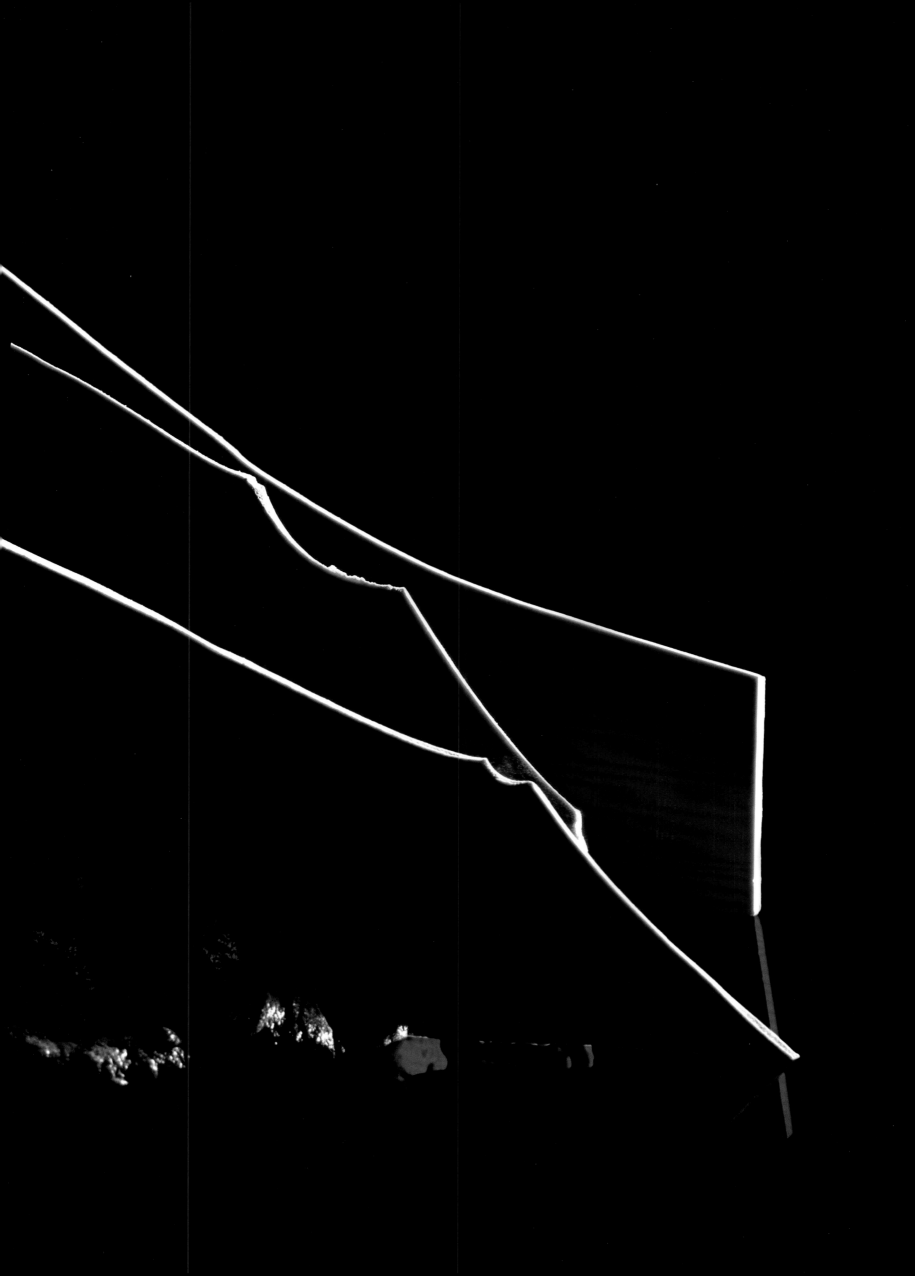

voluptuous

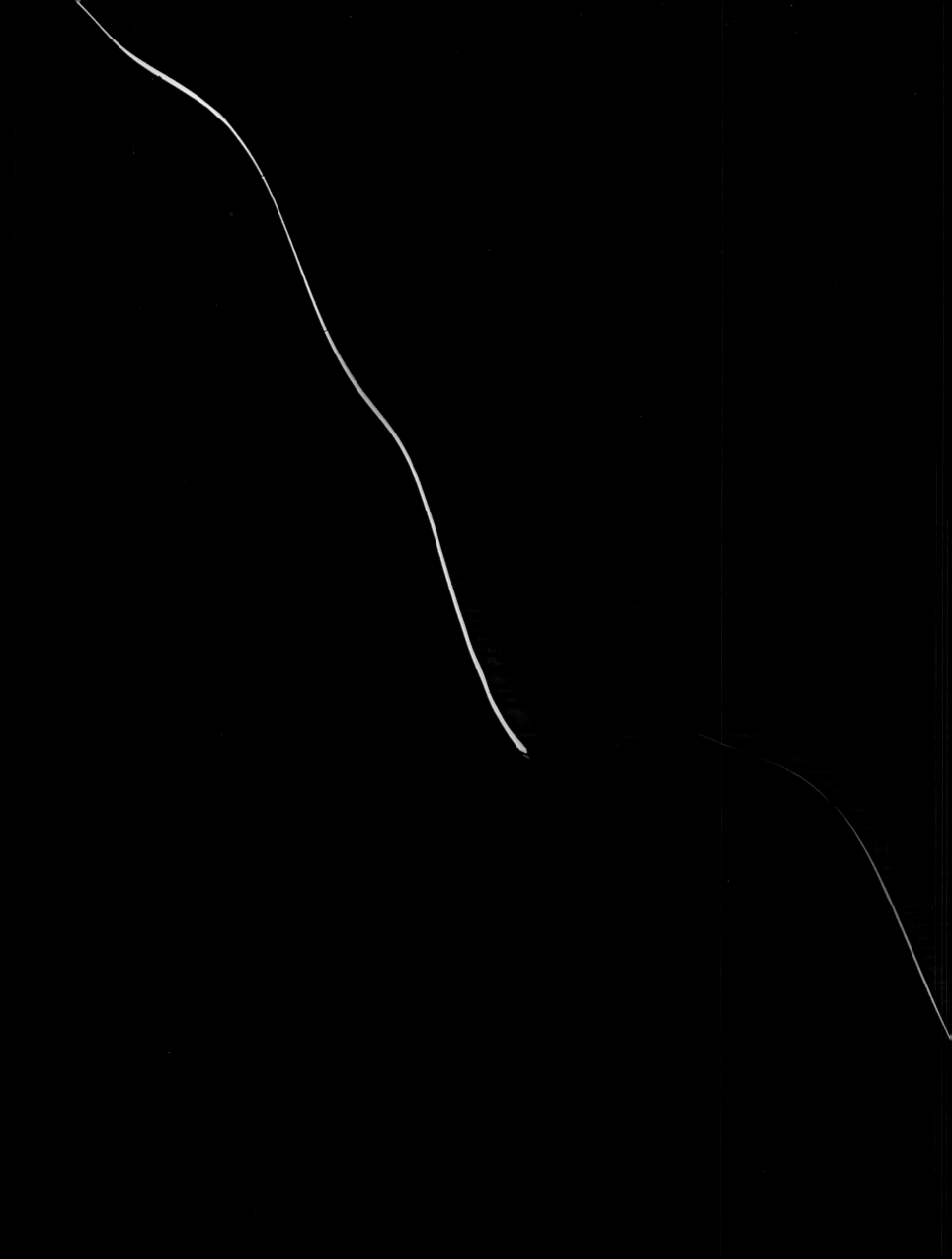

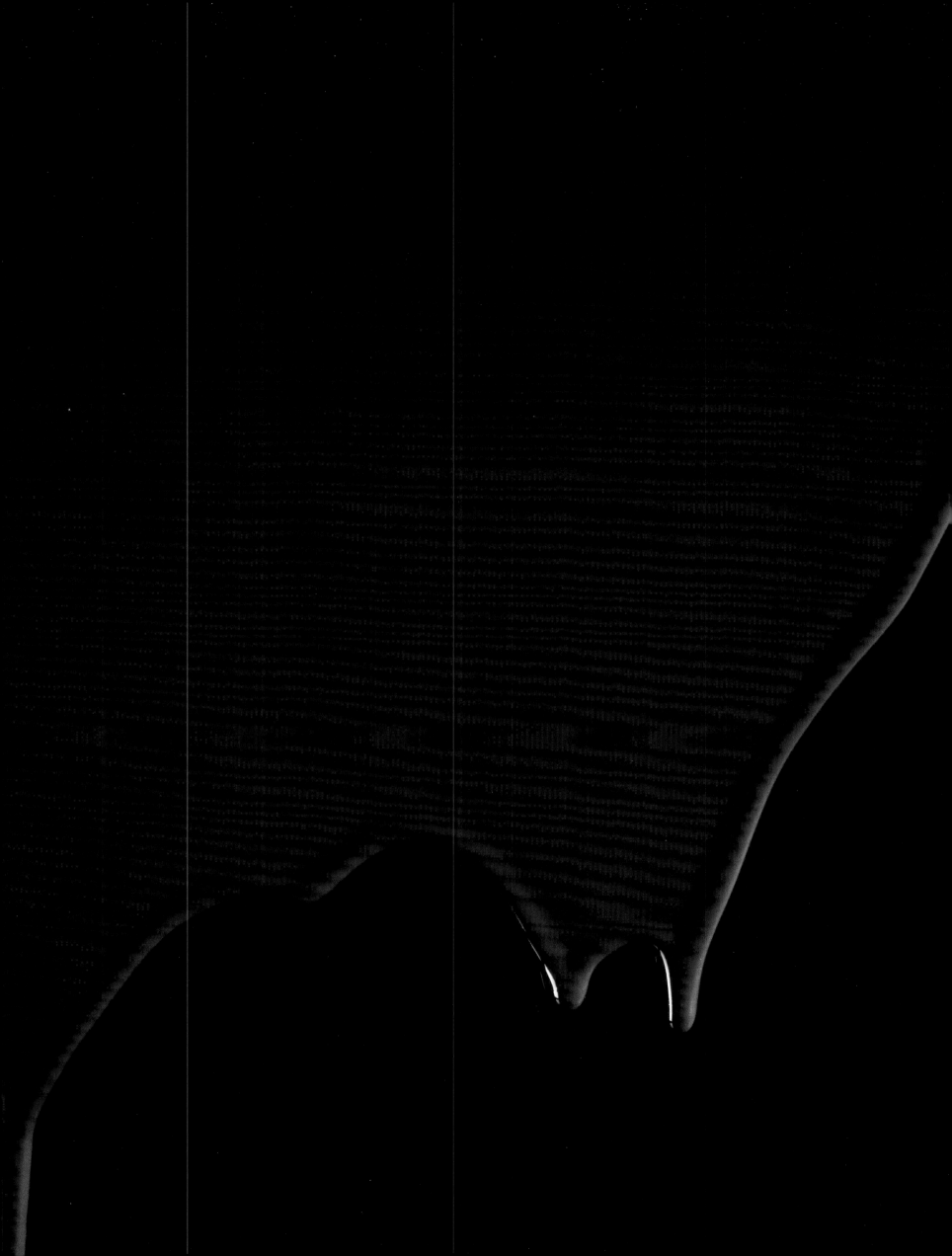

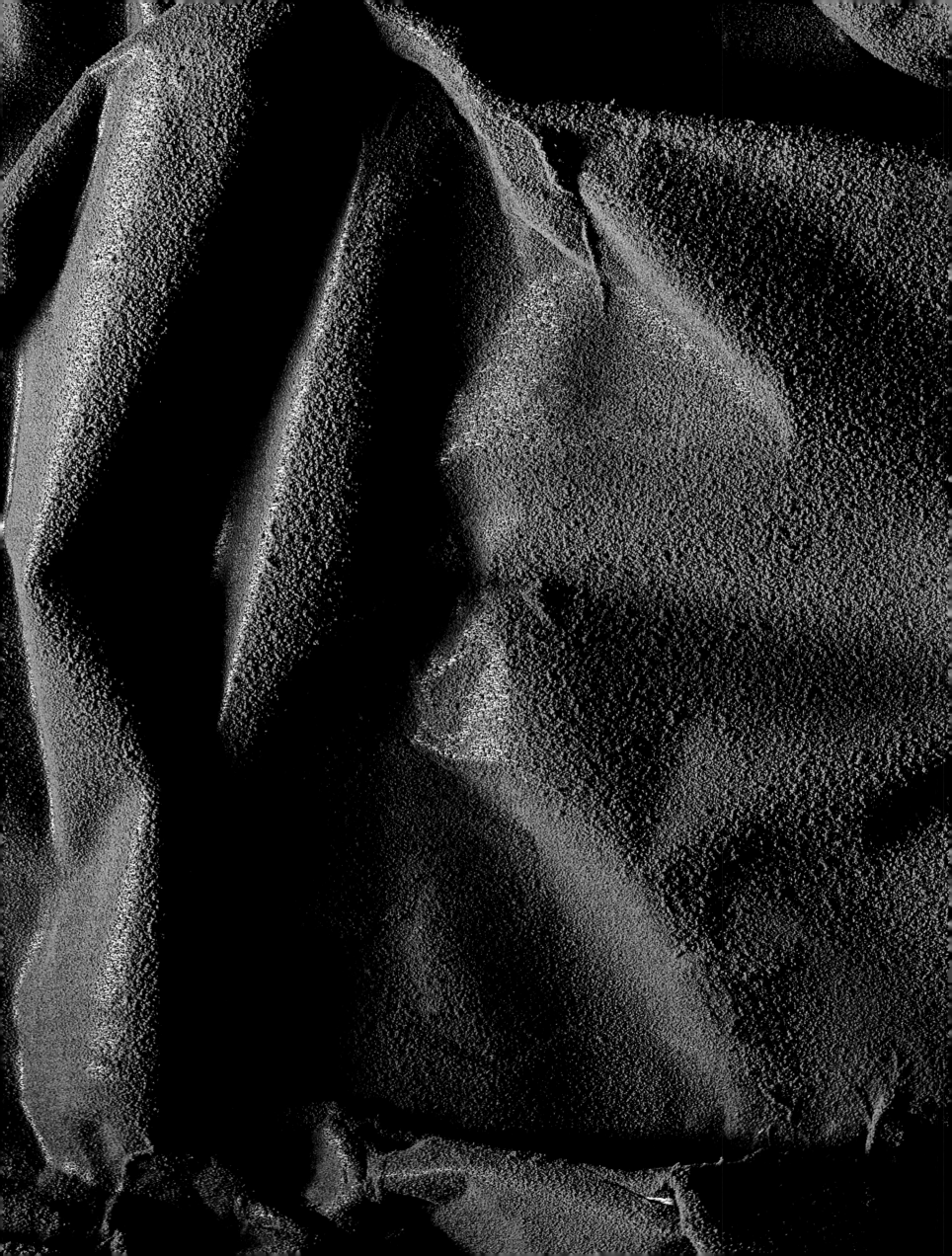

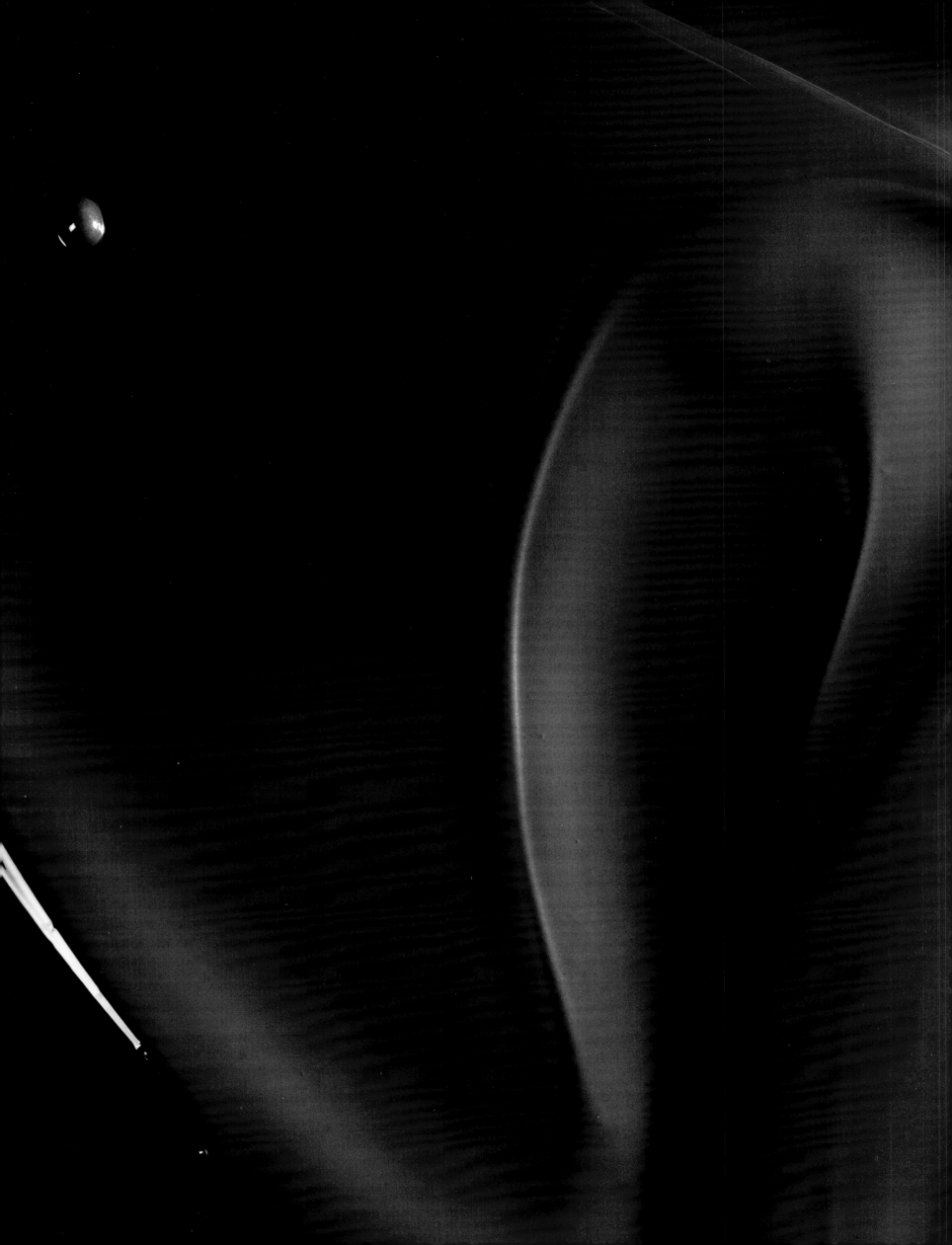

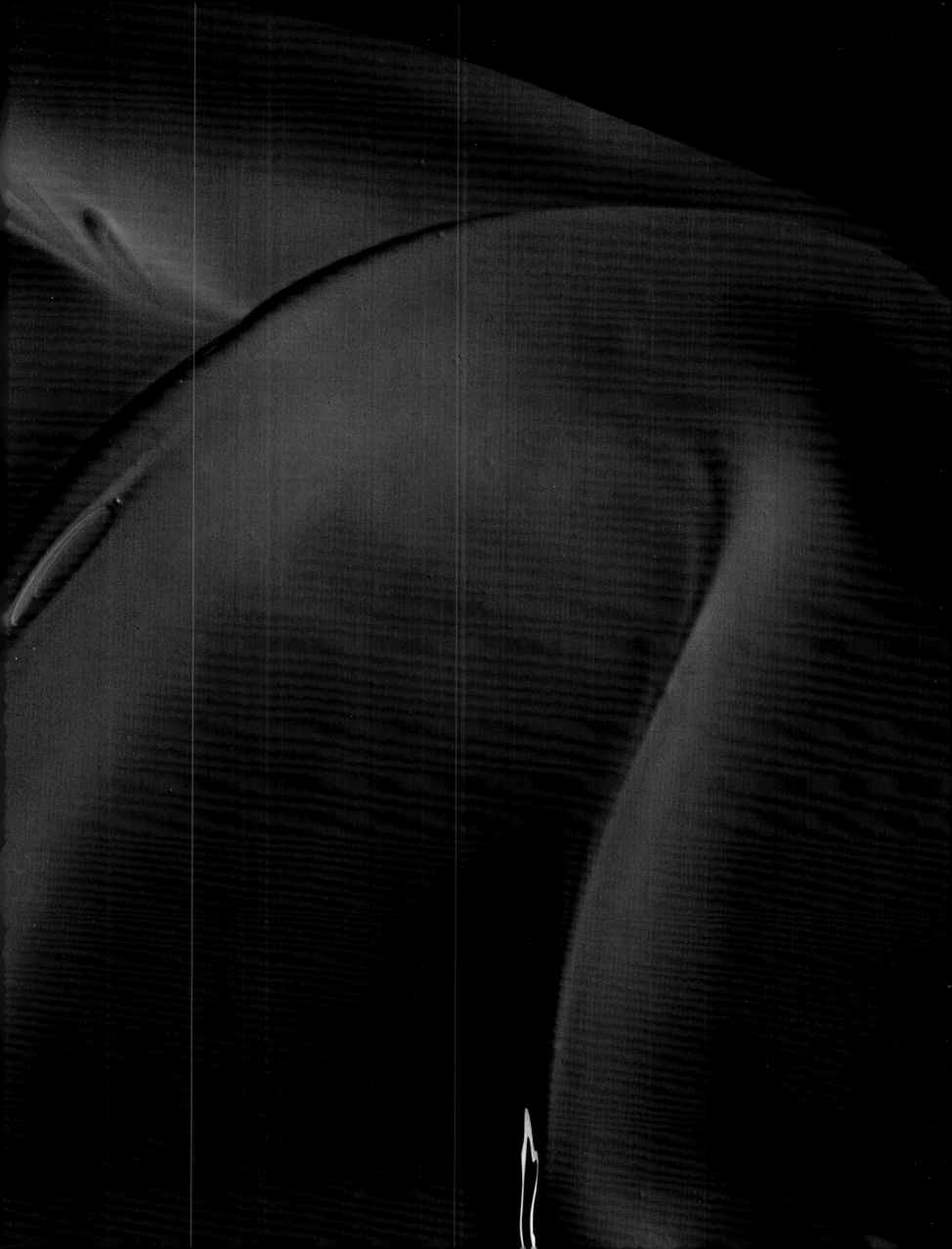

Madeleine Citron Chocolat

Lemon Chocolate Madeleine

Makes 12 madeleines

Ingredients:

Madeleine Batter:

1 1/3 cup (6 oz./170 g) flour
2 teaspoons (1/4 oz./7.5 g) baking
powder
6 tablespoons (3 oz./85 g) butter
6 1/2 tablespoons (3 oz./85 g) *huile
de beurre* (Valrhona) or liquid, clarified
butter
1 organic (untreated) lemon
3/4 cup (5 1/3 oz./150 g) superfine
granulated sugar
3/4 cup (6 oz./170 g) whole eggs
1/4 teaspoon (1.6 g) *Fleur de sel,*
preferably Guérande
2 tablespoons + 1 teaspoon
(1 1/4 oz./35 g) whole milk
Butter for the molds

Chocolate Glaze:

2 3/4 oz. (2 3/4 oz./80 g) Araguani
72% dark chocolate (Valrhona)
7 oz. (200 g) dark chocolate glaze
(Valrhona)
1 1/2 tablespoons (3/4 oz./20 g)
grape seed oil

———

Preparation Time:

20 mins.

Cooking Time:

About 12 mins.

Preparation:

Prepare the madeleine batter: Sift the flour and
baking powder together. Melt the butter and the clarified
butter together to 105°F (40°C). Set aside to cool.
Using a Microplane or fine grater, zest the lemon over
the sugar. Rub the sugar and lemon zest together
between the palms of your hands. In the bowl of a stand
mixer fitted with a whisk, combine the eggs, lemon
with sugar and salt. Add the flour gradually, mixing until
well combined. Stir in the cooled butter and the milk.
Preheat the oven on convection setting to 430°F
(220°C/Gas Mark 7–8). Place a baking sheet in the
oven to until hot.
Meanwhile, brush the madeleine molds lightly with
melted butter. Pour the batter into the madeleine molds,
filling each about one-half full. Place the madeleine
molds on the hot baking sheet and bake in the center
of the oven for eight minutes.
Remove the madeleines from the molds immediately
and place them on a pastry rack to cool.

———

Prepare the chocolate glaze: Chop the chocolate
with a serrated knife and place it in a bain-marie over
simmering water with the dark chocolate glaze to melt
to 113°F (45°C). Stir in the grape seed oil.
Dip the scalloped side of each madeleine into the
chocolate glaze. Place the madeleines on a rack,
chocolate side up, to rest until the chocolate sets. Store
the madeleines side by side in an airtight container.

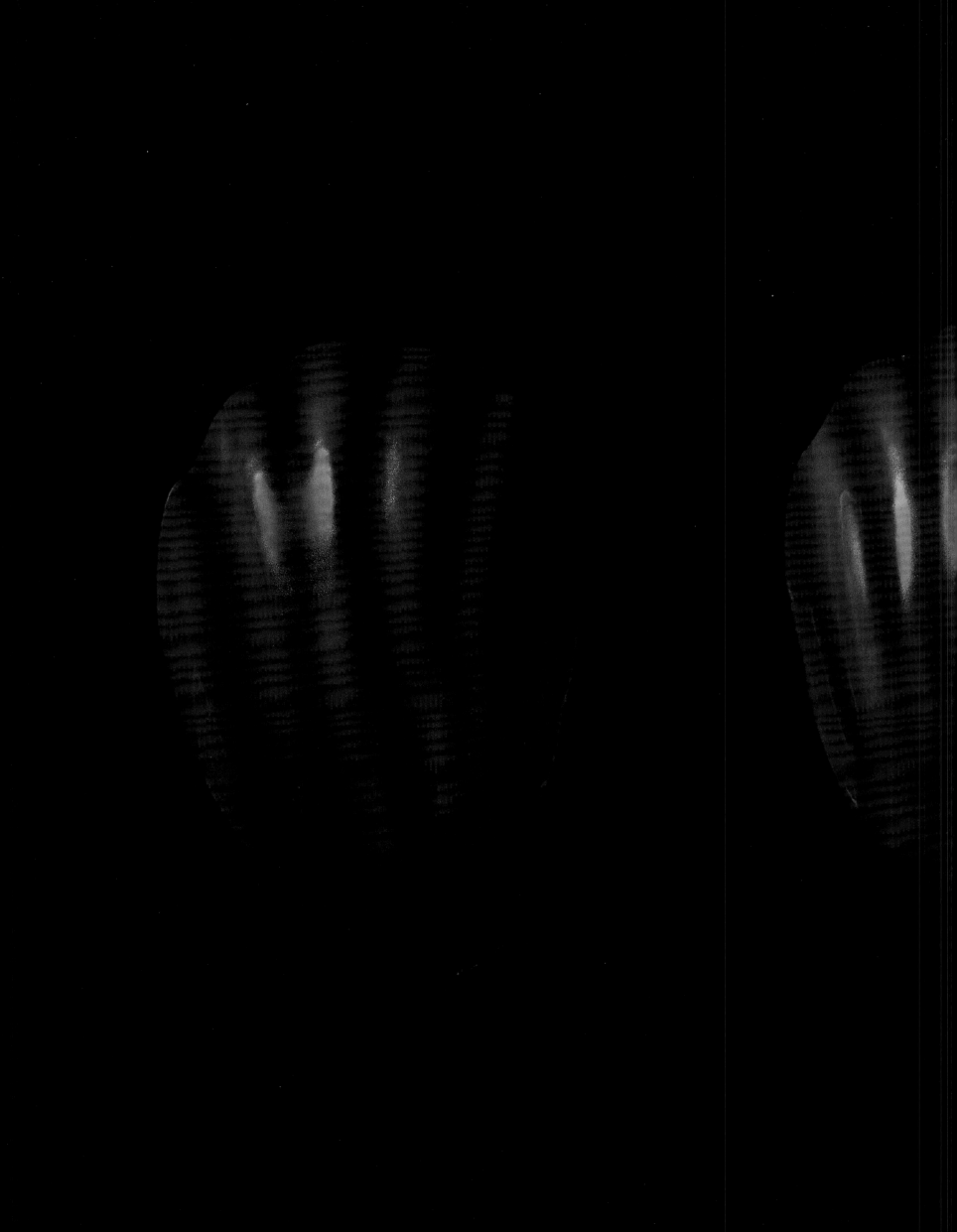

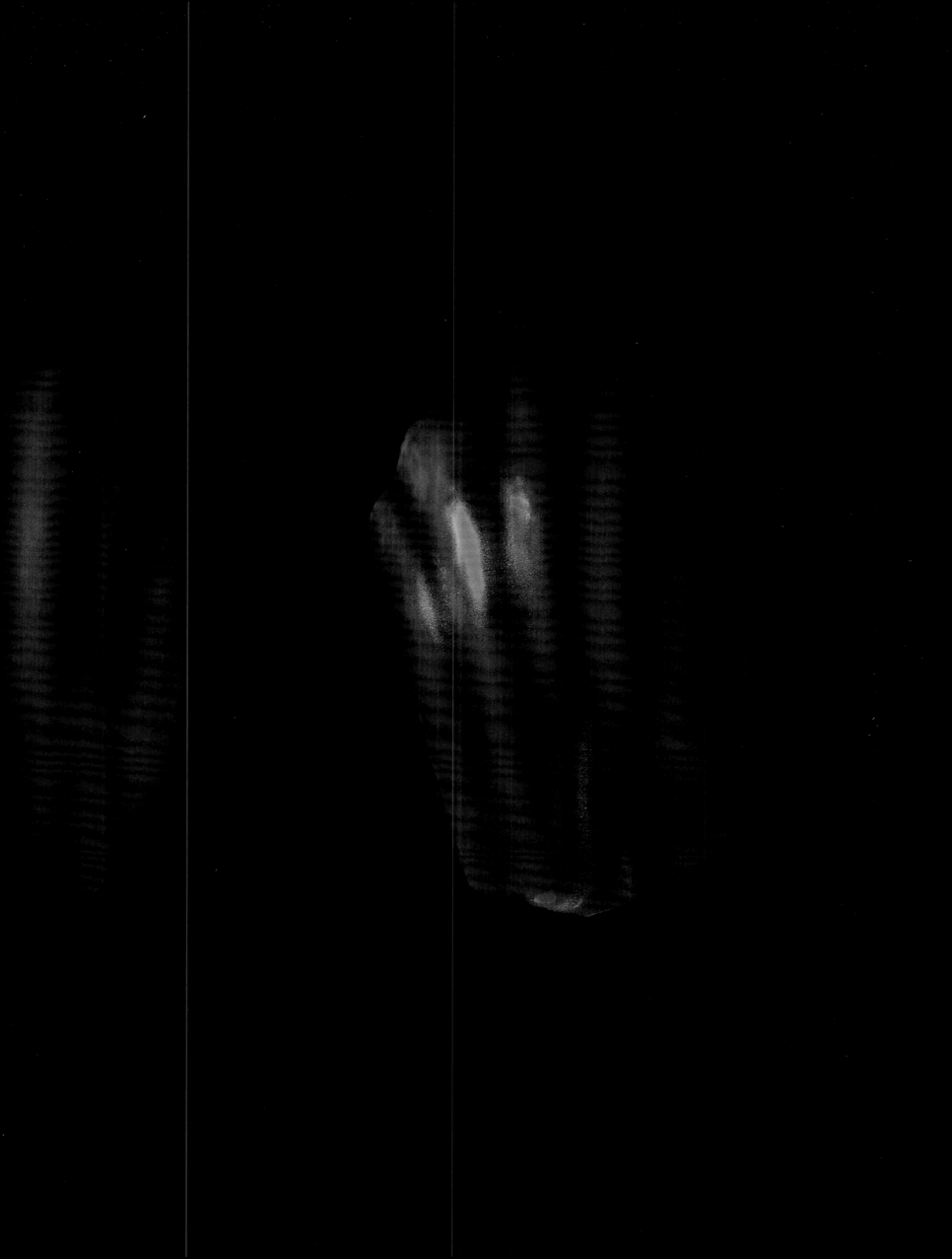

Gaufre et Pâte à Tartiner Plénitude

Waffle with Plénitude Spread

Makes 11 waffles and 1 1/2 lb. (650 g) spread

Ingredients:

Plénitude Spread:

2 3/4 oz. (80 g) Araguani 72% dark chocolate (Valrhona)
1/2 cup (3 1/2 oz./100 g) liquid cream
1 1/4 cup (8 1/2 oz./240 g) superfine sugar
1 tablespoon + 1 teaspoon (2/3 oz./20 g) unsalted butter
1 tablespoon + 1 teaspoon (2/3 oz./20 g) lightly salted butter
3/4 cup + 2 tablespoons (7 oz./200 g) unsweetened evaporated milk, divided

Waffle Batter:

5 1/2 tablespoon (2 3/4 oz./80 g) unsalted butter
2 cups (8 3/4 oz./250 g) flour
1 tablespoon + 2 teaspoons (3/4 oz./20 g) baking powder
1 teaspoon (4 g) *Fleur de sel*, preferably Guérande
4 tablespoons (1 3/4 oz./50 g) superfine sugar, divided
4 egg yolks
1 1/2 cup (12 1/3 oz./350 g) fresh whole milk
6 egg whites

Preparation Time:

25 mins. (1 day in advance);
10 mins. (the same day).

Cooking Time:

About 20 mins. (1 day in advance);
about 20 mins. (the same day).

Chilling Time:

Overnight + 30 mins.

Preparation:

One day in advance, prepare the Plénitude spread:
Chop the chocolate with a serrated knife. Bring the cream to a boil in a saucepan. In a separate saucepan, add the sugar, a little at a time, letting it melt between each addition. Continue cooking until the sugar caramelizes to a reddish brown. Add the unsalted and salted butters to this caramel, and let melt before adding the warm cream. Add, little by little, 3/4 cup (160 g) of the evaporated milk. Continue, cooking until the mixture reaches 223°F (106°C) on a thermometer. Stir the chopped chocolate into the hot mixture. Add the remaining two tablespoons evaporated milk and blend with a hand mixer.
Pour into a jar or a bowl, cover and refrigerate overnight.

The following day, prepare the waffles: Melt the butter over low heat. Set aside to cool.
In a bowl, combine the flour, baking powder, *Fleur de sel* and two tablespoons (25 g) of the sugar. Add the melted butter, egg yolks and milk.
Beat the egg whites until they begin to form soft peaks, add the remaining two tablespoons (25 g) sugar and continue beating until the whites are firm. Using a spatula, fold the whites delicately into the batter, lifting gently from the bottom up and over the whites. Let the batter rest in the refrigerator for thirty minutes before cooking in a waffle iron according to the manufacturer's instructions. Serve with the Plénitude spread.

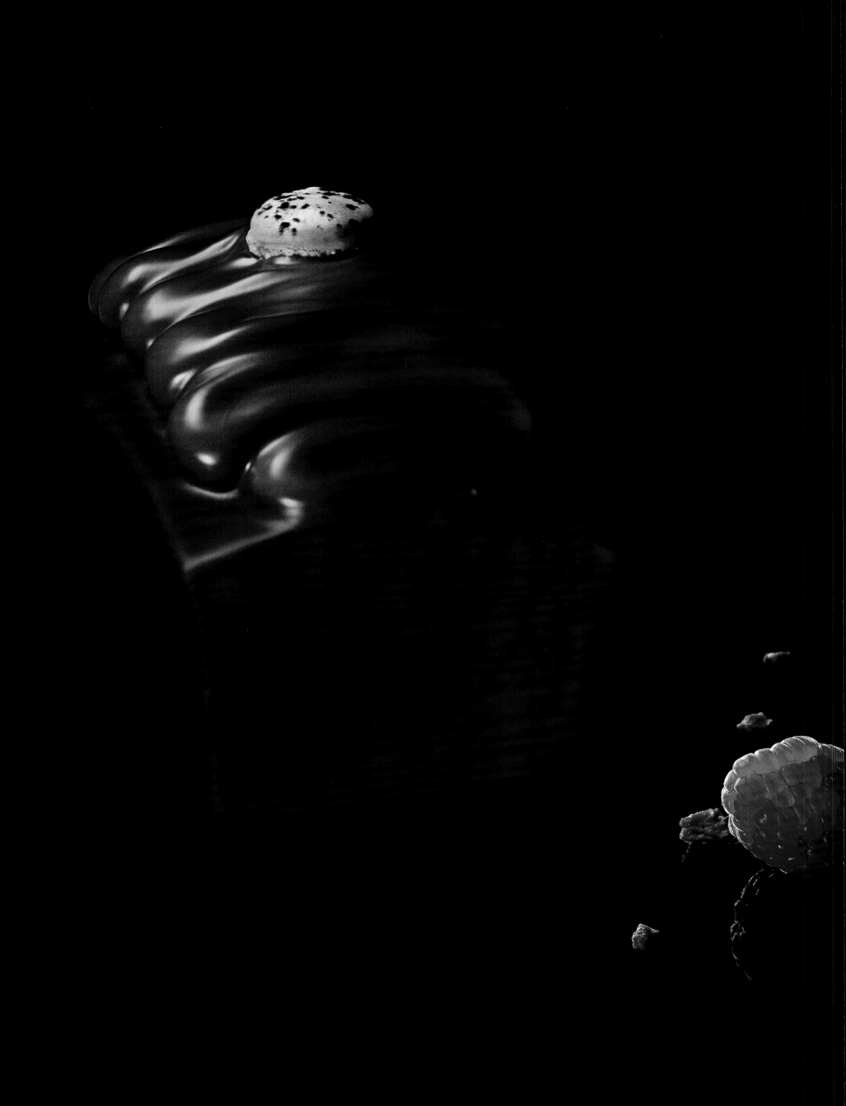

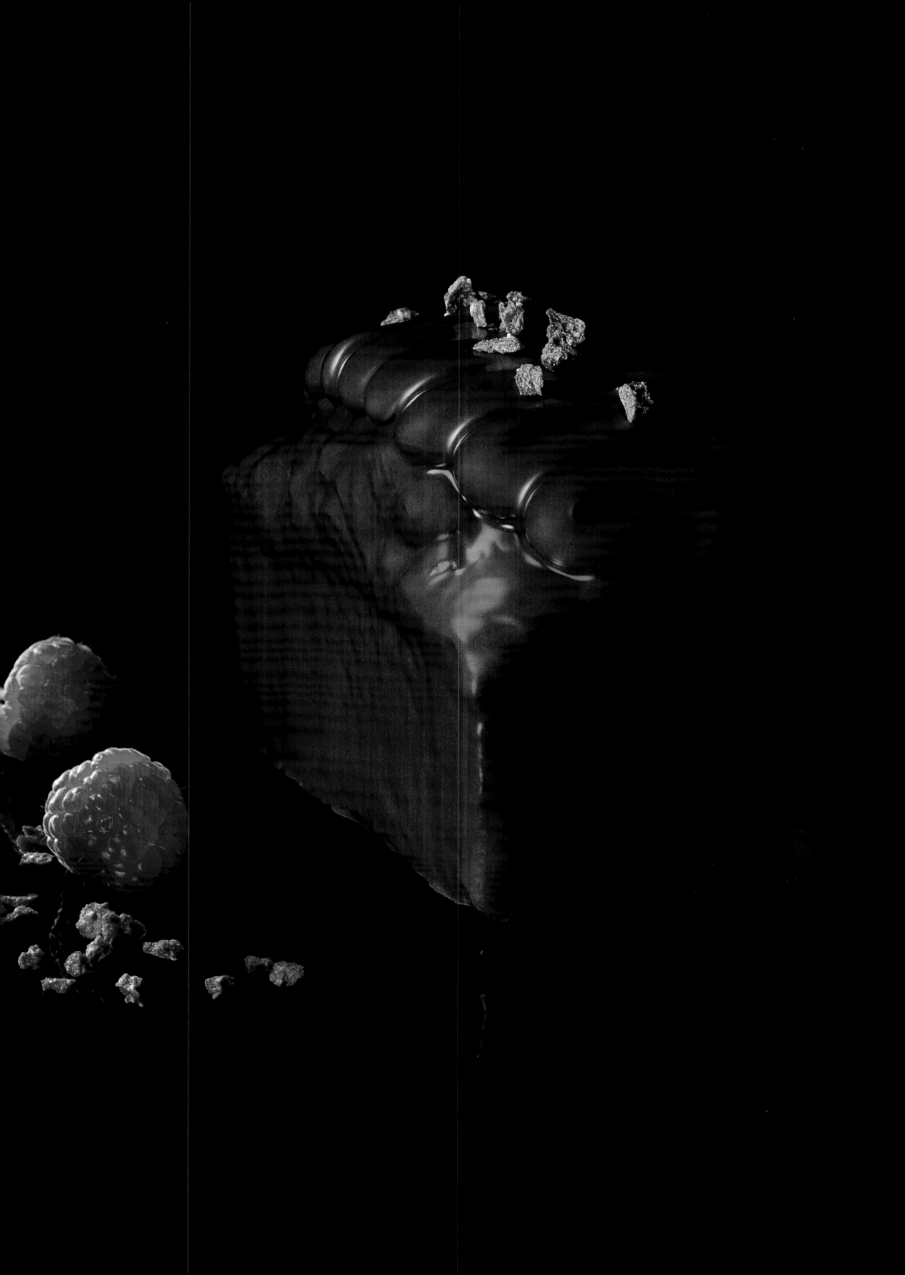

eu
pho
ric

Macaron Infiniment Chocolat

Infiniment Chocolat Macaron

Makes about 72 macarons
(or about 144 shells)

Ingredients:

Macaron Shell:

1 cup (7 2/3 oz./220 g) (or about 8)
"liquefied" egg whites, divided
(see note)
3 1/2 cups (10 1/2 oz./300 g) ground
almonds
2 cups + 5 tablespoons
(10 1/2 oz./300 g) confectioners'
sugar
4 1/4 oz. (120 g) pure cocoa paste
or dark chocolate, 100% cocoa
3/4 teaspoon (4.5 g) carmine red
food coloring
1 1/2 cups (10 1/2 oz./300 g)
superfine sugar
1/3 cup (2 2/3 oz./75 g) mineral water
Cocoa powder

Infiniment Chocolat Ganache:

2/3 cup (5 oz./140 g) butter at room
temperature
12 3/4 oz. (360 g) Guanaja 70% dark
chocolate (Valrhona)
1 1/3 oz. (40 g) pure cocoa paste
(or dark chocolate 100% cocoa)
1 2/3 cups (14 oz./400 g) liquid
cream

Finishing:

Cocoa powder

Preparation Time:

2 mins. (5 days in advance);
one hour (the same day).

Cooking Time:

About 25 mins.

Resting Time:

30 mins.

Chilling Time:

2 h. + 24 h.

Preparation:

Five days in advance,
place the egg whites for
the macaron shells in a
bowl, cover tightly with
plastic film, pierce a few
holes in the film and
refrigerate to liquefy.

**One day in advance,
prepare the macaron
shells:** Sift the ground
almonds and the
confectioners' sugar
together in a bowl. Chop
the cocoa paste and place
in a bowl over a bain-marie
of simmering water to melt
to 122°F (50°C).
Combine 1/2 cup (110 g)
of liquefied egg whites with
the food coloring. Pour
onto the sifted almond
powder–sugar mixture
without mixing.

Combine the sugar and
water in a saucepan and
bring to a boil, monitoring
the temperature with a
thermometer. Meanwhile
place the remaining
1/2 cup (110 g) of liquefied
egg whites in the bowl of
a mixer fitted with a wire
whisk. Once the sugar
syrup has reached 239°F
(115°C), begin beating the
egg whites on high speed.
Once the syrup has
reached 244°F (118°C),
reduce the mixer speed to
medium
and begin pouring the
syrup in a steady stream
into the beaten egg whites.
Continue beating until
the mixture cools to 122°F
(50°C). Using a spatula,
fold the meringue mixture
into the almond–sugar–egg
white mixture. Add the
melted cocoa paste, mixing
until the batter loses a little

volume. Spoon the batter into a pastry bag fitted with a
No. 11 plain tip (1/2 in. diameter).
Line baking sheets with cooking parchment and pipe
out rounds of batter about 1 1/2 in. (3.5 cm) in diameter,
spaced about 3/4 in. apart. Tap the baking sheets gently
on a work surface covered with a kitchen towel to
smooth the surface. Place the cocoa powder in a sifter
and sprinkle lightly over the macaron shells. Set aside
at room temperature for at least thirty minutes to allow
a "skin" to form.
Preheat the oven on convection setting to 355°F
(180°C/Gas Mark 6). Place the baking sheets in the
oven and bake for twelve minutes, opening and closing
the oven door quickly twice during the baking to release
steam. Remove from the oven and slide the macaron
shells onto the work surface.

Prepare the Infiniment Chocolat ganache: Cut the
butter into pieces. Chop the chocolate and cocoa paste
with a serrated knife, and place them in a bowl. Bring
the cream to a boil in a saucepan and pour it, one-third
at a time, over the chocolate and cocoa paste,
stirring from the center out in small, then progressively
larger concentric circles. When the temperature of
the chocolate cools to 95°F–104°F (35°C–40°C),
incorporate, little by little, the butter. Whisk until the
ganache is smooth. Pour into a shallow dish. Press
a sheet of plastic film directly onto the surface of the
chocolate cream and refrigerate until the texture is
creamy. Spoon the ganache into a pastry bag fitted
with a No. 11 plain pastry tip. Turn half of the macaron
shells over, flat side up, on the work surface and
pipe the ganache generously onto each shell. Cover
each with a second macaron shell. Refrigerate for
twenty-four hours.
The following day, remove the macarons from
the refrigerator two hours before serving.

Note: "Liquefied" egg whites are egg whites that have
been allowed to rest for several days to lose their
elasticity. Simply place the egg whites in a bowl, cover
with plastic film, pierce a few holes in the film and
refrigerate for five to seven days.

Sablé Infiniment Chocolat

Infiniment Chocolat Shortbread Cookies

Makes about 120 shortbread cookies

Ingredients:

Infiniment Chocolat Shortbread Dough:

5 1/4 oz. (150 g) Guanaja 70% dark chocolate (Valrhona)
1 1/3 cups (6 oz./175 g) flour
1/4 cup (1 oz./30 g) cocoa powder
1 teaspoon (5 g) baking soda
2/3 cup (5 1/4 oz./150 g) butter at room temperature
1/2 cup (4 1/4 oz./120 g) light brown sugar
1/4 cup (1 3/4 oz./50 g) superfine sugar
3/4 teaspoon (3 g) *Fleur de sel*, preferably Guérande
1/4 teaspoon (2 g) pure natural vanilla extract

———

Preparation Time:

15 mins.

Cooking Time:

11 to 12 mins.

Chilling Time:

2 h.

Preparation:

Chop the chocolate with a serrated knife. Sift the flour, cocoa powder and baking soda together. Place the butter in a bowl and soften with a spatula.
Add the brown sugar, superfine sugar, *Fleur de sel* and vanilla, and combine. Incorporate the flour–cocoa–baking soda mixture, mixing rapidly until combined, without overworking.
Divide the dough into three equal parts. Roll each piece into a cylinder or sausage shape of 1 1/2 in. to 1 3/4 in. (4 cm) diameter by about 16 in. (40 cm) long.
Wrap each in plastic film and refrigerate for two hours. Preheat the oven to 340°F (170°C/Gas Mark 5–6). Remove the plastic film from the dough and slice into rounds of about 1/2 in. (1 cm) thick. Place the cookies on a baking sheet lined with cooking parchment and bake for eleven to twelve minutes. Do not overcook, these shortbread cookies are best when slightly undercooked.

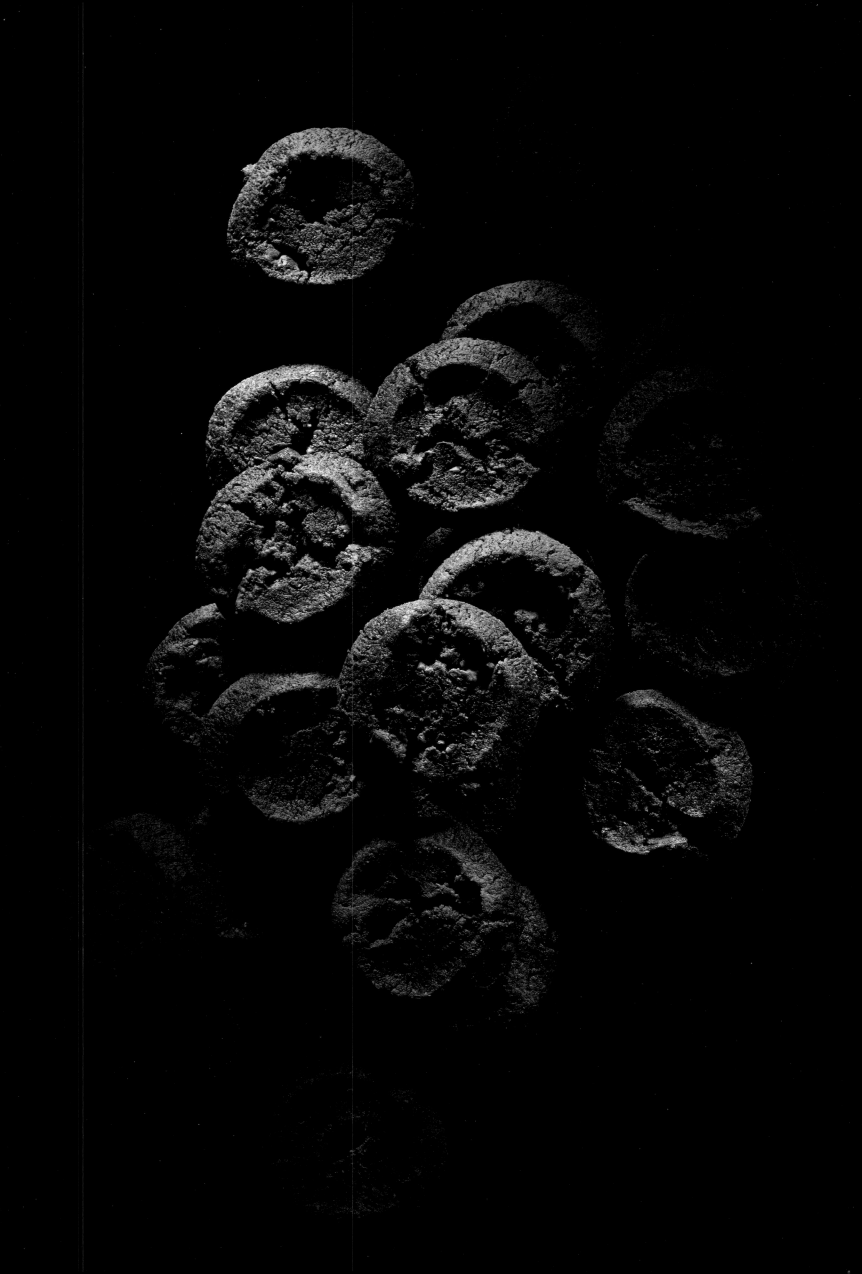

Plaisir Intense

Plaisir Intense

Serves 6 to 8

Ingredients:

Thin Layer of Dark Chocolate:

8 1/2 oz. (240 g) pure Venezuela 64%
dark chocolate (Valrhona)

Venezuela Chocolate Whipped Cream:

1 1/4 oz. (35 g) pure Venezuela 64%
dark chocolate (Valrhona)
1/6 oz. (5 g) pure cocoa paste
(Valrhona)
2/3 cup (6 oz./175 g) liquid cream
1 1/4 teaspoon (5 g) superfine sugar

Smooth Almond Biscuit:

1/2 cup (2 1/2 oz./70 g) whole
blanched almonds
3/4 cup (3 1/2 oz./100 g)
confectioners' sugar
1 cup (3 1/2 oz./100 g) ground
almonds
2 1/2 tablespoons (3/4 oz./20 g) flour
1/2 cup (3 1/2 oz./100 g) egg whites
1 tablespoon + 2 teaspoons
(2/3 oz./20 g) superfine sugar

Flaky Praline with Dark Chocolate:

1 oz. (30 g) pure cocoa paste
(Valrhona)
2 oz. (60 g) almond praline, 60%
almond (Valrhona)
2 oz. (60 g) pure Italian hazelnut paste
(Valrhona)
1 tablespoon + 1 teaspoon
(3/4 oz./20 g) butter
1 1/4 oz./35 g Gavottes Crepe
Dentelle cookies
1 oz. (30 g) cocoa nibs (Valrhona)

Venezuela Chocolate Ganache:

4 3/4 oz. (135 g) pure Venezuela
64% dark chocolate (Valrhona)
3 1/2 tablespoons (1 3/4 oz./50 g)
butter
3/4 cup (6 1/2 oz./185 g) liquid cream

Preparation Time:

20 mins. (1 day in advance);
30 mins. (the same day).

Cooking Time:

About 15 mins. (1 day in advance);
about 40 mins. (the same day).

Chilling Time:

About 2 h.

Preparation:

One day in advance, prepare the thin layer of dark chocolate: Chop the chocolate with a serrated knife and place it in a bowl over a bain-marie of simmering water to melt, stirring gently with a wooden spoon until the temperature of the chocolate reaches 130°F (55°C). Remove the bowl immediately from the bain-marie and place it in a bowl of cold water with four or five ice cubes. Stir the chocolate from time to time, scraping it from the sides of the bowl as it begins to set. Once the chocolate has cooled to 80°F (27°C), return the bowl to the bain-marie to warm slightly, monitoring the temperature carefully with a thermometer until the chocolate warms to between 88°F and 90°F (31°C–32°C). Using a spatula, spread the chocolate in a thin layer on a sheet of rhodoid plastic.* As soon as the chocolate begins to set, cut out two rectangles, each 7 by 3 in. (18 cm x 8 cm). Cover the rectangles with a second sheet of plastic and place a light weight on top to prevent the chocolate from buckling. Break the remaining chocolate into irregular pieces and set aside for the final decoration. Refrigerate overnight.

Prepare the chocolate whipped cream: Chop the chocolate and cocoa paste with a serrated knife, and place them in a bowl over a bain-marie. Bring the cream and sugar to a boil in a saucepan and pour, one-third at a time, over the chocolate, stirring from the center out in small, then progressively larger concentric circles. Cover with a sheet of plastic film, pressing it directly onto the surface of the chocolate cream. Refrigerate overnight.

The following day, prepare the smooth almond biscuit: Preheat the oven on convection setting to 340°F (170°C/Gas Mark 5–6). Spread the whole almonds out on a pastry sheet lined with cooking parchment and toast in the preheated oven for fifteen minutes. Remove from the oven and let the almonds cool before chopping coarsely.
Sift the confectioners' sugar, ground almonds and flour together. In the bowl of a stand mixer fitted with a whisk, beat the egg whites, incorporating the superfine sugar little by little. Remove the bowl from the mixer and using a rubber spatula, delicately fold in the sugar–almond–flour mixture.
Preheat the oven on convection setting to 395°F (200°C/Gas Mark 6–7). Line a baking sheet with cooking parchment. Weigh 7 oz. (200 g) of the batter out onto the baking sheet, and form into a neat rectangle of 8 by 4 in. (20 cm x 10 cm). Sprinkle the chopped roasted hazelnuts over the top of the batter, place in the oven and bake for fifteen minutes. Remove from the oven and let cool.

Prepare the dark flaky praline with dark chocolate: Chop the cocoa paste with a serrated knife, place it in a bowl over a bain-marie of simmering water to melt to 113°F (45°C). Stir in the almond praline, hazelnut paste and butter. Crumble the Gavottes cookies between your fingers and add to the mixture, along with the cocoa nibs. Set aside at room temperature.

Prepare the Venezuela chocolate ganache: Chop the chocolate with a serrated knife and place it in a bowl. Cut the butter into pieces. Bring the cream to a boil in a saucepan and pour, one-third at a time, over the chocolate, stirring from the center out in small, then progressively larger concentric circles. Once the temperature of the mixture has cooled to 140°F (60°C), incorporate, little by little, the pieces of butter. Stir until the mixture is smooth. Pour into a shallow dish. Cover with a sheet of plastic film, pressing the film directly onto the surface of the ganache, and refrigerate until the texture is creamy.

To assemble the chocolate sheets and the ganache, spoon the creamy chocolate ganache into a pastry bag fitted with a basket-weave tip. Place the two thin rectangular sheets of chocolate, shiny side down, on a baking sheet. Pipe the ganache, lengthwise, onto the first sheet of chocolate. Place the second sheet of chocolate on top and pipe with the ganache. Refrigerate until set.

Assemble the smooth almond biscuit and flaky praline with dark chocolate: Using an elbow spatula, spread 3 1/2 oz. (100 g) of the layered praline over the almond biscuit. Invert the sheets of ganache-filled chocolate onto the biscuit, the ganache against the layered praline.

Just before serving, whip the chocolate cream prepared the previous day and spoon it into a pastry bag fitted with a F8 star tip. Pipe the whipped cream in a zigzag pattern on the top of the cake. Decorate the top of the cake with the thin irregular pieces of chocolate, inserting them upright in the whipped cream. Refrigerate for at least one hour before serving.

* Transparent plastic celluloid used in pastry and confectionery.

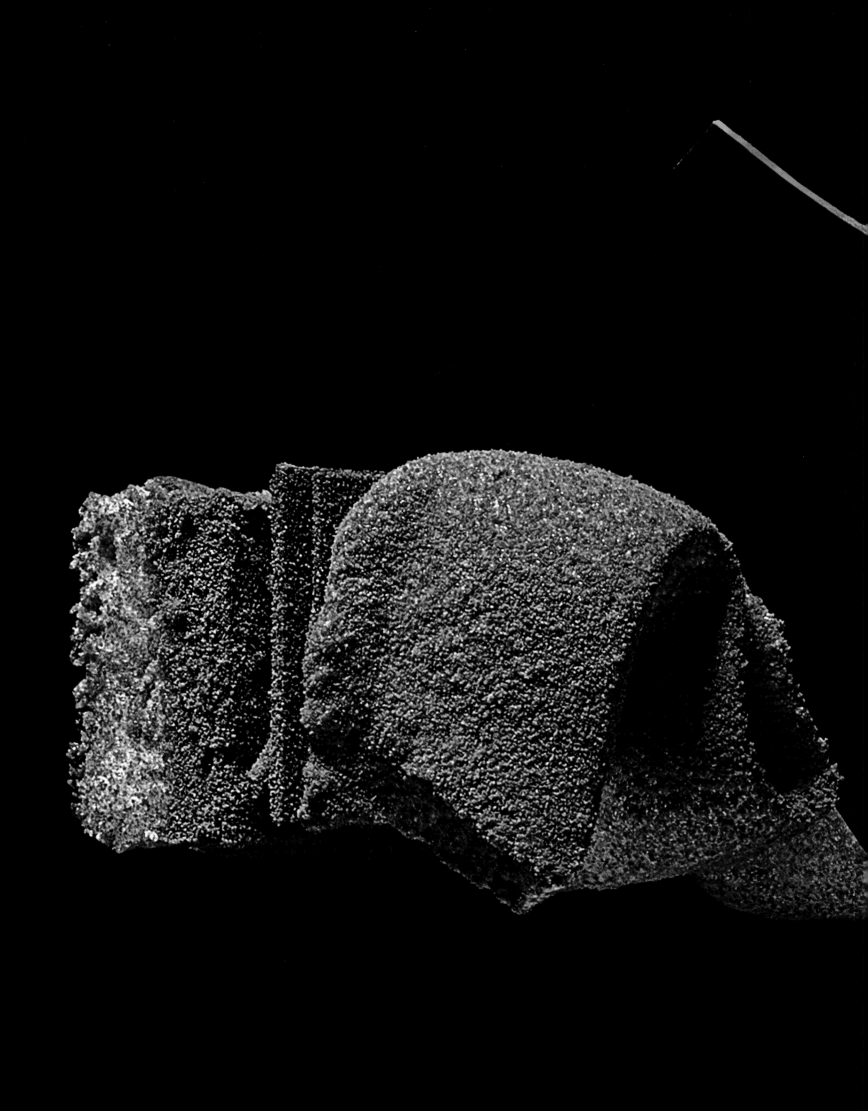

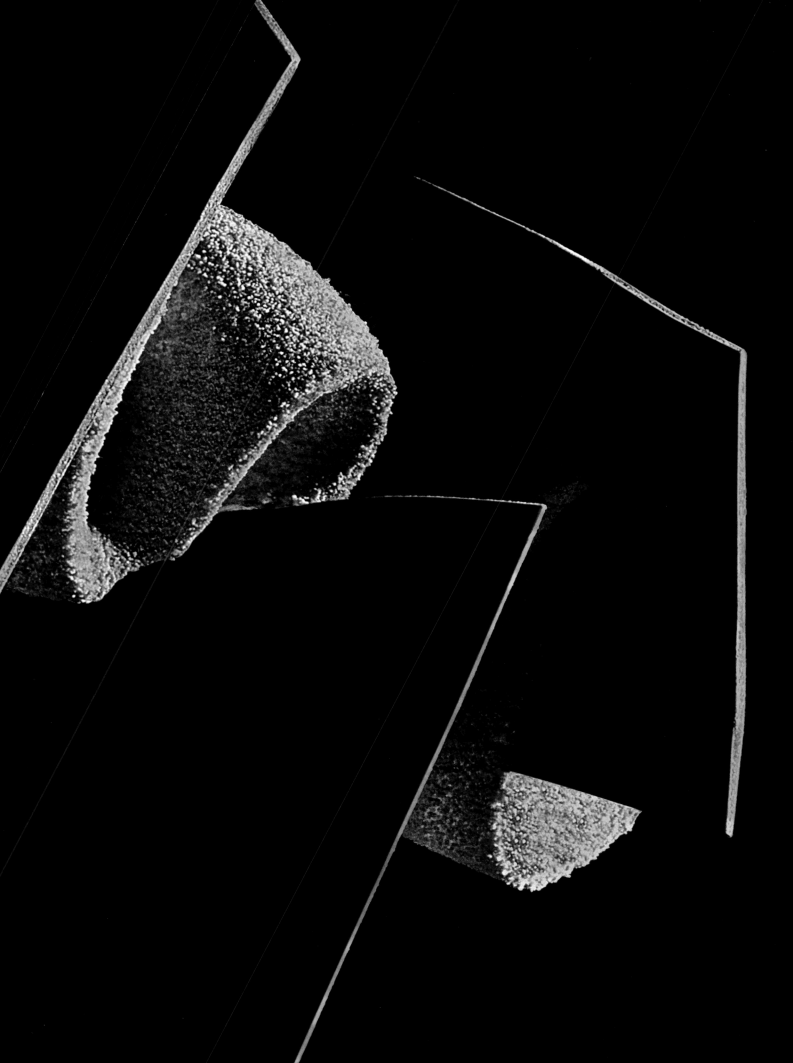

Sensation Chocolat Truffe Noire

Black Truffle Chocolate Sensation

Serves 10

Ingredients:

Black Truffle Custard:

1 1/4 teaspoons (2.5 g) powdered gelatin or 1 1/4 gelatin sheets
2 tablespoons + 1 teaspoon (1 1/2 oz./40 g) egg yolks
1/4 cup (1 3/4 oz./50 g) superfine sugar
2/3 cup (6 oz./170 g) liquid cream
1 tablespoon (1/2 oz./15 g) black truffle juice
1 1/4 oz. (35 g) fresh black truffles
1/4 teaspoon (1.5 g) black truffle aroma

Black Truffle Ice Cream:

1 1/3 cups (11 1/3 oz./320 g) whole milk
1/4 cup (1 oz./30 g) powdered milk, 0% fat
1/2 cup (4 1/2 oz./130 g) liquid cream
1 tablespoon (1/2 oz./15 g) black truffle juice
3 tablespoons (1 3/4 oz./50 g) egg yolks
1/3 cup (2 2/3 oz./75 g) superfine sugar
1 3/4 oz. (50 g) pieces canned black truffles
1/2 teaspoon (3 g) black truffle aroma

Thin Crunchy Chocolate Shell:

17 2/3 oz. (500 g) Caraque 56% chocolate (Valrhona)

Black Truffle Mascarpone Cream:

8 3/4 oz. (250 g) black truffle custard (see recipe above)
1/2 cup (5 3/4 oz./165 g) mascarpone cheese

Caramelized Almonds:

1/2 cup (3 1/2 oz./100 g) blanched whole almonds
1/2 teaspoon (2.5 g) cocoa butter (Valrhona)
1 1/3 tablespoons (2/3 oz./20 g) mineral water
1/3 cup (2 1/4 oz./65 g) superfine sugar

Meringue–Almond Biscuit:

3/4 cup (4 1/2 oz./125 g) blanched whole almonds
1 1/2 cups (6 3/4 oz./190 g) flour
3/4 cup (6 oz./170 g) butter + 3/4 cup (5 3/4 oz./165 g) superfine sugar
1 1/3 cups (10 1/2 oz./295 g) egg whites + 1 cup (6 oz./175 g) superfine sugar

Hot Caraque Chocolate Sauce:

3.5 oz. (100 g) Caraque 56% chocolate (Valrhona)
3/4 cup plus 1 1/2 tablespoons (7 oz./200 g) liquid cream
1/4 cup (1 3/4 oz./50 g) whole milk
2 1/2 teaspoons (1/3 oz./10 g) superfine sugar
1/8 teaspoon (0.5 g) *Fleur de sel*, preferably Guérande

Finishing:

Gold leaf
1 fresh black truffle, about 1 oz. (30 g)

___

Preparation Time:

15 mins. (1 day in advance);
45 mins. (the same day).

Cooking Time:

About 15 mins. (1 day in advance);
about 1 h. 15 mins. (the same day).

Chilling Time:

4 h.

Preparation:

A day in advance, prepare the black truffle custard: Sprinkle the powdered gelatin into a little warm water to dissolve. (If using sheet gelatin, place in a bowl of cold water to soften fifteen minutes, then squeeze out the water.) Whisk the egg yolks with the sugar in a bowl. Combine the cream and truffle juice in a small saucepan, and bring to a boil. Pour this cream–truffle juice mixture over the egg yolk–sugar mixture, whisking briskly. Pour the mixture back into the saucepan and cook, whisking constantly until it reaches 185°F (85°C). Chop the black truffle and stir into the mixture, along with the gelatin and truffle aroma. Mix with a hand blender. Pour into a recipient, cover with a sheet of plastic wrap, pressing the plastic directly onto the surface, and refrigerate overnight.

___

The following day, prepare the black truffle ice cream: Combine the milk, milk powder, cream and truffle juice in a saucepan, and bring to a boil. Whisk the egg yolks and sugar together in a bowl. Pour the hot milk mixture over the egg yolk–sugar mixture, whisking briskly. Pour the mixture back into the saucepan and cook, whisking constantly, until it reaches 185°F (85°C). Transfer the saucepan immediately to a recipient of cold water with ice cubes and let cool, stirring from time to time. Cut the truffles into small cubes and add to the cream, along with the truffle aroma. Mix for two minutes with a hand blender. Cover with a sheet of plastic film, pressing the film directly onto the surface. Refrigerate for four hours. Once chilled, mix again with a hand blender, then process in an ice cream or sorbet machine according to the manufacturer's instructions.

___

Temper the chocolate and prepare the thin crunchy chocolate shell: Chop the chocolate with a serrated knife and place it in a bowl over a bain-marie of simmering water to melt, stirring gently with a wooden spoon until the temperature of the chocolate reaches 130°F (55°C). Remove the bowl immediately from the bain-marie and place it in a bowl of cold water with four or five ice cubes. Stir the chocolate from time to time, scraping it from the sides of the bowl as it begins to set. Once the chocolate has cooled to 80°F (27°C), return the bowl to the bain-marie to warm slightly, monitoring the temperature carefully with a thermometer until the chocolate warms to between 88°F and 90°F (31°C–32°C). Mold the tempered chocolate into twenty half-spheres, each 3 in. (8 cm) in diameter. Let the chocolate set. Unmold the spheres, cover with plastic film and refrigerate.

___

Prepare the caramelized almonds: Preheat the oven to 340°F (170°C/Gas Mark 5–6). Spread the almonds on a baking sheet lined with cooking parchment. Place in the oven and toast the almonds for fifteen minutes. Chop the cocoa butter. Combine the water and sugar in a saucepan and cook to 245°F (118°C). Add the roasted almonds, stirring and cooking until the caramel turns reddish amber. Stir in the cocoa butter and pour the mixture onto a baking sheet lined with a silicon pastry sheet, spreading out evenly. Let cool. Chop coarsely.

Prepare the black truffle mascarpone cream:
In the bowl of a mixer fitted with a whisk, soften the mascarpone, then incorporate 8 3/4 oz. (250 g) of the black truffle custard. Whisk for a few minutes. Refrigerate.

Prepare the meringue–almond biscuit: Preheat the oven to 340°F (170°C/Gas Mark 5–6). Spread the almonds out evenly on a baking sheet lined with cooking parchment. Place in the oven to toast for fifteen minutes. Remove and let cool. Chop coarsely.
Sift the flour. In the bowl of a mixer fitted with a paddle, soften the butter, then add 3/4 cup of the superfine sugar and mix for two minutes. In a separate bowl, combine the egg whites and the remaining cup of sugar, and whip to stiff peaks. Delicately incorporate, one-third at a time, the whipped egg whites with the butter–sugar mixture. Incorporate the flour. Preheat the oven on convection setting to 340°F (170°C/Gas Mark 5–6). Pour the biscuit batter out onto a baking sheet lined with cooking parchment and using an elbow spatula, form the batter into a 14 1/2 x 11-in. (37 cm x 28 cm) rectangle. Sprinkle with the chopped almonds, place in the oven and cook for thirty-five minutes. Remove and let cool before cutting into 1/3-in. (1 cm) cubes.

Prepare the hot Caraque chocolate sauce: Chop the chocolate with a serrated knife and place it in a bowl. Bring the cream, milk, sugar and *Fleur de sel* to a boil in a saucepan, and pour, one-third at a time, over the chocolate, stirring from the center out in small, then progressively larger concentric circles. Mix with a hand blender. Keep warm over a bain-marie of simmering water.

Sprinkle gold leaf over the exterior of half of the chocolate shells. To stabilize the remaining chocolate shells, slide the rounded side very briefly over a hot baking sheet, then place each shell immediately in the center of a shallow serving dish. Fill each chocolate shell with the black truffle mascarpone cream. Sprinkle with cubes of almond meringue biscuit and chopped caramelized almonds. Add a scoop of black truffle ice cream. Using a truffle grater, grate a few slices of fresh

black truffle over each serving. Place the open side of the second half of the chocolate shells quickly and lightly on a hot baking sheet, and position each sphere directly over a filled shell, holding gently until the sphere adheres to the filled bottom half.

Serve immediately, pouring a little hot Caraque chocolate sauce over each serving.

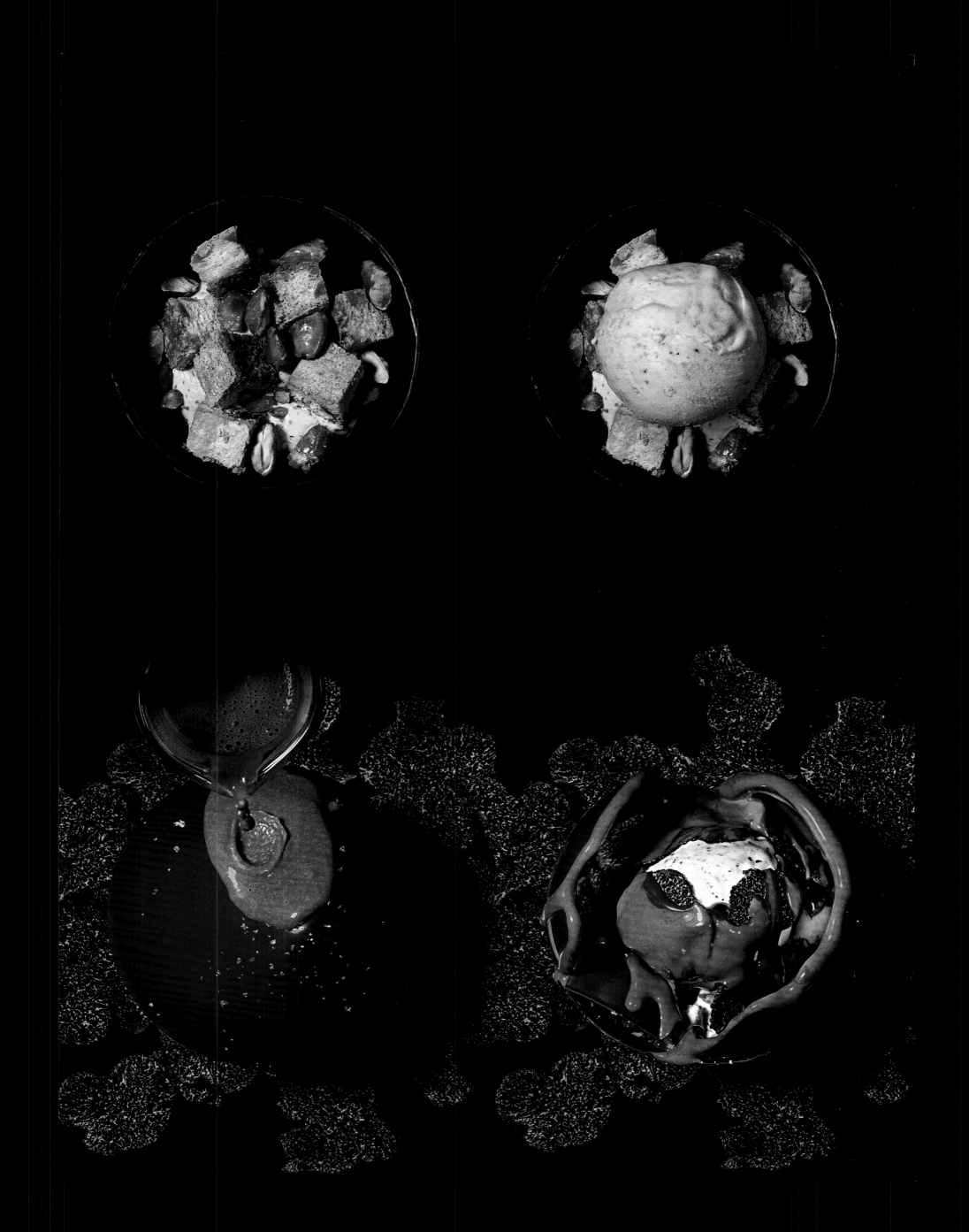

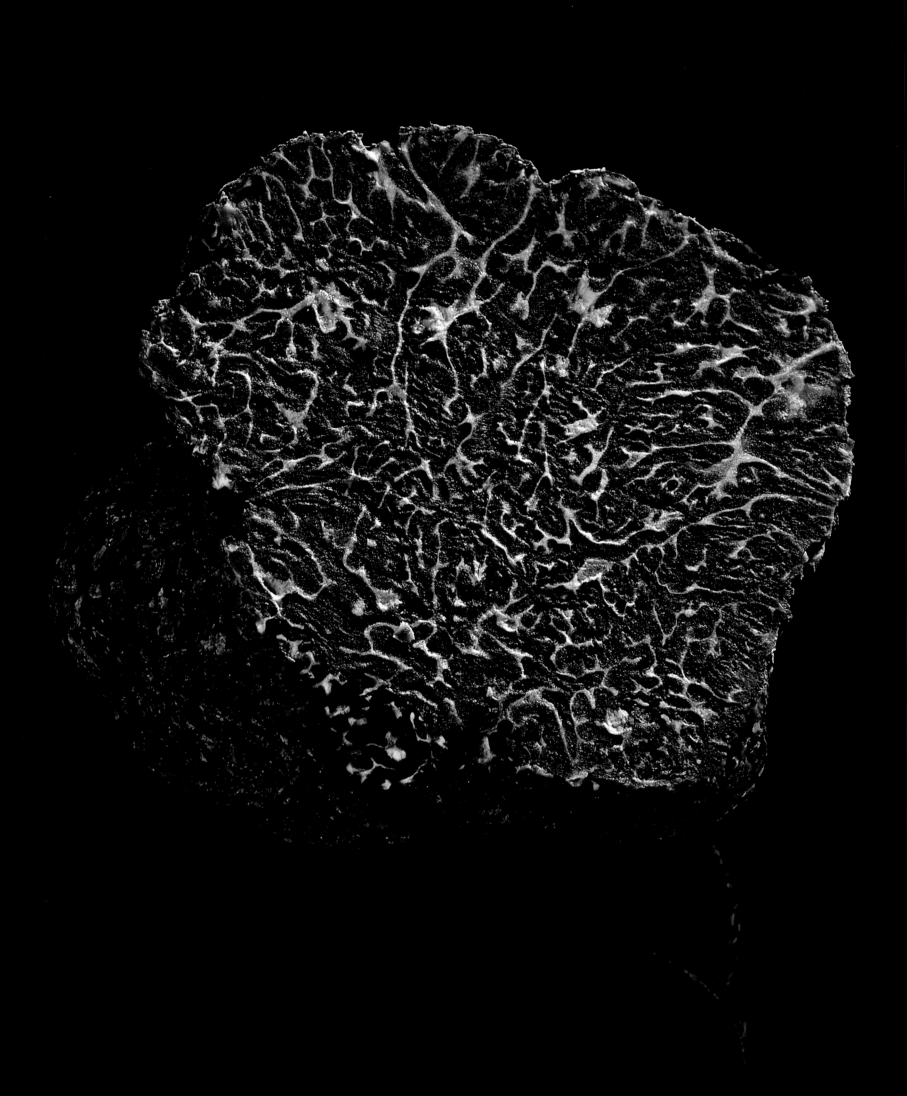

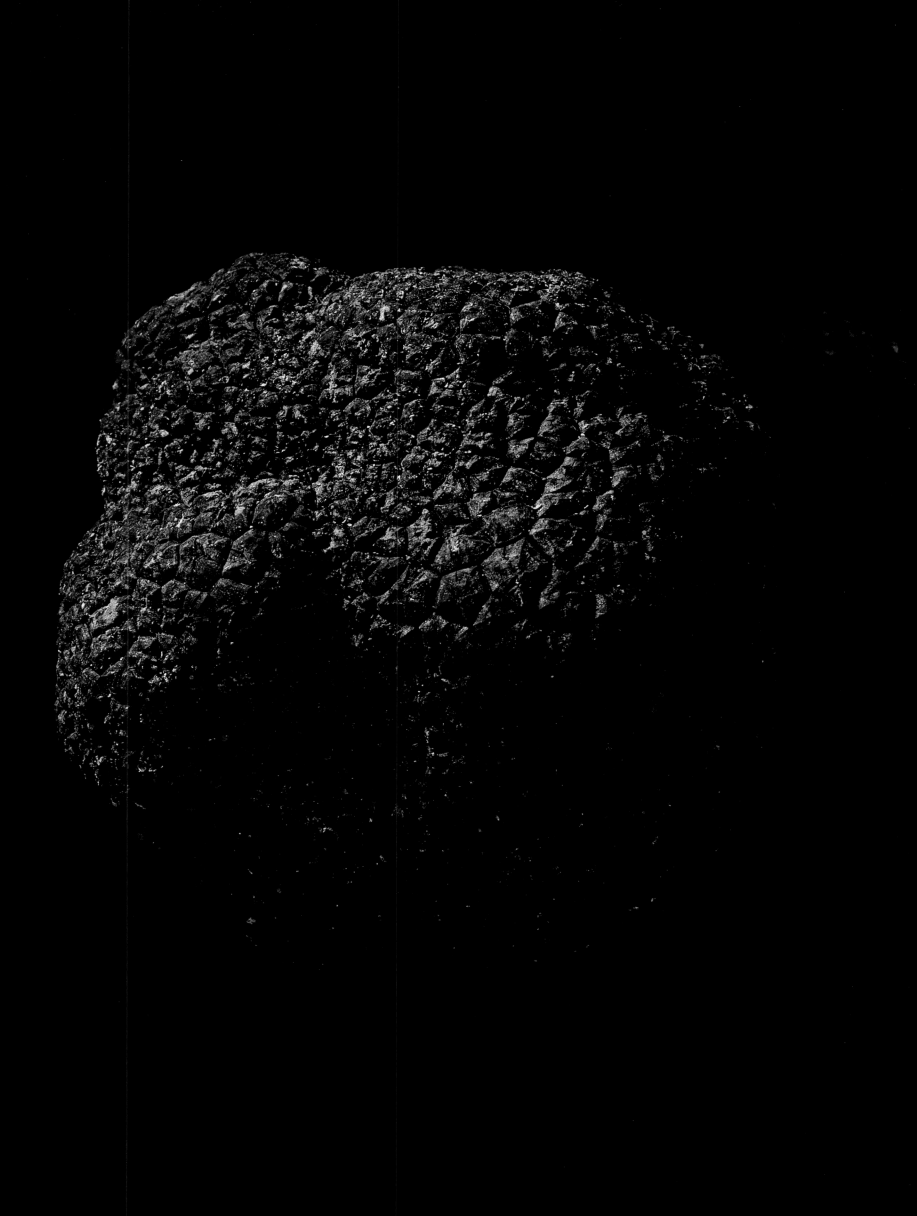

Nougatine Infiniment Chocolat

Infiniment Chocolat Nougatine

Makes about 60 nougatine squares

Ingredients:

Infiniment Chocolat Nougatine:

6 1/2 oz. (185 g) slivered almonds
1 1/4 oz. (35 g) cocoa nibs
1 cup + 3 tablespoons (8 oz./225 g)
superfine sugar
1 1/2 teaspoons (6 g) pectin NH
2 2/3 oz. (75 g) cocoa paste, 100%
cocoa (Valrhona)
3 tablespoons + 1 teaspoon
(2 2/3 oz./75 g) glucose syrup or corn
syrup
5 tablespoons (2 2/3 oz./75 g) whole
milk
5 tablespoons (2 2/3 oz./75 g) lightly
salted butter
Fleur de sel, preferably Guérande
Black Sarawak pepper

**Chocolate Coating and
Finishing:**

3 1/3 lb. (1.5 kg) Mexique 64% dark
chocolate (Valrhona)
3 1/2 oz. (100 g) cocoa nibs, crushed

———

Preparation Time:

1 h. 30 mins.

Cooking Time:

1 h.

Freezing Time:

30 mins.

Drying Time:

24 h.

Preparation:

Preheat the oven to 300°F (150°C/Gas Mark 3).
Spread the slivered almonds over a baking sheet lined
with cooking parchment. Place in the oven to toast for
fifteen minutes, stirring and turning every five minutes.
Remove from the oven and cover with aluminum foil
to keep warm. Spread the cocoa nibs between two
sheets of cooking parchment and use a rolling pin
to crush them.
Combine the sugar and pectin in a bowl. Chop the
cocoa paste with a serrated knife and combine it with
the glucose syrup, milk and butter in a bowl over a
bain-marie of simmering water. Heat to 113°F–122°F
(45°C–50°C). Add the sugar–pectin mixture and heat
to 217°F (103°C). Add the warm roasted almonds and
crushed cocoa nibs.
Using a spatula, spread the nougatine out onto a sheet
of cooking parchment. Cover with a second sheet
of cooking parchment and using a rolling pin, roll the
nougatine out in an even layer. Place the nougatine
on two baking sheets and place in the freezer for
thirty minutes.
Preheat the oven on convection setting to 338°F
(170°C/Gas Mark 5–6). Remove the sheets of nougatine
from the freezer, remove the top sheet of parchment,
and sprinkle with a few grains of *Fleur de sel* and a little
freshly ground pepper.
Place one baking sheet in the oven and cook for
fifteen minutes, turning the sheet around after
seven minutes. Remove from the oven and transfer the
nougatine to a cutting board. Cover the nougatine with
a sheet of cooking parchment. Using a rolling pin, roll
to a uniform thickness. Remove the parchment, cut the
nougatine into 1 1/4-in. (3 cm) cubes. Cover again with
the sheet of cooking parchment and use the rolling pin
to eliminate any uneven waves from the surface.
Place the second baking sheet of nougatine in the oven
preheated to 338°F (170°C/Gas Mark 5–6) and proceed
in the same manner as for the first sheet.

———

Temper the chocolate for the coating: Chop the
chocolate with a serrated knife and place it in a bowl
over a bain-marie of simmering water to melt, stirring
gently with a wooden spoon, until the temperature of the
chocolate reaches 130°F (55°C). Remove the bowl
immediately from the bain-marie and place it in a bowl of
cold water with four or five ice cubes. Stir the chocolate
from time to time, scraping it from the sides of the bowl
as it begins to set. Once the chocolate has cooled to
80°F (27°C), return the bowl to the bain-marie to warm
slightly, monitoring the temperature carefully with a
thermometer until the chocolate warms to 88°F–90°F
(31°C–32°C). Spread several sheets of rhodoid plastic*
on a flat work surface. Dip a first nougatine square in the

chocolate, remove with a three-tined chocolate dipping fork, lifting toward the edge of the bowl, then dipping the square once again in the chocolate, lifting two or three times in a pumping motion to coat. Remove the square with the fork, resting it on the edge of the bowl and tapping lightly to remove any excess chocolate. Finish by scraping the bottom of the fork along the edge of the bowl. Place the chocolate nougatine on the plastic. Sprinkle a few pieces of crushed chocolate nibs on the corner of each square.

Continue in the same manner for the remaining nougatine, taking care to return the chocolate to the bain-marie from time to time to maintain the temperature between 88°F–90°F (31°C–32°C). Let the nougatine squares dry at room temperature overnight.
The following day, arrange the nougatine in an airtight container and store at between 59°F–64°F (15°C–18°C), in a dry, odor-free place.

* Transparent plastic celluloid used in pastry and confectionery.

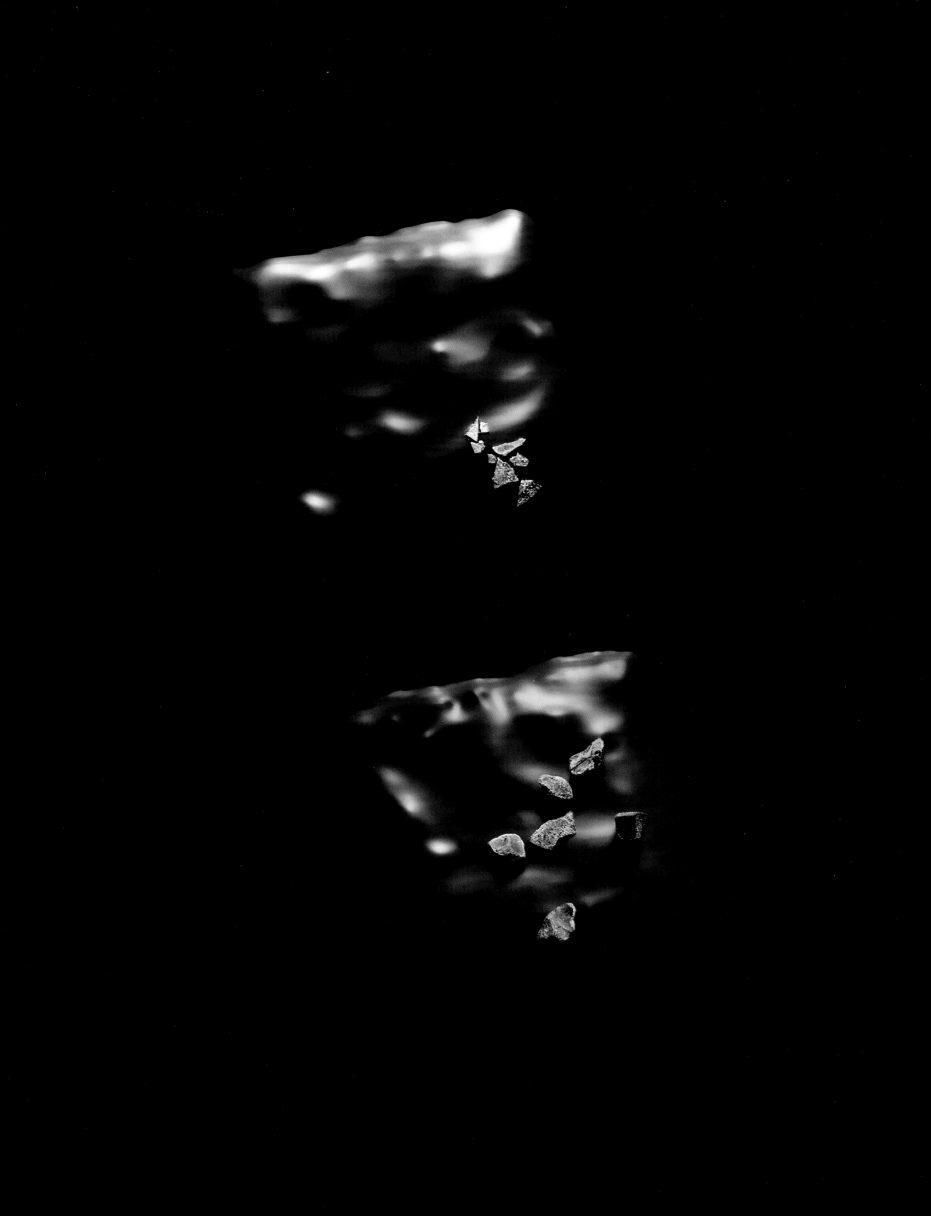

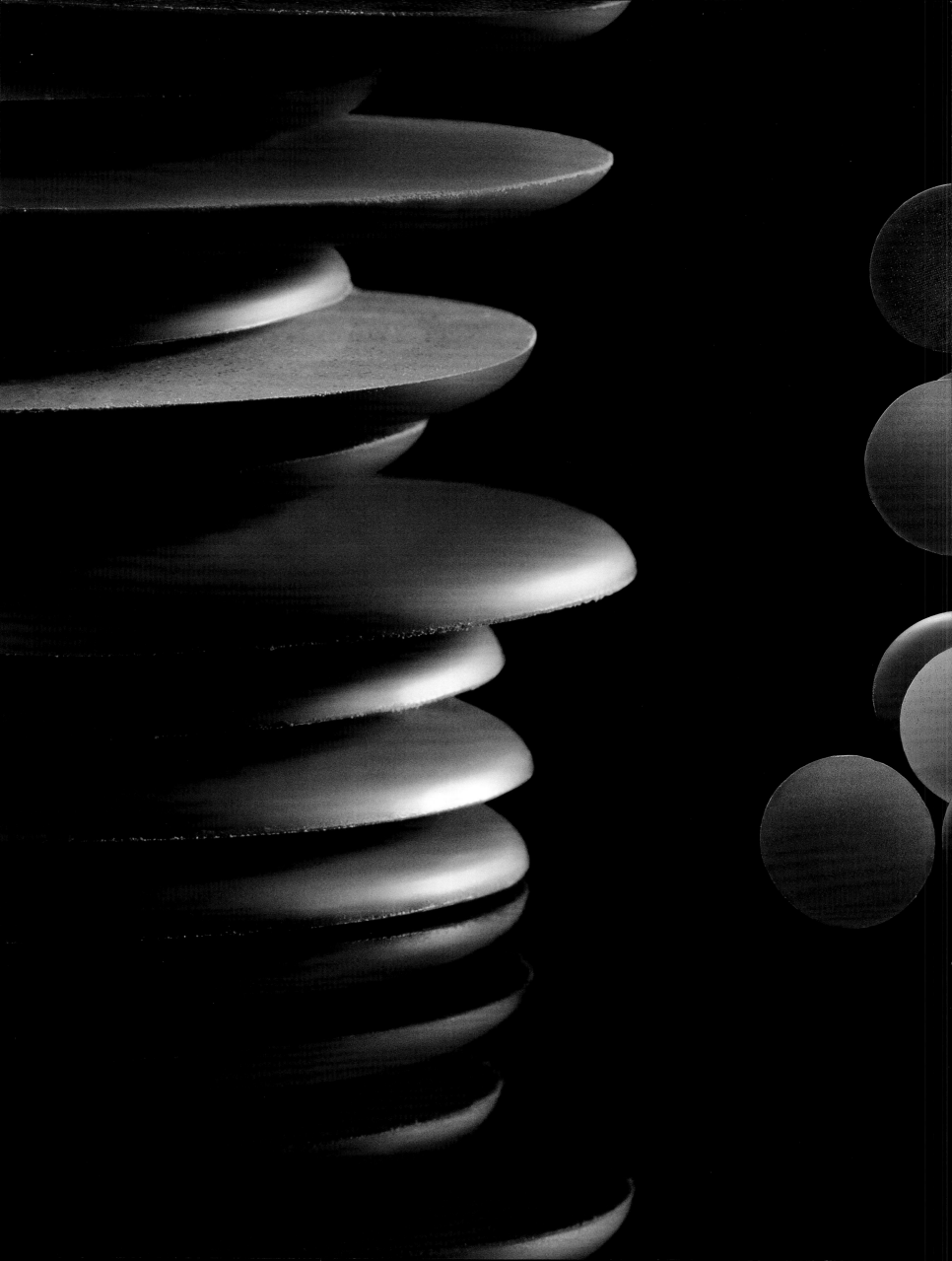

Cake Chocolat Banane et Gingembre

Banana, Ginger and Chocolate Cake

Makes 2 rectangular cakes, each
7 1/2 x 3 in. (19 cm x 8 cm)

Ingredients:

Fleur de sel Chocolate Cubes:

1/2 teaspoon (2.3 g) *Fleur de sel*,
preferably Guérande
4 1/4 oz. (120 g) extra-bitter 67%
chocolate

Cake Batter:

1 banana
Lemon juice 2 3/4 oz (80 g) candied
ginger
1 1/3 cups (6 oz./170 g) flour
6 1/2 tablespoons (1 1/2 oz./45 g)
cocoa powder
1 1/4 teaspoons (5 g) baking powder
1 cup (7 1/2 oz./210 g) butter
1 cup (7 1/2 oz./210 g) superfine
sugar
4 large eggs
3 oz. (90 g) *Fleur de sel* chocolate
cubes (see recipe above)
Melted butter and flour for the cake
molds

Imbibing Syrup:

1/4 cup (2 oz./55 g) superfine sugar
2/3 cup (5 oz./140 g) mineral water

Chocolate Glaze:

5 2/3 oz. (160 g) Araguani 72% dark
chocolate (Valrhona)
14 oz. (400 g) dark chocolate glaze
(Valrhona)
3 tablespoons (1 1/3 oz./40 g) grape
seed oil

Finishing:

Candied ginger
4 rounds of semi-dried banana

Preparation Time:

40 mins.

Cooking Time:

About 3 h.

Chilling Time:

3 h.

Preparation:

**Prepare the chocolate
cubes:** Crush the *Fleur de
sel* to a powder with a
rolling pin. Sift through a
fine sieve.
Chop the chocolate with a
serrated knife and place it
in a bowl over a bain-marie
of simmering water to heat
until melted. Stir the sifted
salt into the chocolate.
Pour the chocolate into
a shallow dish lined
with plastic film, to form a
layer of about 1/3 to 1/2 in.
(1 cm) thick. Tap the dish
gently against the work
surface to distribute
the chocolate evenly in
the dish. Refrigerate for
at least three hours.
Once firm, cut the
chocolate into cubes of
about 1/3 to 1/2 in. Set
them aside, separating the
cubes to prevent them from
sticking together.

Prepare the cake batter:
Preheat the oven to 140°F
(60°C/Gas Mark 1–2). Peel
the banana. Cut it in half,
lengthwise. Place in a
baking dish, sprinkle with
drops of lemon juice. Place
in the oven to dry for about
one and a half hours.
Remove the banana from the
oven and increase the oven
temperature, on convection
setting, to 340°F (170°C/Gas
Mark 5–6).
Set aside four rounds of the
semi-dried banana and
a little of the candied ginger
for the decoration. Chop
the remaining banana and
the candied ginger into
small cubes.
Sift the flour, cocoa powder
and baking powder
together into a bowl. Add
the cubes of banana and

candied ginger. Place the butter in the bowl of a mixer
fitted with a paddle attachment and mix for about
three minutes until the butter is creamy. Add the sugar
and mix for five minutes, incorporating the eggs one
at a time. Remove the bowl from the mixer and add the
flour–cocoa mixture, folding with a spatula. Fold in
3 oz. (90 g) of the chocolate cubes. Brush the two
rectangular (7 1/2 x 3 in./19 cm x 8 cm) cake molds
with melted butter and sprinkle them with a little flour.
Invert the molds and tap out excess flour.

Divide the batter equally among the two molds. Place
in the oven and cook for ten minutes. Reduce the oven
temperature to 320°F (160°C/Gas Mark 5–6) and bake
for an additional forty minutes. Insert the tip of a knife
in the center of the cakes to verify the cooking. If the
knife comes out clean the cakes are ready.

Prepare the imbibing syrup: Bring the sugar and water
to a boil in a saucepan.
Prepare the chocolate glaze: Chop the chocolate with
a serrated knife and combine it with the chocolate glaze
in a bowl over a bain-marie to melt to 113°F (45°C).
Stir in the grape seed oil.

Remove the cakes from the oven and unmold
immediately onto a rack placed over a rimmed baking
sheet. While the cakes are still hot, pour the sugar
syrup over them three times. Set the cakes aside
to drain and cool.
Bring the chocolate glaze to 105°F (40°C), reheating
in a bain-marie or microwave if necessary. Pour it evenly
over the cakes, and let drain. Decorate the top of the
cakes with the reserved banana slices and candied
ginger.

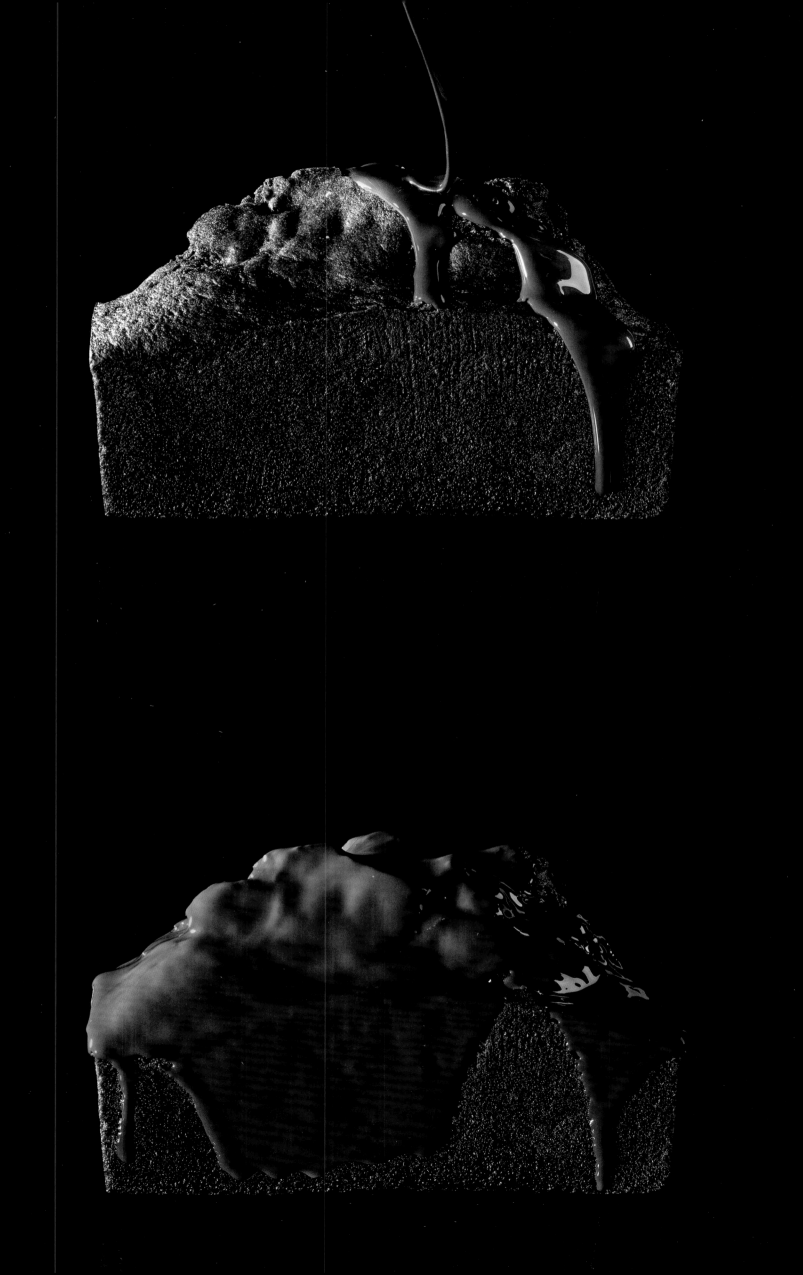

gour
met

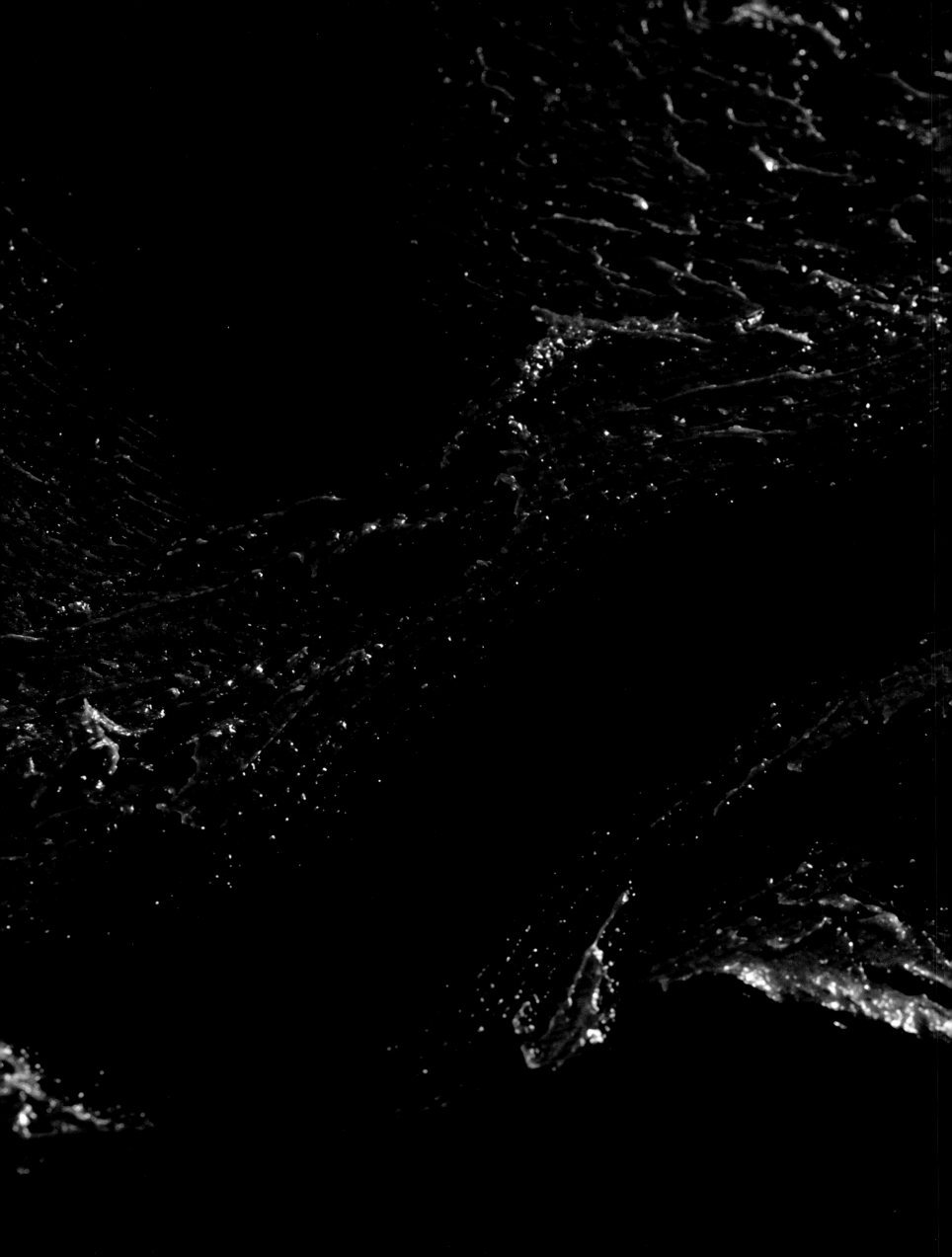

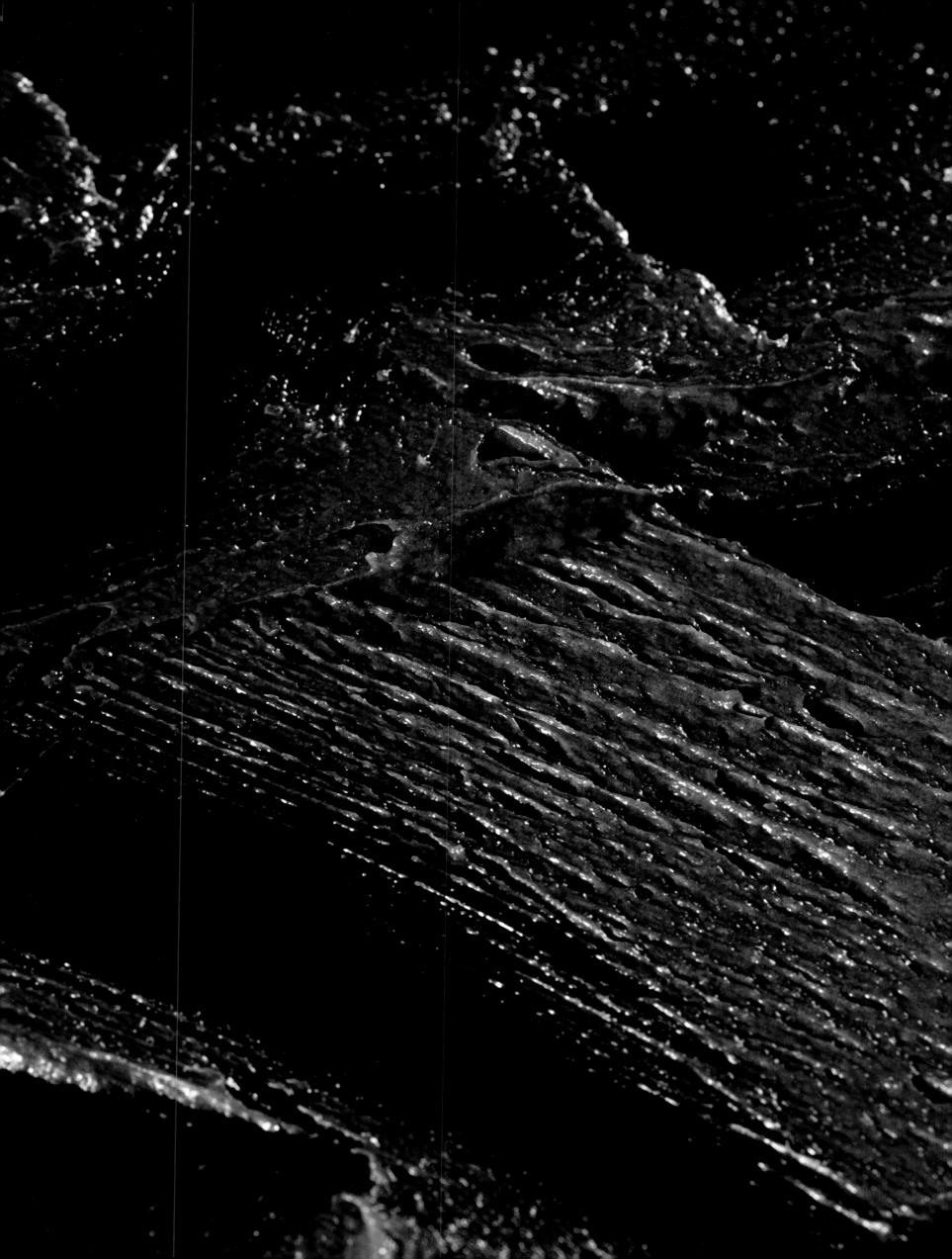

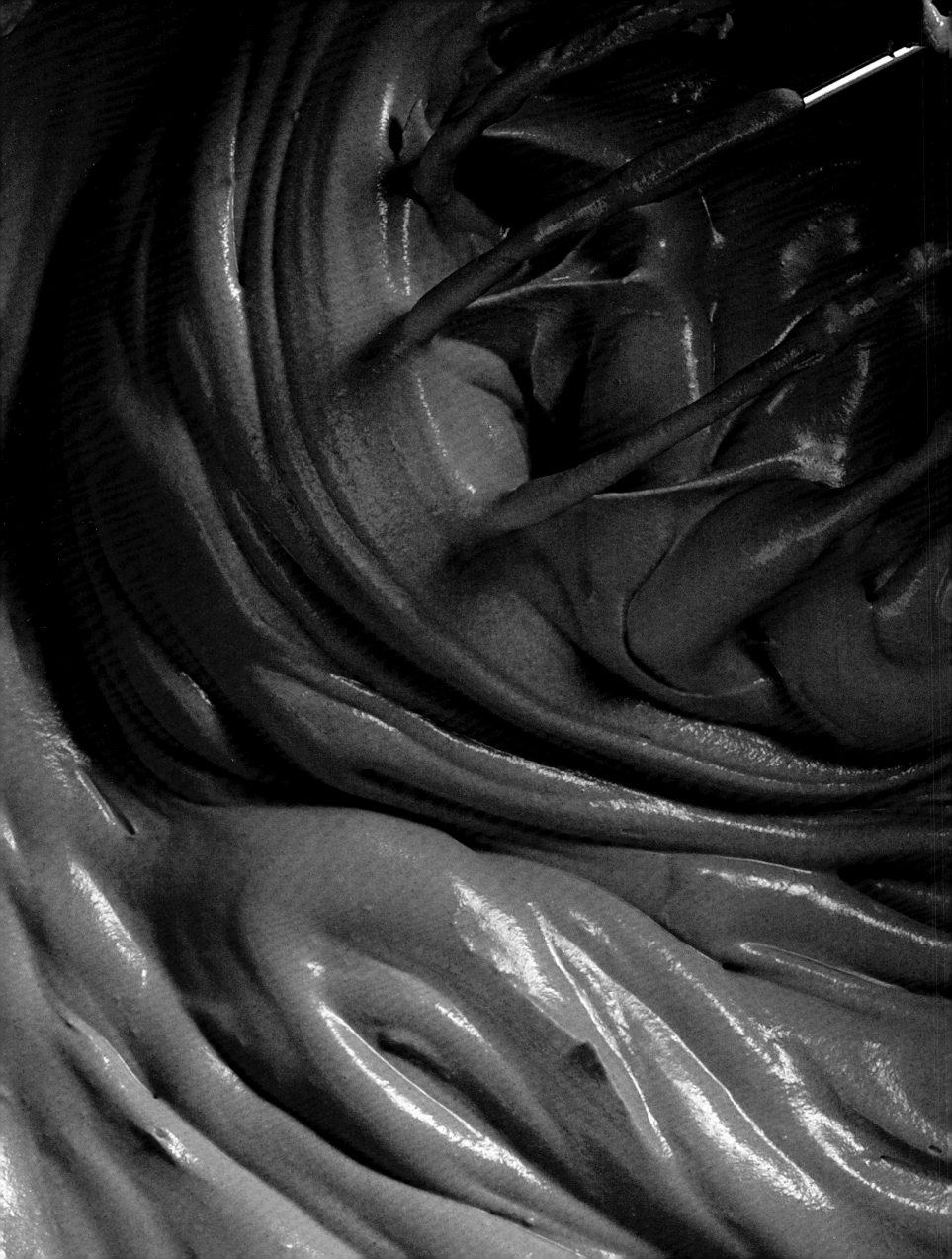

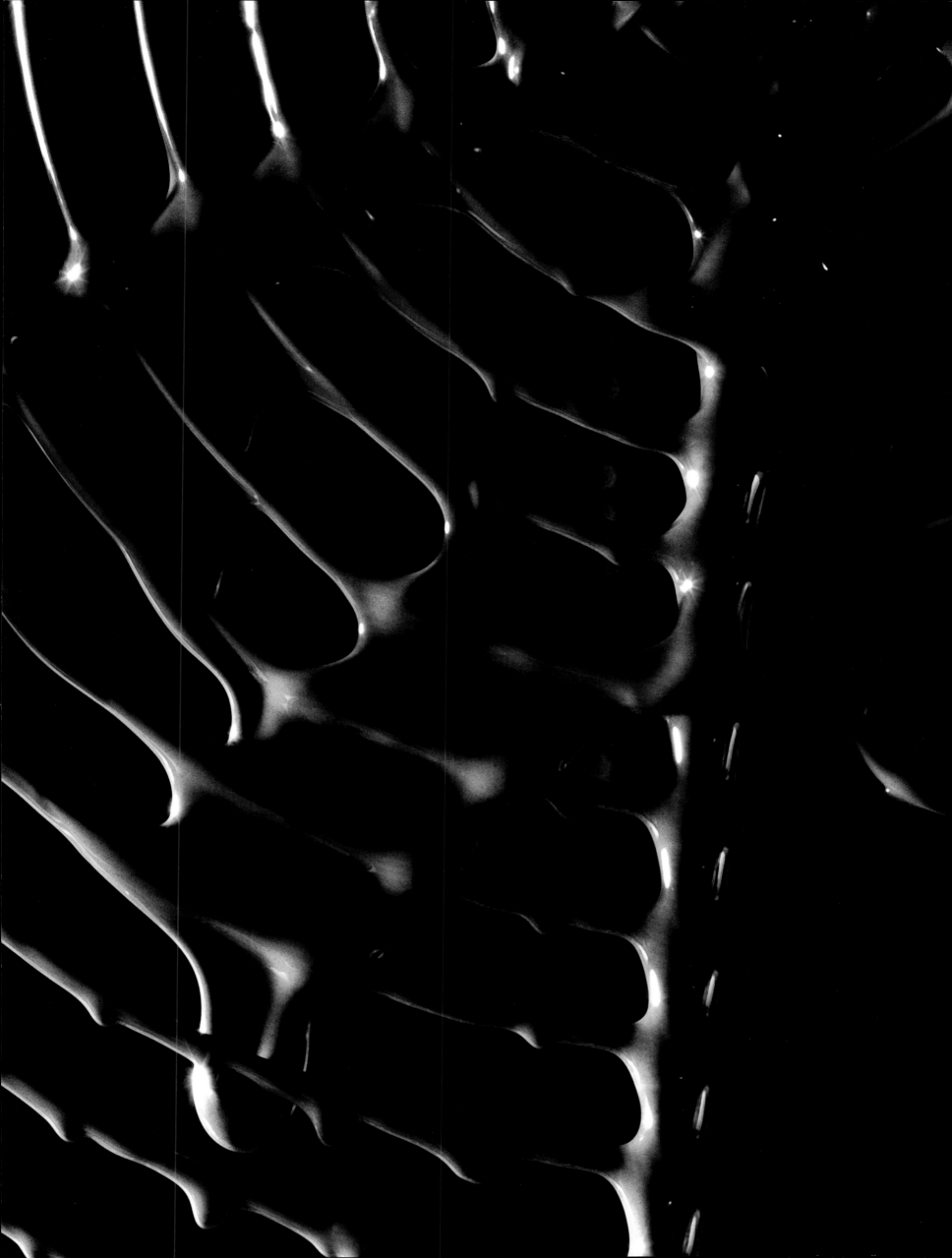

"A pinch of *Fleur de sel* puts sugar on a pedestal."

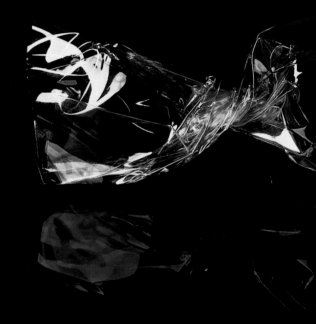

Miss Gla'Gla Plénitude

Miss Gla'Gla Plénitude Ice Cream Bars

Makes 18 ice cream bars

Ingredients:

Salted Butter Caramel Brittle:

2 tablespoons + 1 teaspoon
(1 3/4 oz./50 g) glucose syrup or corn
syrup
1/4 cup (1 3/4 oz./50 g) superfine
sugar
3 1/2 tablespoons (1 3/4 oz./50 g)
lightly salted butter

Salted Butter Caramel Ice
Cream:

3 1/2 tablespoons + 7 tablespoons
(5 oz./150 g) liquid cream
1 cup + 1/2 cup (9 oz./260 g)
superfine sugar
2 1/2 tablespoons (1 1/4 oz./35 g)
lightly salted butter
2 cups (17 2/3 oz./500 g) whole milk
3 1/2 tablespoons (2 oz./60 g) egg
yolks
1 3/4 oz. (50 g) salted butter caramel
brittle (see recipe above)

Dark Chocolate Chips
Fleur de sel:

10 1/2 oz. (300 g) Guanaja 70% dark
chocolate (Valrhona)
1 1/2 teaspoons (6 g) *Fleur de sel*,
preferably Guérande

Chocolate Ice Cream with *Fleur
de sel* Dark Chocolate Chips:

4 3/4 oz (135 g) Guanaja 70% dark
chocolate (Valrhona)
2 cups (17 2/3 oz./500 g) whole milk
3 tablespoons (22.5 g) milk powder,
0% fat
4 tablespoons (1 3/4 oz./50 g)
superfine sugar
2 2/3 oz. (75 g) *Fleur de sel* dark
chocolate slivers (see recipe above)

Chocolate Macaron Rectangular
Shells:

1 3/4 cups (5 1/4 oz./150 g) ground
almonds
1 cup + 2 1/2 tablespoons
(5 1/4 oz./150 g) confectioners' sugar
2 oz. (60 g) pure cocoa paste
(Valrhona)
1/2 cup (4 oz./110 g) or about
4 "liquefied" egg whites, divided
(see note)
4 drops (0.25 g) carmine red food
coloring
3/4 cup (5 1/4 oz./150 g) superfine
sugar
2 tablespoons + 1 teaspoon
(1 1/4 oz./35 g) mineral water

Caramel Macaron Rectangular
Shells:

1 3/4 cup (5 1/4 oz./150 g) ground
almonds
1 cup + 2 1/2 tablespoons
(5 1/4 oz./150 g) confectioners' sugar
1/2 cup (4 oz./110 g) or about
4 "liquefied" egg whites, divided
(see note)

5 drops egg yolk yellow food coloring
1 1/3 teaspoons (7.5 g) coffee
extract, preferably Trablit
3/4 cup (5 1/4 oz./150 g) superfine
sugar
2 tablespoons + 1 teaspoon mineral
water

Finishing:

Apricot jam

———

Preparation Time:

2 mins. (5 days in advance);
15 mins. (1 day in advance);
about 2 h. 30 mins. (the same day).

Cooking Time:

About 40 mins.

Resting Time:

5 h.

Chilling Time:

2 h. + 24 h.

Freezing Time:

2 x 2 h.

Preparation:

Five days in advance, place the egg whites for the
chocolate and caramel macaron rectangles
in a bowl, cover the bowl tightly with plastic film,
pierce a few holes in the film and refrigerate to liquefy.

One day in advance, prepare the caramel brittle:
Place the glucose or corn syrup in a small saucepan to
melt, stir in the sugar. Let caramelize to a uniform amber
color. Add the butter immediately, stirring, and bring
to a boil. Pour the mixture out onto a silicone pastry
sheet to cool. Once cooled, break the brittle into pieces
using a rolling pin. Place the caramel brittle pieces
in a processor and pulse to chop the brittle to smaller
pieces. Store the brittle pieces in an airtight container
at room temperature until using.

———

**The same day, prepare the salted butter caramel ice
cream:** Whip 3 1/2 tablespoons (1 3/4 oz./50 g) of the
liquid cream. Pour one cup (6 1/4 oz./175 g) of the
sugar, little by little, into a saucepan, letting it melt after
each addition, and cook until caramelized to a uniform
amber color. Add the butter immediately and remove
from the heat. Stir in the whipped cream. In a second
saucepan, combine the milk and the remaining
seven tablespoons (100 g) cream, and bring to a boil. In
a third saucepan, whisk the egg yolks with the remaining
1/3 cup (85 g) sugar. Pour the caramel over the milk–cream
mixture, stirring briskly. Pour this caramel over the egg
yolk–sugar mixture, stirring, and heat, stirring constantly
to 185°F (85°C). Place the saucepan in a recipient of
ice-cold water to cool the mixture, stirring constantly for
four to five minutes. Mix with a hand blender, then pour
the mixture into an ice cream machine and process
according to the manufacturer's instructions. Meanwhile,
place a stainless steel container of approximately
12 x 6 in. by 4 in. deep (30 cm x 15 cm x 10 cm) in the
freezer for twenty minutes. Incorporate 1 3/4 oz. (50 g)
of the caramel brittle in the ice cream when processed
and pour the ice cream into the chilled container,
smooth the surface and return it to the freezer.

———

Prepare the *Fleur de sel* dark chocolate slivers:
Crush the *Fleur de sel* with a rolling pin. Sift through a
fine sieve. Chop the chocolate with a serrated knife and
place it in a bowl over a bain-marie of simmering water
to melt, stirring gently with a wooden spoon until the
temperature of the chocolate reaches 130°F (55°C).
Remove the bowl immediately from the bain-marie and
place it in a bowl of cold water with four or five ice
cubes. Stir the chocolate from time to time, scraping it
from the sides of the bowl as it begins to set. Once the
chocolate has cooled to 80°F (27°C), return the bowl to
the bain-marie to warm slightly, monitoring the

temperature carefully with a thermometer until the chocolate warms to between 88°F and 90°F (31°C–32°C). Stir in the sifted *Fleur de sel*. Place a sheet of rhodoid plastic* on a work surface. Pour the chocolate onto the plastic and use a spatula to spread into a thin, even layer. Cover the chocolate with a second sheet of rhodoid and top with light weights to keep the chocolate flat. Refrigerate until the following day.

Prepare the chocolate ice cream with *Fleur de sel* dark chocolate slivers: Fill a large bowl with water and ice cubes. Place a smaller bowl in the ice-cold bain-marie.
Chop the chocolate using a serrated knife. Combine the milk, milk powder and sugar in a saucepan, and bring to a boil. Add the chocolate, whisking briskly. Bring back to a boil, whisking constantly for thirty seconds. Pour the mixture into the bowl set over the ice-cold bain-marie. Let cool, stirring from time to time. Once cooled, process the mixture in an ice cream machine according to the manufacturer's instructions. Fold 2 2/3 oz. (75 g) of the *Fleur de sel* dark chocolate slivers delicately into the chocolate ice cream and pour into the stainless steel container on top of the salted butter caramel ice cream. Return the container to the freezer for one hour.

Prepare the marble mixture of caramel and chocolate ice creams: Place a stainless steel rectangular pastry frame, 21 1/2 x 4 1/2 x 1 in. (55 cm x 11.5 cm x 2.5 cm) on a pastry sheet lined with cooking parchment. Place the container of ice creams next to the frame. Using an ice cream spatula, scoop out a large spoonful of the two ice creams, dipping down vertically to the bottom of the container. Spread the ice cream over the bottom of the pastry frame, packing the ice cream lightly and swirling the spatula two or three times. Continue in the same manner with the remaining ice cream, pressing down lightly and swirling between each addition to create a marbled effect. Smooth the top with the spatula and cover with plastic film. Store in the freezer until the macaron rectangles are baked.

Prepare the rectangular chocolate macaron shells: Make a stencil for the macarons, cutting a 6 x 2-in. (15 cm x 5 cm) rectangle out of a piece of cardboard (about 1/16 in. thick). Draw a neat rectangle of about 4 3/4 x 1 1/2 in. in the center of the cardboard and cut out. Proceed in the same manner to make thirty-six rectangular stencils.
Sift the ground almonds and confectioners' sugar together. Chop the cocoa paste with a serrated knife and place it in a bowl over a bain-marie of simmering water to melt to 122°F (50°C). Combine 1/4 cup (55 g)

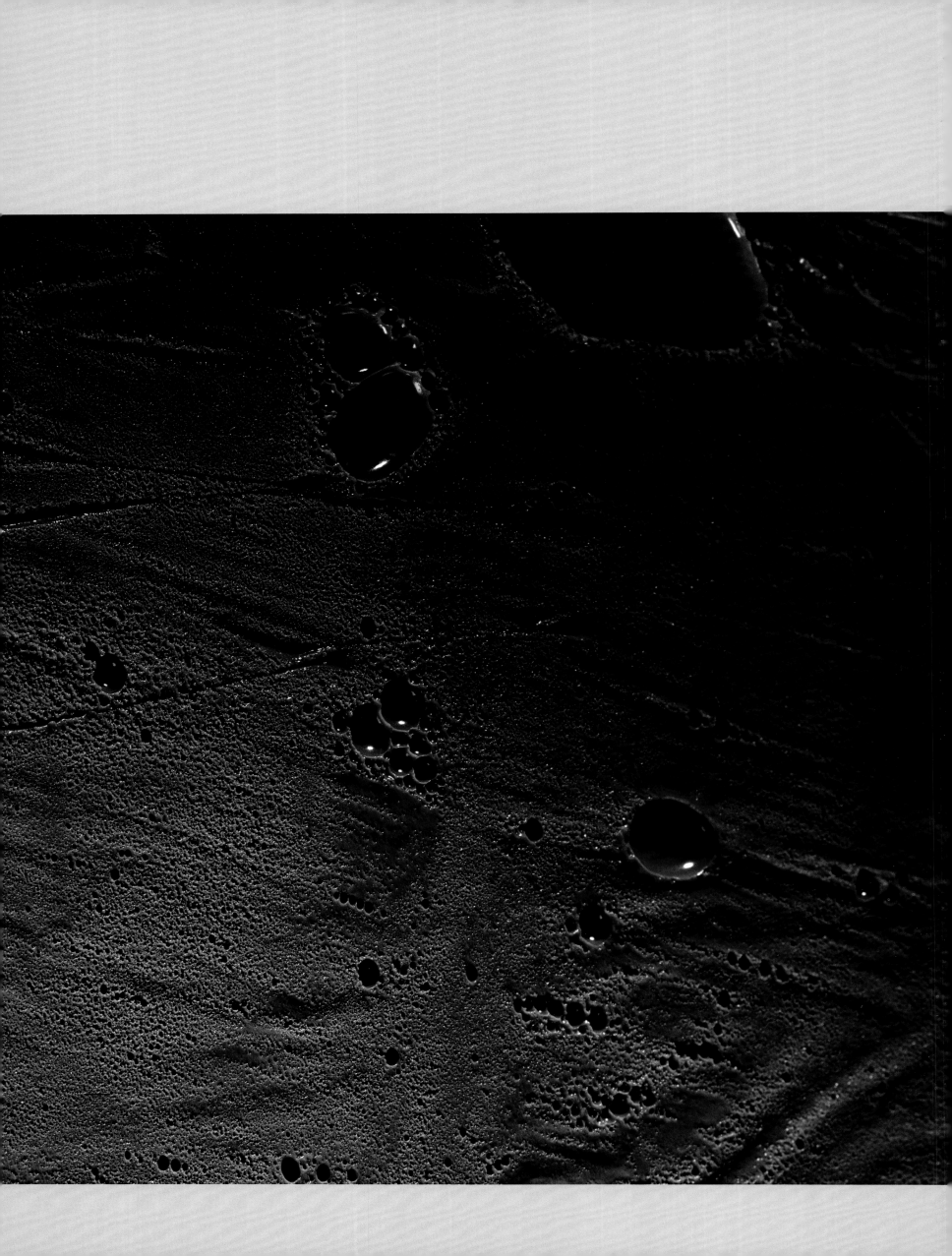

of liquefied egg whites with the food coloring. Pour onto the sifted almond powder–sugar mixture, without mixing.

Combine the sugar and water in a saucepan, and bring to a boil, monitoring the temperature with a thermometer. Meanwhile place the remaining 1/4 cup (55 g) of liquefied egg whites in the bowl of a mixer fitted with a wire whisk. Once the sugar syrup has reached 239°F (115°C), begin beating the egg whites on high speed. When the syrup reaches 244°F (118°C), reduce the mixer speed to medium and begin pouring the syrup in a steady stream into the egg whites. Continue beating until the mixture cools to 122°F (50°C). At this temperature, fold the meringue mixture into the almond–sugar–egg white mixture using a spatula. Add the melted cocoa paste, folding until the mixture loses a little of its volume. Spoon the batter into a pastry bag fitted with a No. 11 plain tip (1/2 in. diameter). Place the first rectangular stencil on a baking sheet lined with cooking parchment and pipe a little of the macaron batter into the center of the rectangle, spreading it out in a thin layer, smoothing the top with a spatula and scraping off any excess batter. Carefully remove the stencil and proceed in the same manner to make a total of thirty-six rectangles. Let rest at room temperature for five hours to allow a "skin" to form. Preheat the oven on convection setting to 300°F (150°C/Gas Mark 3). Place the baking sheets in the oven and cook for ten minutes, opening and closing the oven door quickly twice during the baking to release steam. Remove from the oven and slide the macaron rectangles onto a rack. When cooled, place in the freezer for thirty minutes.

Prepare the rectangular caramel macaron shells: Sift the ground almonds and confectioners' sugar together. Combine 1/4 cup (55 g) of liquefied egg whites with the food coloring and the coffee extract. Pour onto the sifted almond powder–sugar mixture, without mixing. Combine the sugar and water in a saucepan, and bring to a boil, monitoring the temperature with a thermometer. Meanwhile place the remaining 1/4 cup (55 g) of liquefied egg whites in the bowl of a mixer fitted with a wire whisk. Once the sugar syrup has reached 239°F (115°C), begin beating the egg whites on high speed. Once the syrup has reached 244°F (118°C), reduce the mixer speed to medium and begin pouring the syrup in a steady stream into the egg whites. Continue beating until the mixture cools to 122°F (50°C). At this temperature, fold the meringue mixture into the almond–sugar–egg white mixture, using a spatula and folding until the mixture loses some of its volume. Spoon the batter into a pastry bag fitted with a No. 11 plain tip (1/2 in. diameter). Prepare baking sheets lined with cooking parchment and proceed in the same manner as for the chocolate macaron shells, piping the batter into the rectangular stencils, spreading in a thin layer and removing the stencil to make thirty-six macaron shells. Set aside at room temperature for five hours to allow a "skin" to form.

Preheat the oven on convection setting to 300°F (150°C/Gas Mark 3). Place the baking sheets in the oven and cook for ten minutes, opening and closing the oven door quickly twice during the baking to release steam. Remove from the oven and slide the macaron shells onto a rack. Once cooled, place in the freezer for thirty minutes. Meanwhile, remove the ice cream from the freezer and run the blade of a small knife between the steel frame and the ice cream. Remove the frame and cut the ice cream into rectangles of 4 1/2 x 1 in. Return them to the freezer for thirty minutes.

To assemble: Heat the apricot jam in a small saucepan, and strain it through a fine sieve. Arrange the chocolate and caramel macaron shells, flat side up, on a work surface and brush each lightly with the apricot jam. Place an ice cream bar on a chocolate macaron shell and top with a caramel shell. Serve immediately, or freeze until just before serving. The bars can be stored in the freezer for several days.

* Transparent plastic celluloid used in pastry and confectionery.

Note: "Liquefied" egg whites are egg whites that have been allowed to rest for several days to lose their elasticity. Simply place the egg whites in a bowl, cover with plastic film, pierce a few holes in the film, and refrigerate for five to seven days.

PH Cube Infiniment Café Iapar Rouge du Brésil

Infiniment Café Iapar Rouge du Brésil PH Cubes

Makes about 100 PH Cubes

Ingredients:

Infiniment Café Iapar Rouge du Brésil Coffee Ganache:

1 1/4 oz. (35 g) Iapar Rouge du Brésil coffee beans
1 1/2 cups (13 1/3 oz./380 g) liquid cream
13 1/2 oz. (385 g) Caraque 56% chocolate (Valrhona)
8 1/2 oz. (240 g) Jivara 40% milk chocolate (Valrhona) or milk chocolate, 40% cocoa
1 1/2 tablespoons (1 1/4 oz./35 g) glucose syrup or corn syrup
3 1/2 tablespoons (1 3/4 oz./50 g) butter

Pre-Coating of PH Cubes:

10 1/2 oz. (300 g) Mexique 64% dark chocolate (Valrhona)

Final Coating of PH Cubes:

2 1/4 lb. (1 kg) Mexique 64% dark chocolate (Valrhona)

Preparation Time:

About 1 h. (2 days in advance);
about 1 h. (1 day in advance and the same day).

Cooking Time:

A few minutes (2 days in advance);
a few minutes (1 day in advance and the same day).

Resting Time:

2 x 24 h.

Preparation:

Two days in advance, prepare the coffee ganache: Grind the coffee beans in a coffee grinder. Bring the cream to a boil in a saucepan. Add the ground coffee, remove from the heat and set aside to infuse for three minutes. Strain. Chop the Caraque and Jivara chocolates with a serrated knife, and place them in a bowl with the glucose or corn syrup over a bain-marie of simmering water to heat to 113°F (45°C). Bring the coffee-infused cream back to a boil and pour, one-third at a time, over the chocolate, stirring from the center out in small, then progressively larger concentric circles.

Cut the butter into pieces. Once the temperature of the chocolate has reached 95°F–105°F (35°C–40°C), incorporate, little by little, the butter pieces. Whisk until the ganache is smooth.

Place a stainless steel square pastry frame, 6 3/4 in. x 6 3/4 in. and 1/2 in. deep (17 cm x 17 cm x 12 mm), on a silicon pastry sheet. Pour the coffee–chocolate ganache into the pastry frame, spreading the mixture out in an even layer with an elbow spatula. Allow to set at room temperature overnight.

The next day, temper the chocolate and proceed with the pre-coating: Chop the 10 1/2 oz. (300 g) of chocolate with a serrated knife, place it in a bowl over a bain-marie of simmering water to melt, stirring gently with a wooden spoon until the temperature of the chocolate reaches 130°F (55°C). Remove the bowl immediately from the bain-marie and place it in a bowl of cold water with four or five ice cubes. Stir the chocolate from time to time, scraping it from the sides of the bowl as it begins to set. Once the chocolate has cooled to 80°F (27°C), return the bowl to the bain-marie to warm slightly, monitoring the temperature carefully with a thermometer until the chocolate warms to between 88°F and 90°F (31°C–32°C). Using an elbow spatula, spread a thin, even layer of the tempered chocolate over the ganache in the pastry frame. Smooth the surface and let set at room temperature for about twenty minutes. Turn the pastry frame over carefully, the pre-coated side down, on the silicon pastry sheet and spread a thin coat of the chocolate over the other side. Smooth the surface and let set for twenty minutes at room temperature.

Carefully remove the pastry frame, running the blade of a small knife dipped in hot water around the inner edges between the ganache and the pastry frame. Cut into 2/3-in. (15 mm) cubes. Separate the cubes and place them, well spaced out, on a pastry sheet.

Store at room temperature between 60°F and 65°F (16°C–18°C) overnight.

The following day, proceed with the final coating:
Chop the 2 1/4 lb. (1 kg) of chocolate with a serrated knife, place it in a bowl over a bain-marie of simmering water to melt, stirring gently with a wooden spoon until the temperature of the chocolate reaches 130°F (55°C). Remove the bowl immediately from the bain-marie and place it in a bowl of cold water with four or five ice cubes. Stir the chocolate from time to time, scraping it from the sides of the bowl as it begins to set. Once the chocolate has cooled to 80°F (27°C), return the bowl to the bain-marie to warm slightly, monitoring the temperature carefully with a thermometer until the chocolate warms to between 88°F and 90°F (31°C–32°C).
Spread several sheets of rhodoid plastic* on a flat work surface. Dip a first cube of the coffee–chocolate ganache in the chocolate, remove with a three-tined chocolate dipping fork, lifting toward the edge of the bowl, then dipping the bar once again in the chocolate, lifting two or three times in a pumping motion to coat. Remove the cube with the fork, resting it on the edge of the bowl, and tapping lightly to remove any excess chocolate. Finish by scraping the bottom of the fork along the edge of the bowl. Place the chocolate cube on the plastic.
Continue in the same manner for the remaining chocolate cubes, taking care to return the chocolate to the bain-marie from time to time to maintain the temperature between 88°F–90°F (31°C–32°C).
Let the cubes dry at room temperature overnight. Store the PH Cubes in an airtight container at between 60°F and 65°F (16°C–18°C), away from humidity and odors.

* Transparent plastic celluloid used in pastry and confectionery.

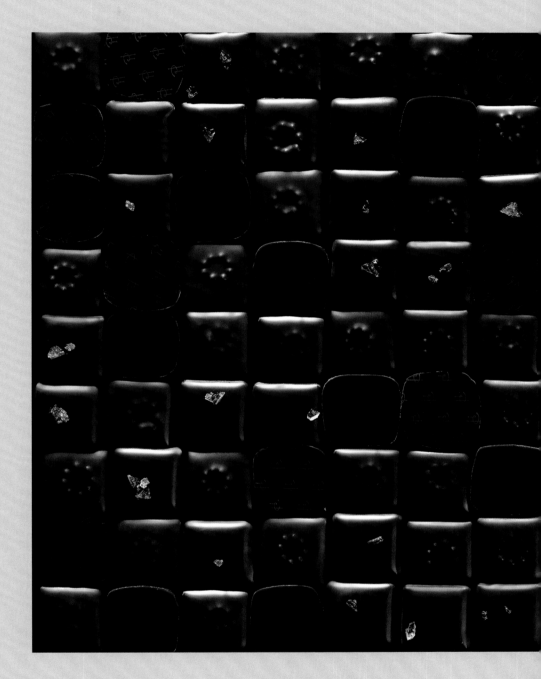

"The format and the perception of the flavor are inextricably linked."

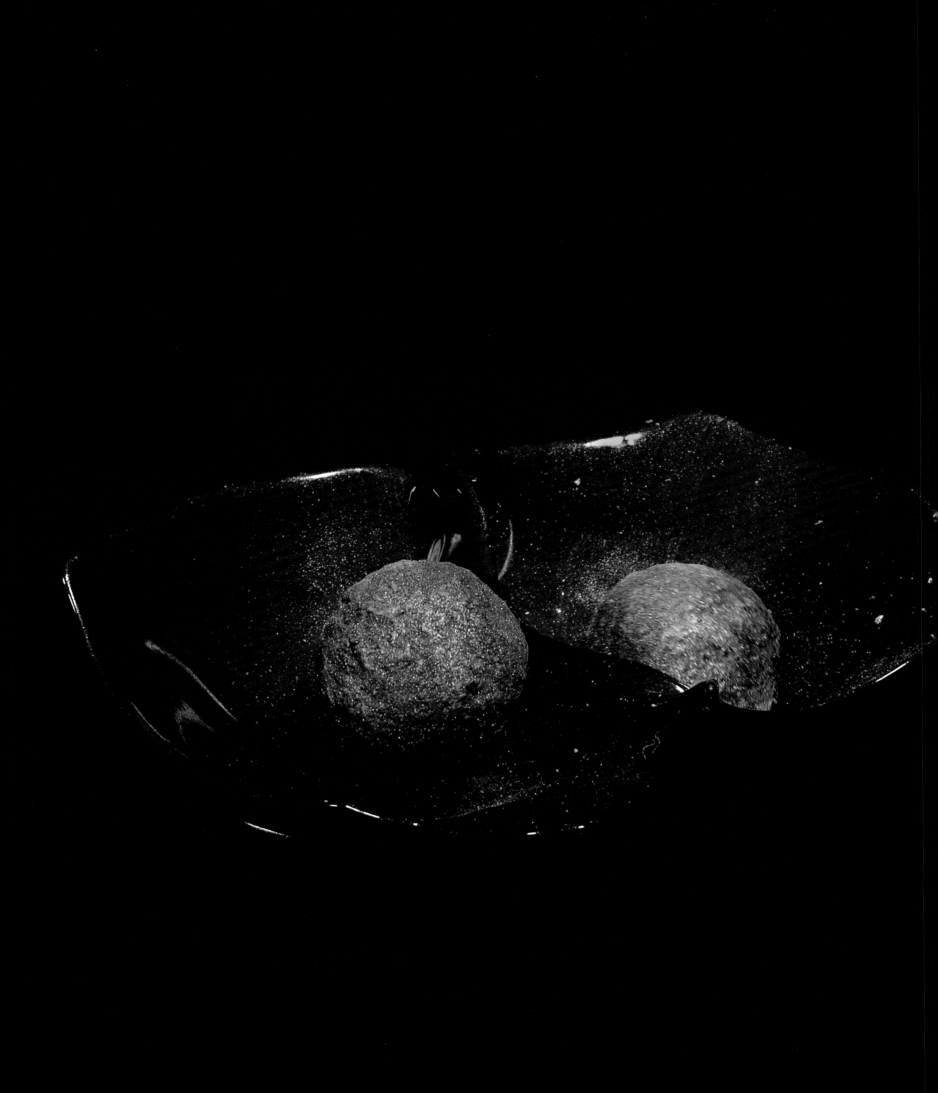

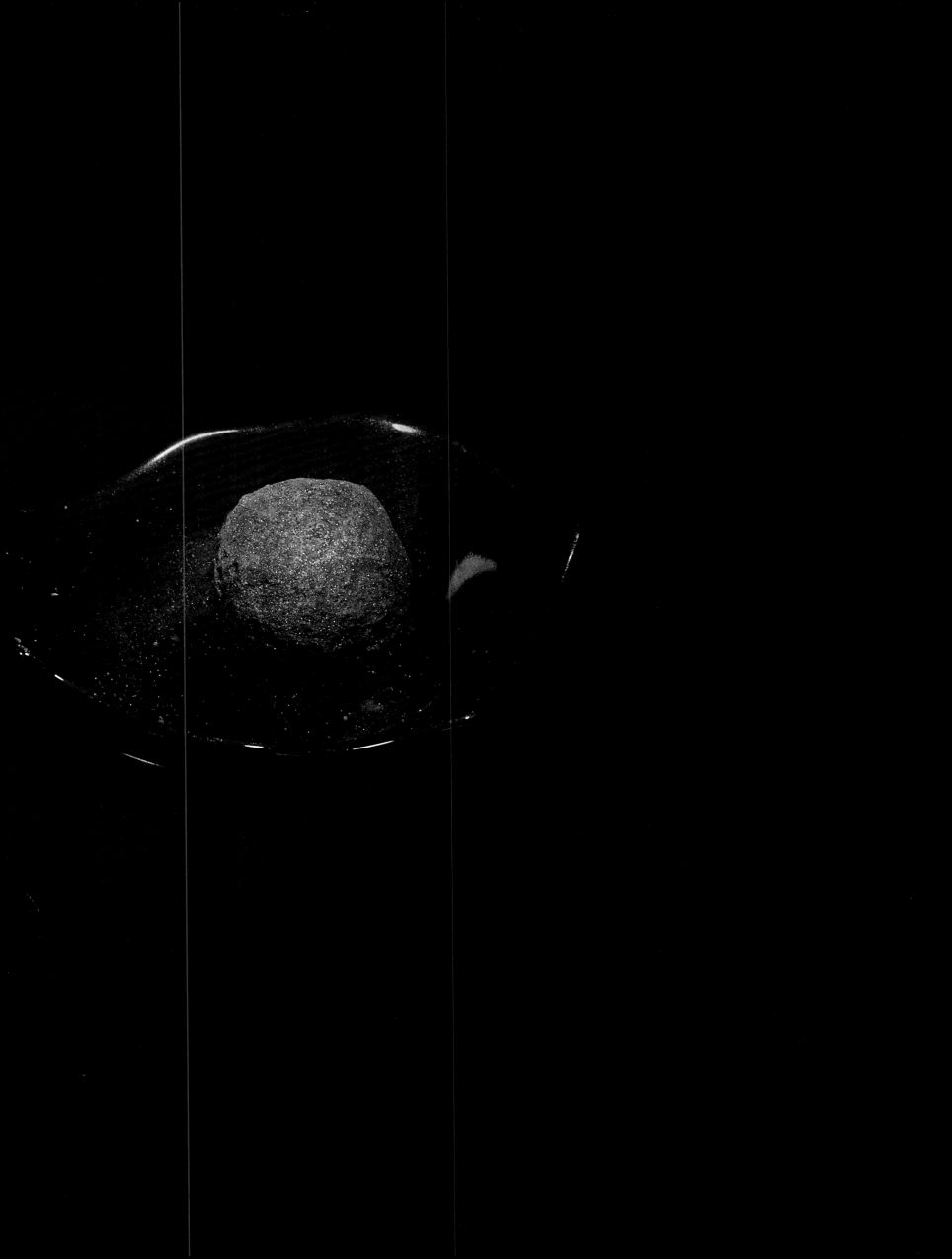

Dre
am

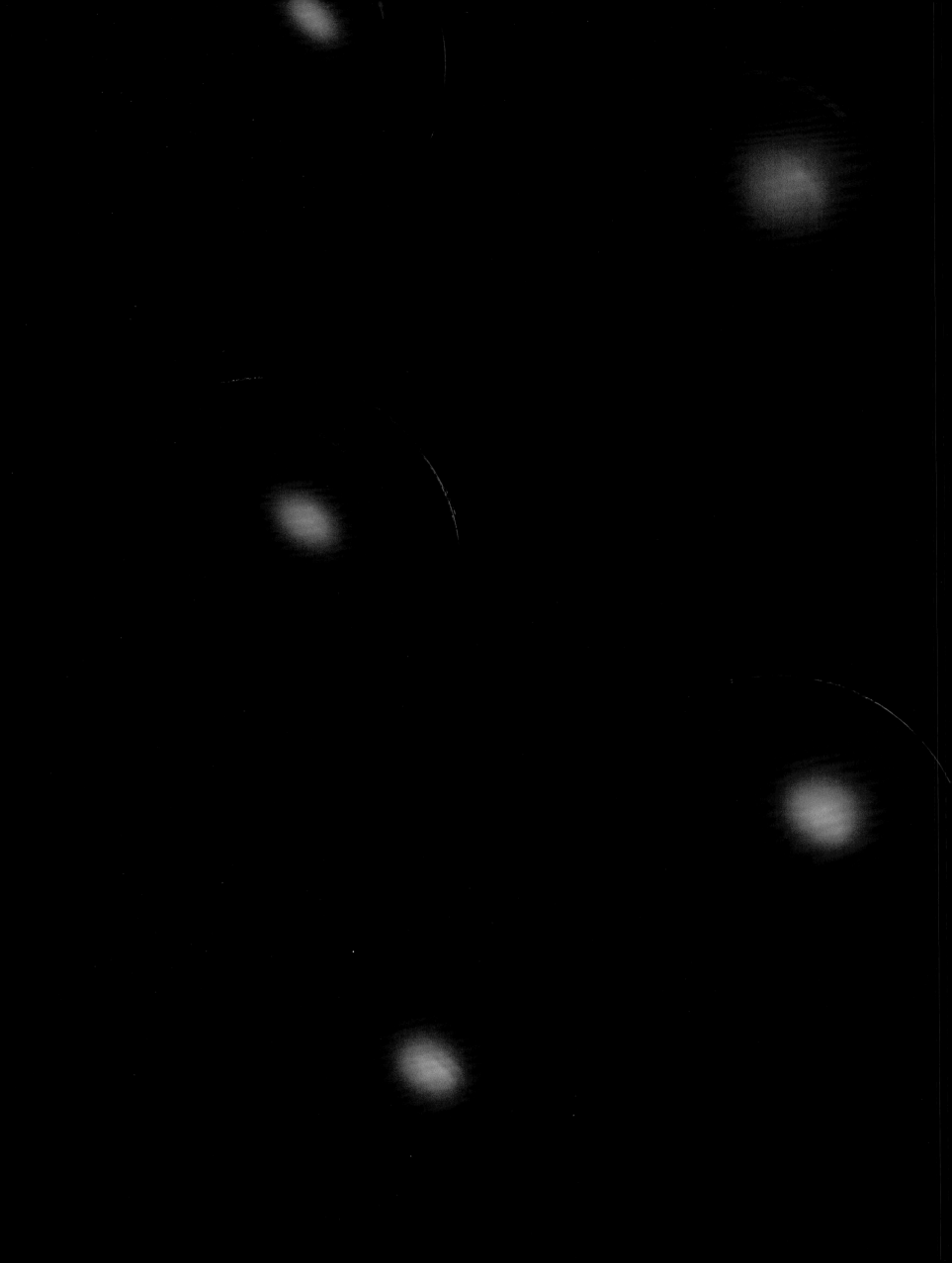

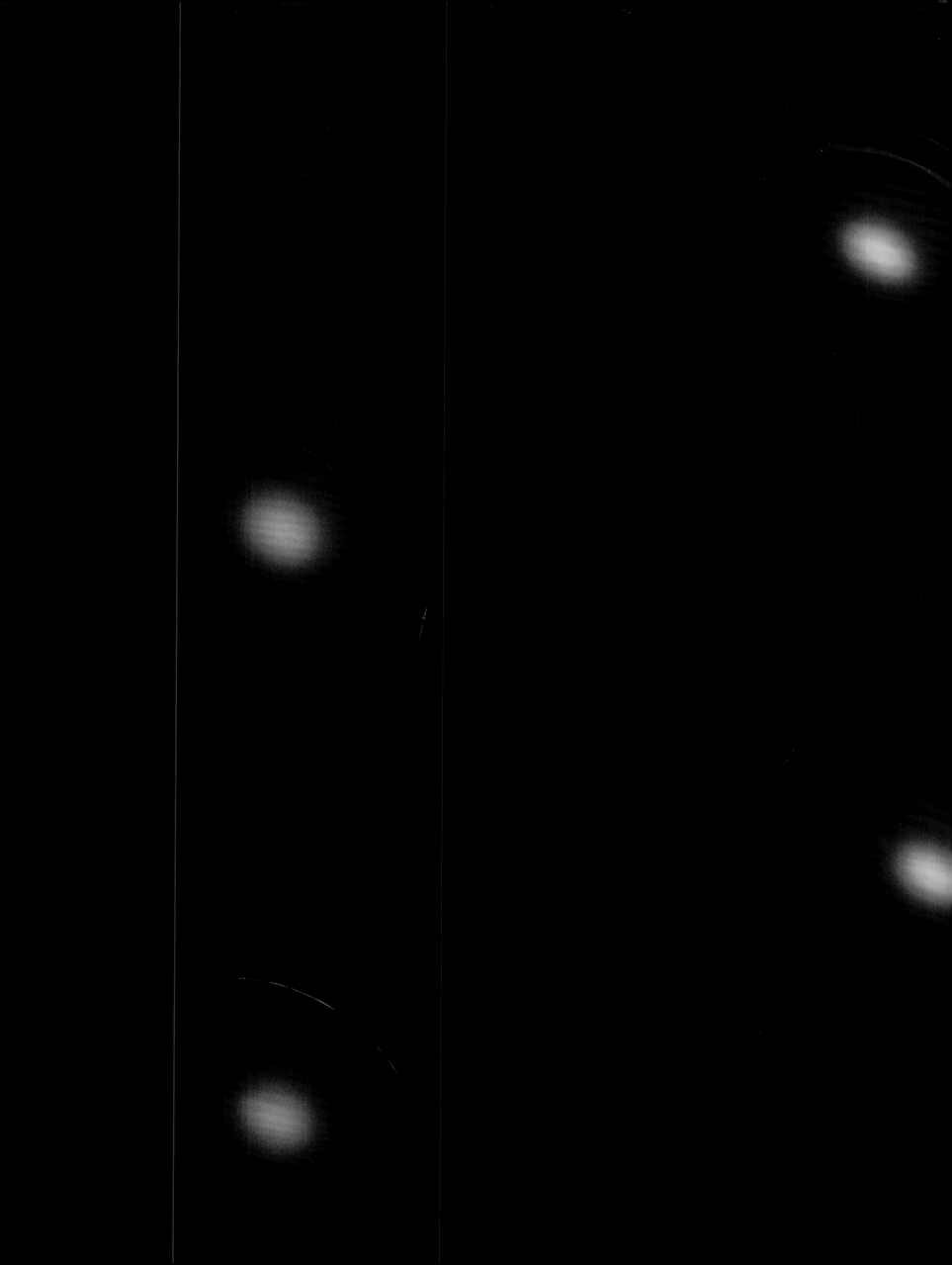

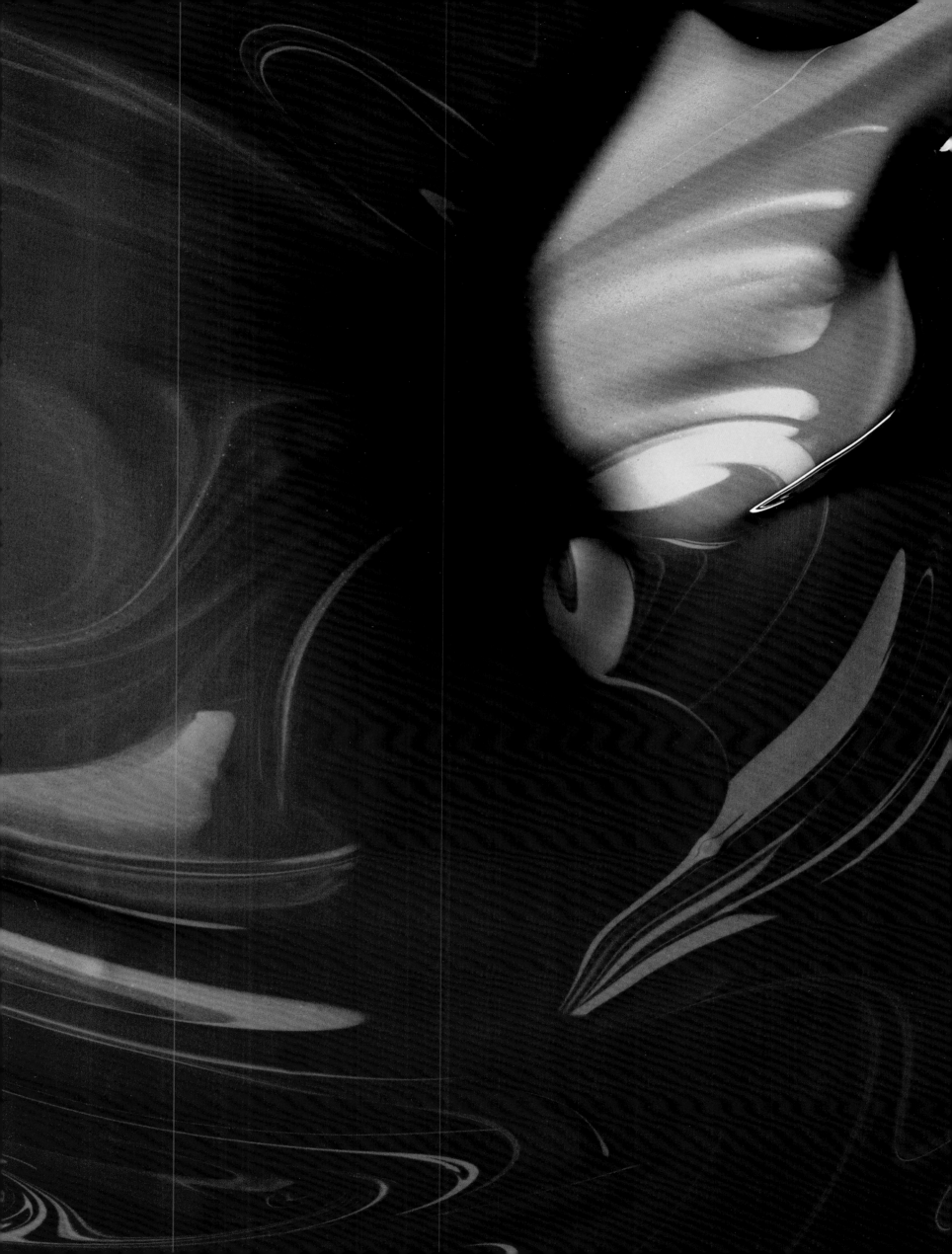

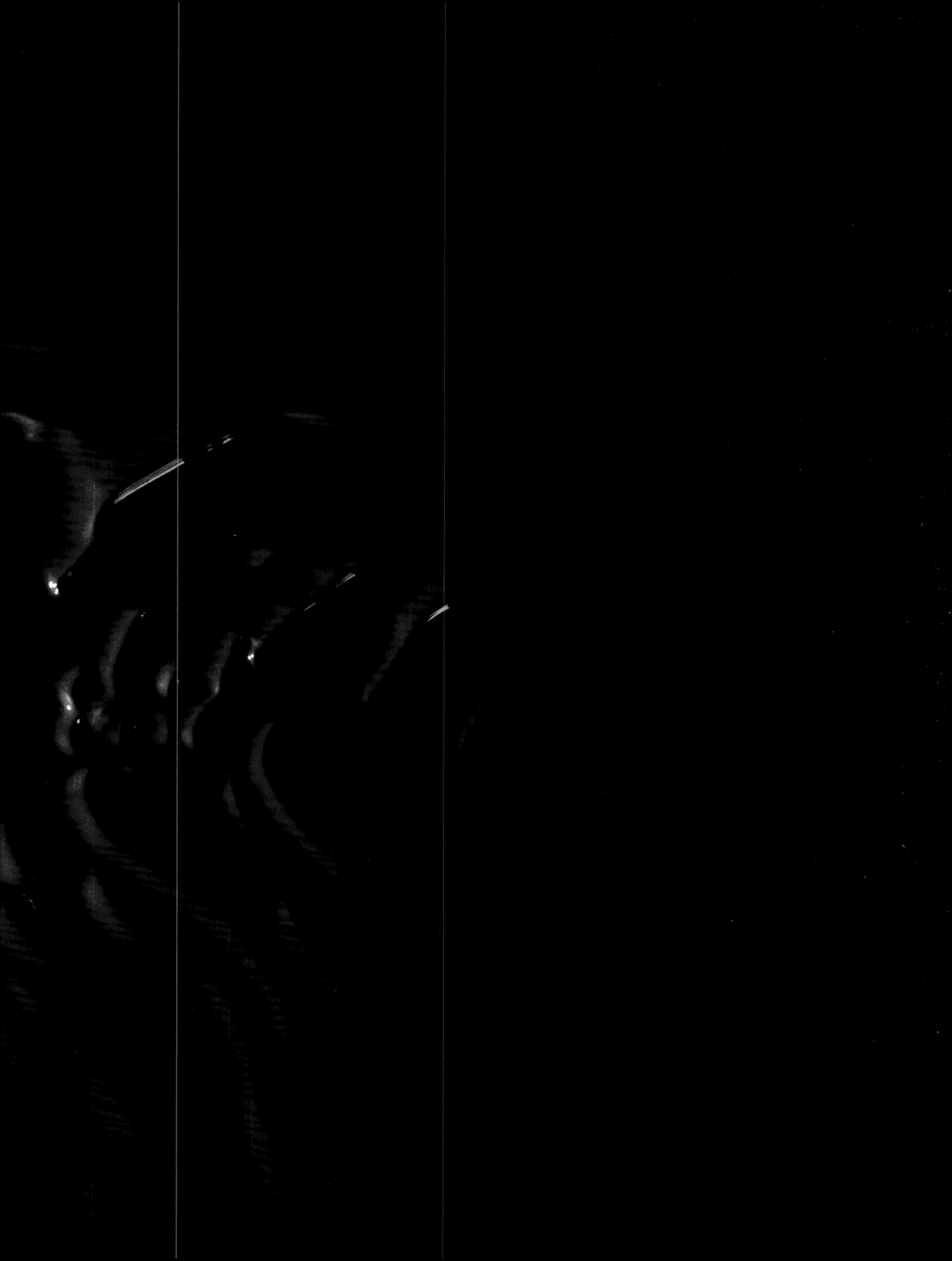

Coupe glacée Infiniment Chocolat

Infiniment Chocolat Ice Cream

Serves 10

Ingredients:

Fleur de sel Dark Chocolate Fragments:

1 1/2 teaspoons (6 g) _Fleur de sel_, preferably Guérande
10 1/2 oz (300 g) Araguani 72% dark chocolate (Valrhona)

Chocolate Whipped Cream:

5 oz. (140 g) Guanaja 70% dark chocolate (Valrhona)
2/3 oz. (20 g) pure cocoa paste (Valrhona)
3 cups (24 2/3 oz./700 g) liquid cream
2 1/2 tablespoons (1 oz./30 g) superfine sugar

Dark Chocolate Ice Cream:

2 lb. (960 g) Manjari 64% dark chocolate (Valrhona)
1 1/4 cups (10 1/2 oz./300 g) whole milk
1 cup (4 1/4 oz./120 g) milk powder, 0% fat
1 1/2 cups (10 1/2 oz./300 g) superfine sugar

Roasted Almond Brownies:

1/2 cup (3 1/2 oz./100 g) whole blanched almonds
7 tablespoons + 2 teaspoons (2 oz./60 g) flour
2 1/2 oz. (70 g) Guanaja 70% dark chocolate (Valrhona)
1/2 cup (4 1/3 oz./125 g) butter
2/3 cup (4 1/3 oz./125 g) superfine sugar
1/2 cup (3 1/2 oz./100 g) eggs

Cold Chocolate Soup:

10 1/2 oz. (300 g) Guanaja 70% dark chocolate (Valrhona)
3 cups (26 1/2 oz./750 g) mineral water
2 1/2 tablespoons (1 oz./30 g) superfine sugar
1/4 teaspoon (1.5 g) _Fleur de sel_, preferably Guérande

Finishing:

Gold leaf

———

Preparation Time:

30 mins. (1 day in advance);
30 mins. (the same day).

Cooking Time:

5 mins. (1 day in advance);
35 mins. (the same day).

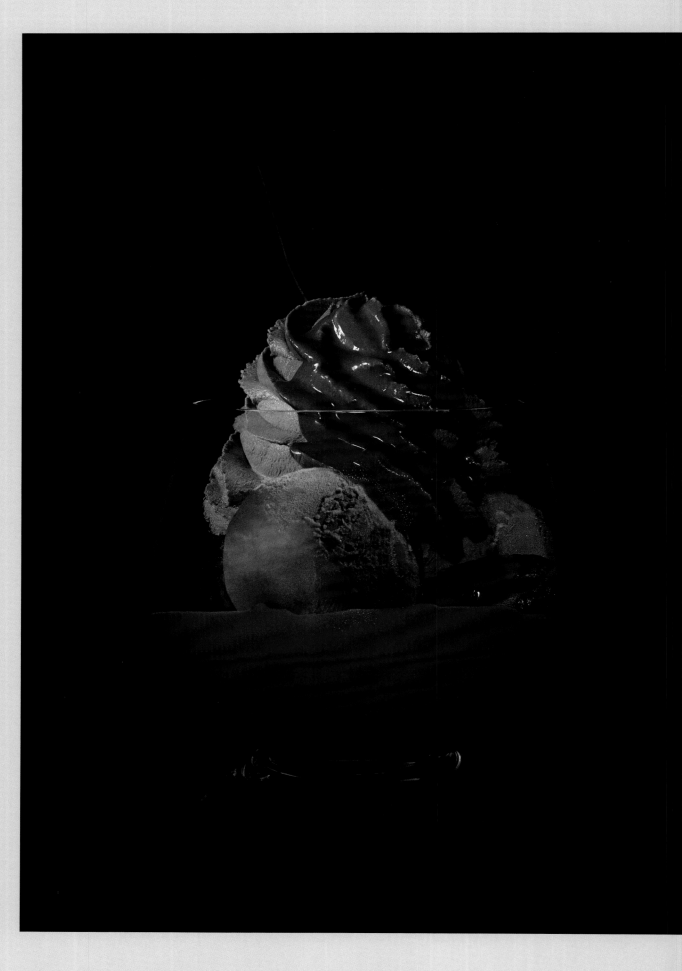

Preparation:

A day in advance, prepare the chocolate sheet for the chocolate slivers: Crush the *Fleur de sel* with a rolling pin. Sift through a fine sieve. Chop the chocolate with a serrated knife and place it in a bowl over a bain-marie of simmering water to melt, stirring gently with a wooden spoon until the temperature of the chocolate reaches 130°F (55°C). Remove the bowl immediately from the bain-marie and place it in a bowl of cold water with four or five ice cubes. Stir the chocolate from time to time, scraping it from the sides of the bowl as it begins to set. Once the chocolate has cooled to 80°F (27°C), return the bowl to the bain marie to warm slightly, monitoring the temperature carefully with a thermometer until the chocolate warms to between 88°F and 90°F (31°C–32°C). Stir in sifted *Fleur de sel* into the chocolate. Place a large sheet of rhodoid plastic* on a work surface. Pour the chocolate onto the plastic and spread into a thin, even layer with a spatula. Cover the chocolate with a second sheet of rhodoid and top with light weights to keep the sheet of chocolate flat. Refrigerate until the following day.

Also a day in advance, prepare the chocolate whipped cream: Chop the chocolate and cocoa paste with a serrated knife. Place them in a bowl over a bain-marie of simmering water to melt. Combine the cream and sugar in a saucepan, and bring to a boil. Pour the cream, one-third at a time, over the chocolate, stirring from the center out in small, then progressively larger concentric circles. Press a sheet of plastic film directly onto the surface of the cream and refrigerate overnight.

The following day, prepare the chocolate ice cream: Place a bowl over a recipient of cold water with a few ice cubes. Chop the chocolate with a serrated knife. Combine the milk, milk powder and the sugar in a saucepan, and bring to a boil. Add the chopped chocolate, whisking briskly. Bring the mixture back to a boil, whisking continually for thirty seconds. Pour the chocolate into the bowl over the ice-cold bain-marie and let cool, stirring from time to time. Once cooled, process the chocolate mixture in an ice cream machine according to the manufacturer's instructions.

Prepare the brownies: Preheat the oven on convection setting to 340°F (170°C/Gas Mark 5–6). Spread the almonds on a baking sheet lined with cooking parchment. Place in the oven to toast the almonds for fifteen minutes. Remove from the oven and let the almonds cool before chopping coarsely. Reduce the oven temperature to 320°F (160°C/Gas Mark 5–6). Sift the flour and add the chopped almonds. Chop the chocolate with a serrated knife and place it in a bowl over a bain-marie of simmering water to melt to 113°F (45°C). Cut the butter into pieces and place it in the bowl of a mixer fitted with the paddle attachment. Add the sugar, melted chocolate, eggs and flour–almond mixture, and mix until well combined. Spread the batter out evenly in a 2/3 in. (1.5 cm) thick layer. Place in the oven and bake for twelve minutes. Remove and let cool before cutting into 2/3-in. (1.5 cm) cubes.

Prepare the cold chocolate soup: Chop the chocolate with a serrated knife and place it in a bowl. Combine the mineral water, sugar and salt in a saucepan, and bring to a boil. Pour this syrup, one-third at a time, over the chocolate, stirring from the center out in small, then progressively larger concentric circles. Mix with a hand blender. Refrigerate.

To assemble: Just before serving, remove the *Fleur de sel* chocolate sheet from the refrigerator and break it into irregular pieces. Whip the chilled chocolate cream and spoon it into a pastry bag fitted with a F8 star tip. Place several brownie cubes in the bottom of individual sundae glasses. Spoon about 1/3 cup (80 g) of the cold chocolate soup into each glass, sprinkle with more chocolate cubes. Add three scoops of the chocolate ice cream and top with a rosette of chocolate whipped cream. Place a *Fleur de sel* chocolate fragment in the cream and top each serving with a piece of gold leaf. Serve immediately, accompanied by the remaining chocolate soup.

* Transparent plastic celluloid used in pastry and confectionery.

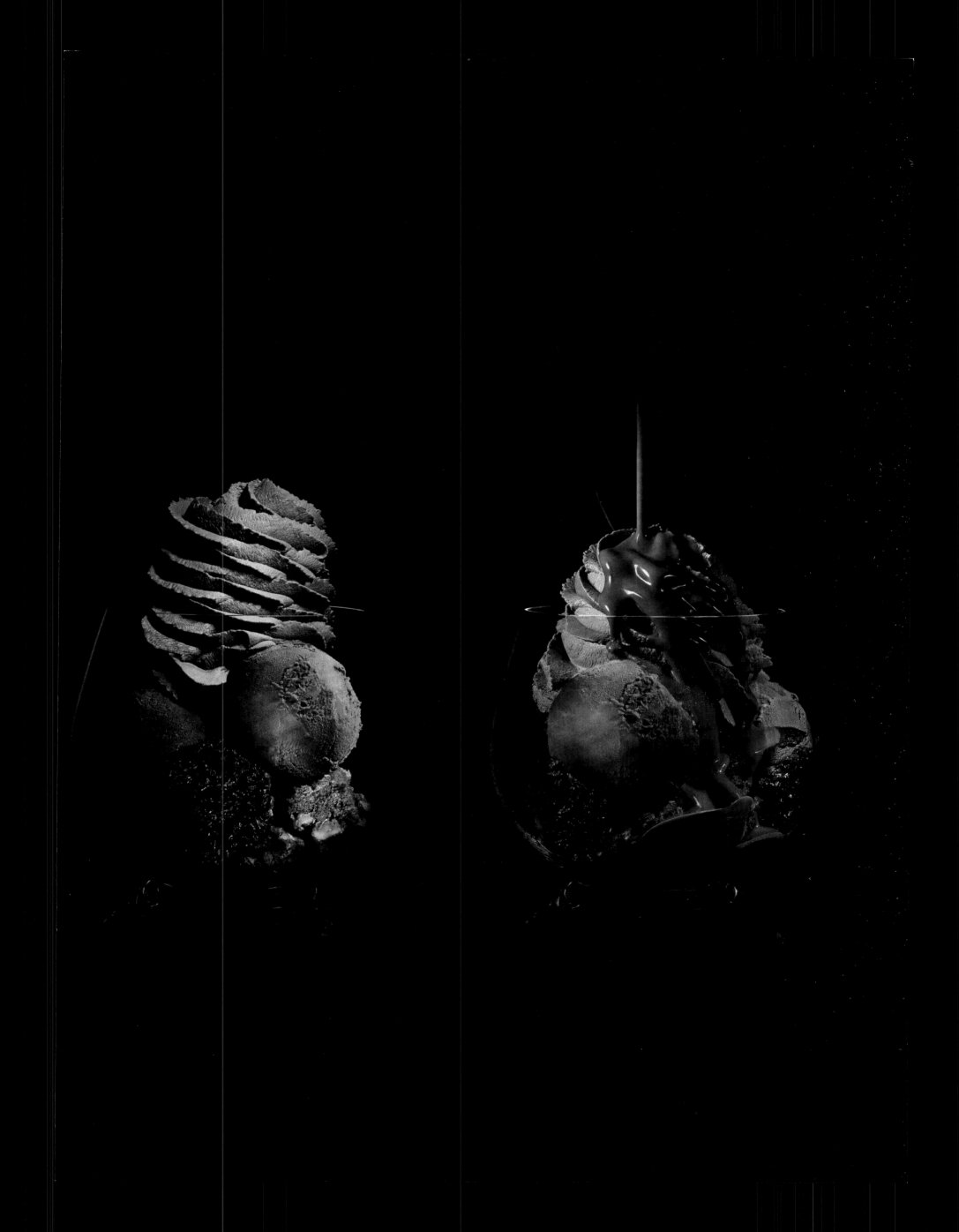

"Unlike the fine coating that professional chocolate makers look for, I like it to be a little bit thicker, part and parcel of the taste of the chocolate bonbon."

"Behind each of my creations lies a hidden and extremely precise architecture of taste."

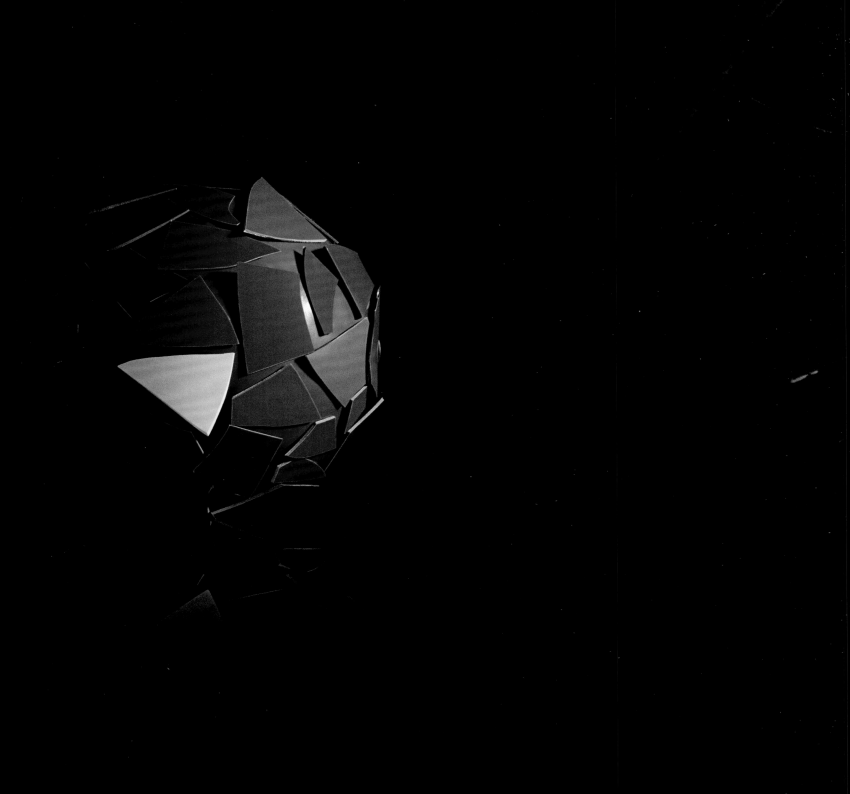

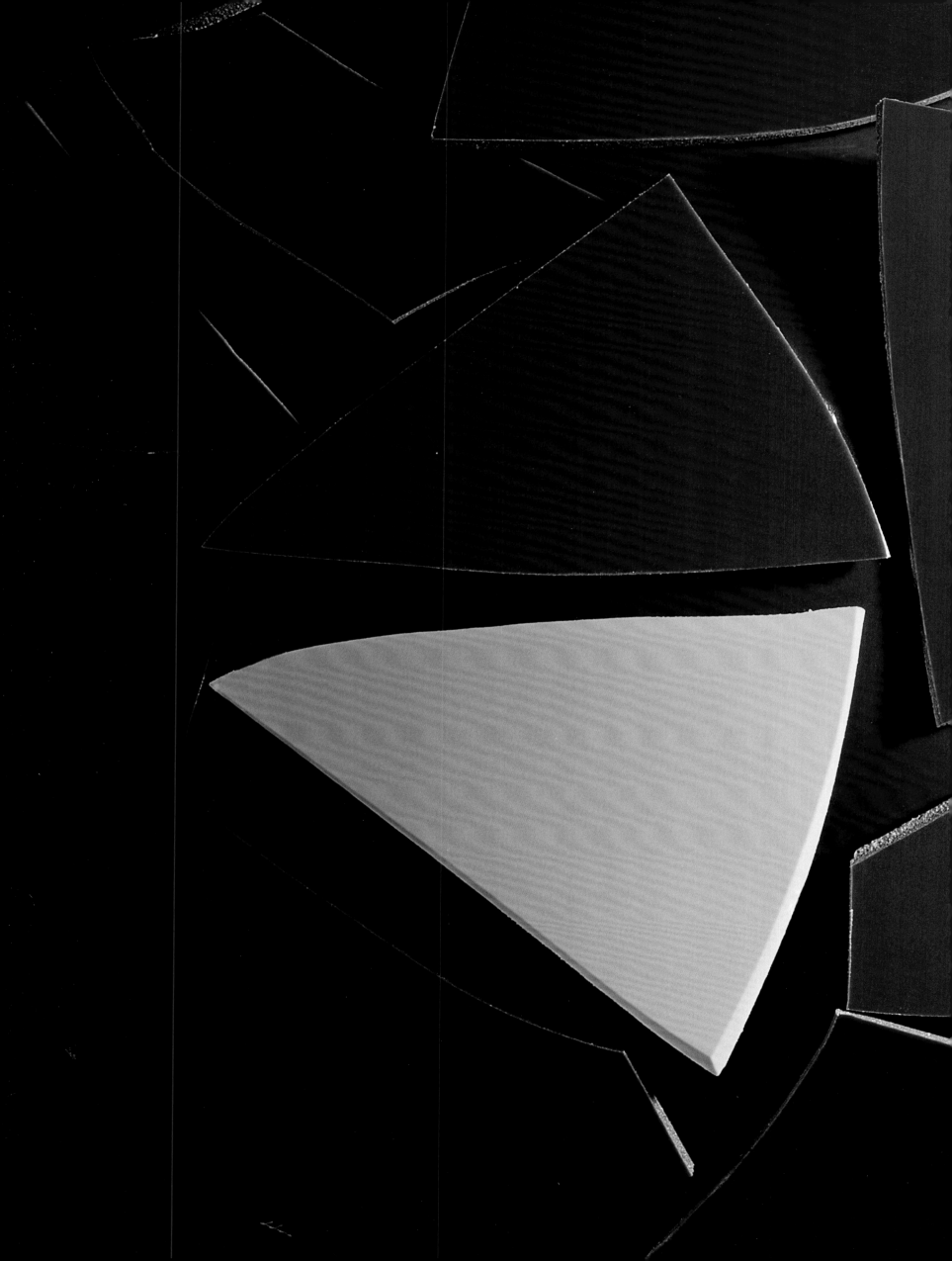

"Crunchy, smooth, crispy, melting, creamy…
The Cerise sur le Gâteau is all of these at once."

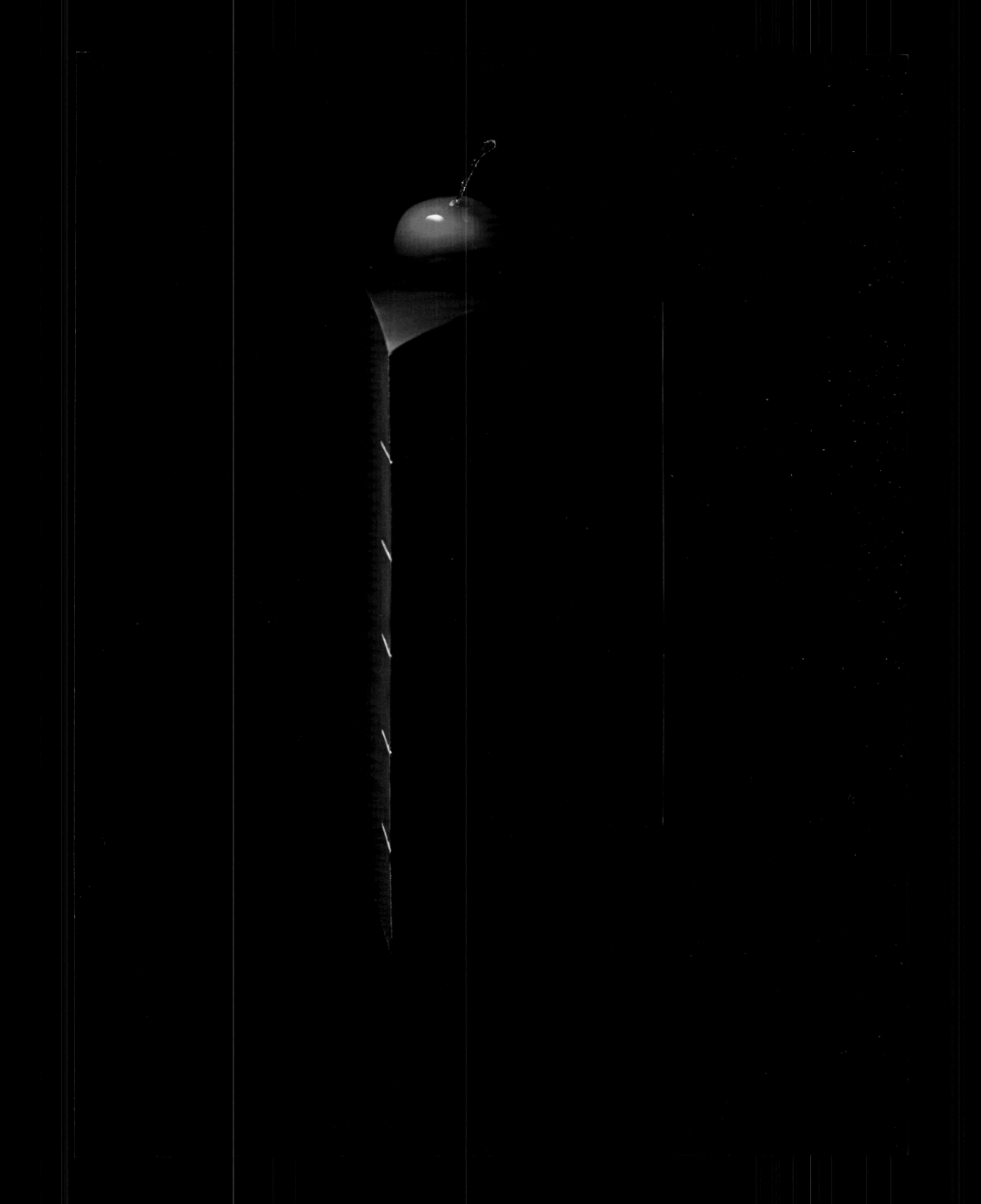

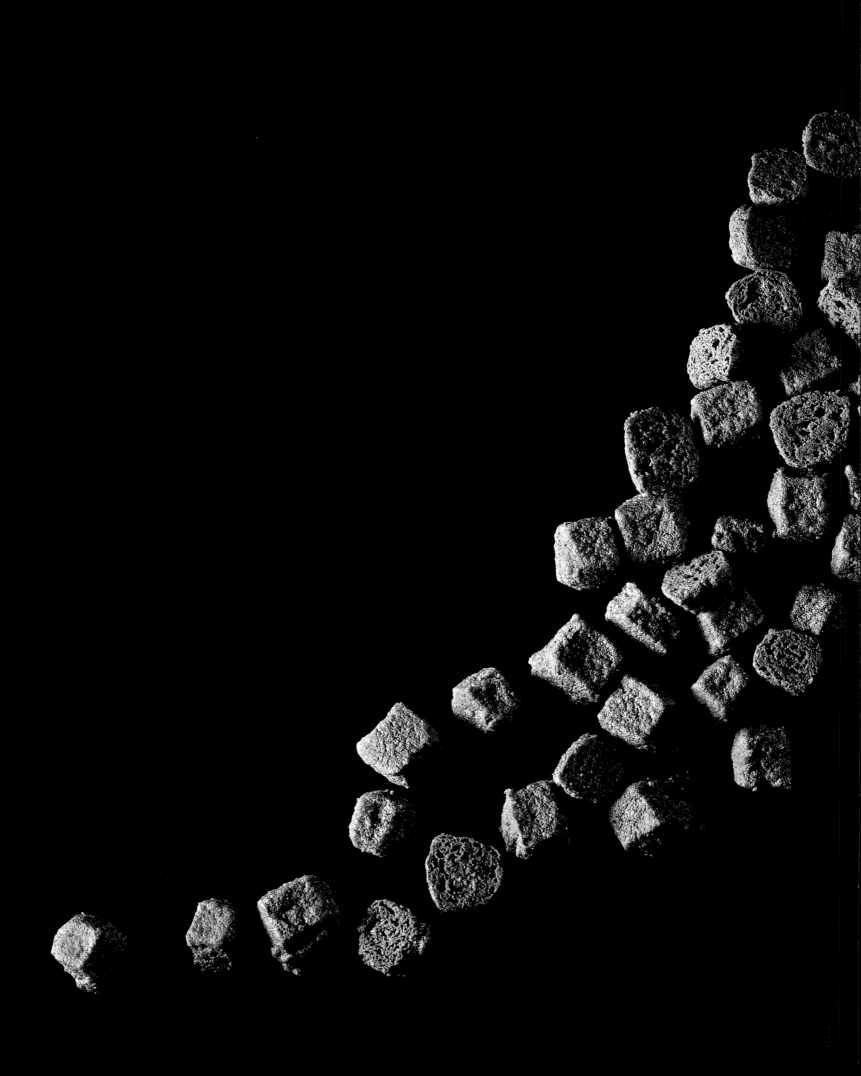

Émotion Infiniment Chocolat

Infiniment Chocolat Emotion

Makes 10 tall, slim glasses about 4 in. 10cm high, (5 2/3 oz./160 g capacity)

Ingredients:

Fleur de sel Dark Chocolate Fragments:

1 1/2 teaspoons (6 g) *Fleur de sel*, preferably Guérande
10 1/2 oz (300 g) Araguani 72% dark chocolate (Valrhona)

Araguani Chocolate Whipped Cream:

1 1/2 oz. (45 g) Araguani 72% dark chocolate (Valrhona)
1/6 oz. (5 g) pure cocoa paste (Valrhona)
3/4 cup (6 oz./175 g) liquid cream
2 teaspoons (1/4 oz./7.5 g) superfine sugar

Fleur de sel Chocolate Shortbread Dough:

5 1/4 oz. (150 g) Araguani 72% dark chocolate (Valrhona)
1 1/2 cups (6 oz./175 g) flour
1/4 cup (1 oz./30 g) cocoa powder (Valrhona)
1 teaspoon (5 g) baking soda
2/3 cup (5 1/4 oz./150 g) butter at room temperature
1/2 cup (4 1/4 oz./120 g) light brown sugar
1/4 cup (1 3/4 oz./50 g) superfine sugar
1 teaspoon (5 g) *Fleur de sel*, preferably Guérande
1/2 teaspoon (2 g) pure vanilla extract (natural)

Araguani Chocolate Gelée:

6 3/4 oz. (190 g) Araguani 72% dark chocolate (Valrhona)
3 tablespoons + 1 teaspoon (1 1/2 oz./40 g) superfine sugar
1/2 teaspoon (2 g) fruit pectin X58
2 1/2 cups (21 oz./600 g) whole milk

Araguani Chocolate Cake Batter:

2 oz. (60 g) Araguani 72% dark chocolate (Valrhona)
1 tablespoon + 2 teaspoons (3/4 oz./25 g) butter
1 1/2 tablespoons (3/4 oz./24 g) egg yolk + 1 tablespoon (1/2 oz./13 g) superfine sugar
2 tablespoons + 2 teaspoons (1 1/4 oz./36 g) egg whites + 1 tablespoon (1/2 oz./12 g superfine sugar)

Finishing:

Gold leaf

Preparation Time:

35 mins. (1 day in advance);
40 mins. (the same day).

Cooking Time:

8 mins. (1 day in advance);
about 30 mins. (the same day).

Chilling Time:

4 h. + 1 h. (the same day)

Preparation:

One day in advance, prepare the chocolate sheet for the chocolate slivers: Crush the *Fleur de sel* with a rolling pin. Sift with a fine sieve. Chop the chocolate with a serrated knife and place it in a bowl over a bain-marie of simmering water to melt, stirring gently with a wooden spoon until the temperature of the chocolate reaches 130°F (55°C). Once the temperature is reached, remove the bowl immediately from the bain-marie and place it in a bowl of cold water with four or five ice cubes. Stir the chocolate from time to time, scraping it from the sides of the bowl as it begins to set. Once the chocolate has cooled to 80°F (27°C), return the bowl to the bain-marie to warm slightly, monitoring the temperature carefully with a thermometer until the chocolate warms to between 88°F and 90°F (31°C–32°C). Stir in the sifted *Fleur de sel*. Place a large sheet of rhodoid plastic* on a work surface. Pour the chocolate onto the plastic and use a spatula to spread it into a thin, even layer. Cover the chocolate with a second sheet of rhodoid, and top with light weights to keep the sheet of chocolate flat. Refrigerate until the following day.

Also a day in advance, prepare the chocolate whipped cream: Chop the chocolate and cocoa paste with a serrated knife. Place in a bowl over a bain-marie of simmering water to melt. Combine the cream and sugar in a saucepan, and bring to a boil. Pour the cream, one-third at a time, over the chocolate, stirring from the center out in small, then progressively larger concentric circles. Mix with a hand blender. Press a sheet of plastic film directly onto the surface of the cream and refrigerate overnight.

The following day, prepare the *Fleur de sel* chocolate shortbread dough: Chop the chocolate with a serrated knife. Sift the flour, cocoa powder and baking soda together. Cut the butter into pieces, place it in the bowl of a mixer fitted with a plastic paddle. Mix until the butter is creamy. Add the brown sugar, superfine sugar, salt and vanilla, and combine. Incorporate the flour–cocoa–soda mixture, mixing rapidly until combined, without overworking. If the dough is overworked, it will lose its flaky texture. Roll the dough into a ball and wrap in plastic film. Flatten gently, refrigerate and let rest for at least four hours.

Prepare the Araguani chocolate gelée: Chop the chocolate with a serrated knife and place it in a bowl. Combine the sugar and pectin. In a saucepan, heat the milk to 104°F (40°C), then stir in the sugar–pectin mixture. Bring to a boil and pour, one-third at a time, over the chocolate, stirring from the center out in small, then progressively larger concentric circles.

Spoon about 2 oz. (60 g) of the chocolate jelly into each serving glass, place the glasses on a tray and refrigerate.

Prepare the *Fleur de sel* chocolate shortbread cubes:
On a lightly floured work surface, roll out the shortbread dough to about 1/4 in. (7 mm) thick. Let rest in the refrigerator for one hour.
Preheat the oven on convection setting to 330°F (165°C/Gas Mark 5–6). Cut the shortbread dough into 1/4-in. cubes. Place the cubes on a baking sheet lined with parchment, leaving about 1/2 in. between each. Place in the oven and cook for eight minutes.

Prepare the Araguani chocolate cake batter:
Chop the chocolate with a serrated knife and place it in a bowl over a bain-marie of simmering water to melt to 105°F (40°C). Remove the bowl from the bain-marie and stir in the butter. In the bowl of a mixer fitted with a whisk, combine the egg yolks with one heaping tablespoon of the sugar, and beat until the mixture thickens and turns light yellow. In a separate bowl, whisk the egg whites to stiff peaks, adding the remaining one tablespoon sugar, little by little. Pour the blanched egg yolks over the chocolate–butter mixture and whisk to blend. Incorporate the whipped egg whites, folding them in delicately, lifting and turning the mixture with a rubber spatula.
Preheat the oven on convection setting to 320°F (160°C/Gas Mark 5–6). Pour the batter in a 1/3-in. layer onto a pastry sheet lined with cooking parchment. Place in the oven and cook for fifteen minutes. Remove from the oven, let the cake cool, then cut it into 1/3-in. cubes.

To assemble: Break the *Fleur de sel* chocolate sheet into irregular pieces or fragments. Just before serving, remove the chocolate cream from the refrigerator and whip. Spoon into a pastry bag fitted with a F8 star tip.

In a bowl, combine equal quantities of the chocolate cake cubes and the *Fleur de sel* chocolate shortbread cubes. Sprinkle 3/4 oz. (20 g) of the mixed cubes over the chocolate gelée in each serving glass. Decorate each serving with the chocolate whipped cream. Plant a few *Fleur de sel* chocolate slivers in the whipped cream and decorate with gold leaf. Keep the glasses refrigerated until serving.

* Transparent plastic celluloid used in pastry and confectionery.

Macaron Plaisir Sucré

Plaisir Sucré Macaron

Makes about 72 macarons (or about 144 shells)

Ingredients:

Flaky Hazelnut Praline Cubes:

2 tablespoons (3/4 oz./20 g) whole hazelnuts with their skins
1 1/2 oz. (45 g) Jivara 40% milk chocolate (Valrhona) or milk chocolate, 40% cocoa
2 1/3 oz. (65 g) hazelnut praline
3 1/2 oz. (100 g) pure Italian hazelnut paste (Valrhona)
1 1/2 tablespoons (3/4 oz./20 g) butter
3 oz. (85 g) Gavottes Crepe Dentelle cookies, crumbled

Macaron Shells:

1 cup (7 2/3 oz./220 g) or about 8 "liquefied" egg whites, divided (see note)
3 1/2 cups (10 1/2 oz./300 g) ground almonds
2 1/3 cups (10 1/2 oz./300 g) confectioners' sugar
2 oz. (60 g) pure cocoa paste (or dark chocolate, 100% cocoa)
1/2 tablespoon (1/3 oz./10 g) coffee extract
1/2 teaspoon (2 g) lemon yellow food coloring
1 1/2 cups (10 1/2 oz./300 g) superfine sugar
1/3 cup (2 2/3 oz./75 g) mineral water
A few Gavottes Crepe Dentelle cookies

Milk Chocolate Ganache:

9 1/2 oz. (270 g) Jivara 40% milk chocolate (Valrhona) or milk chocolate, 40% cocoa
1 1/4 cups (10 1/2 oz./300 g) liquid cream

Preparation Time:

2 mins. (5 days in advance);
about 1 h. (the same day).

Cooking Time:

About 40 mins.

Resting Time:

30 mins.

Chilling Time:

1 h. + 2 h. + 24 h.
Freezing time: 2 h.

Preparation:

Five days in advance, place the egg whites for the macaron shells in a bowl, cover the bowl tightly with plastic film, pierce a few holes in the film and refrigerate to liquefy.

One day in advance, prepare the flaky hazelnut praline cubes: Preheat the oven to 340°F (170°C/Gas Mark 5–6). Spread the hazelnuts on a baking sheet, place them in the oven and toast for fifteen minutes, stirring occasionally. Remove the hot hazelnuts from the oven, transfer to a drum sieve and rub to eliminate the skins. Place the nuts in a plastic bag on a work surface and using a rolling pin, crush to medium-sized pieces. Chop the chocolate with a serrated knife and place it in a bain-marie over simmering water to melt. Chop the hazelnut praline and add to the chocolate, along with the hazelnut paste. Cut the butter into pieces and add it to the mixture, stirring until well mixed. Add the hazelnut pieces and the crumbled Gavottes cookies. Line a shallow baking dish with plastic film and pour the chocolate mixture out in an even layer a little less than 1/4 in. thick (4 mm). Smooth the surface. Refrigerate for one hour, then transfer to the freezer for two hours. Turn the frozen mixture out onto a work surface, remove the plastic film, cut into neat 2/3-in. (1.5 cm) squares. Return the squares to the freezer.

Prepare the batter for the macaron shells: Sift the ground almonds and the confectioners' sugar together. Chop the cocoa paste in a bowl over a bain-marie of simmering water to melt to 120°F (50°C). Combine 1/2 cup (110 g) of the liquefied egg whites with the coffee extract and the food coloring. Add to the sifted almond powder–sugar mixture, without mixing. Combine the sugar and water in a saucepan, and bring to a boil, monitoring the temperature with a thermometer. Meanwhile place the remaining 1/2 cup (110 g) of liquefied egg whites in the bowl of a mixer fitted with a wire whisk. Once the sugar syrup has reached 239°F (115°C), begin beating the egg whites on high speed. Once the syrup has reached 244°F (118°C), reduce the mixer speed to medium and begin pouring the syrup in a steady stream into the egg whites. Continue beating until the mixture cools to 122°F (50°C). Using a spatula, fold the meringue mixture into the almond–sugar mixture. Add the melted cocoa paste, folding until the mixture loses a little volume. Transfer the batter into a pastry bag fitted with a No. 11 plain tip (1/2 in. diameter).

Line baking sheets with cooking parchment and pipe out rounds of batter about 1 1/2 in. (3.5 cm) in diameter, spaced about 3/4 in. apart. Tap the baking sheets gently on a work surface covered with a kitchen towel to smooth the surface. Crumble a few Gavottes cookies between your fingers and sprinkle over the macarons. Set aside at room temperature for at least thirty minutes to allow a "skin" to form.

Preheat the oven on convection setting to 355°F (180°C/ Gas Mark 6). Place the baking sheets in the oven and cook for twelve minutes, opening and closing the oven door quickly twice during the baking to release steam. Remove from the oven and slide the macaron shells onto the work surface.

Prepare the milk chocolate ganache: Chop the chocolate with a serrated knife and place it in a bowl. Bring the cream to a boil in a saucepan and pour, one-third at a time, over the chocolate, stirring from the center out in small, then progressively larger concentric circles.

Pour the mixture into a shallow baking dish. Press a sheet of plastic film directly onto the surface of the ganache. Refrigerate until the texture is creamy.

Spoon the ganache into a pastry bag fitted with a No. 11 plain pastry tip. Turn half of the macaron shells over, flat side up on the work surface and pipe the ganache onto each shell. Place a frozen hazelnut praline cube in the center of each macaron, pressing down lightly. Pipe a dot of ganache on top of each praline cube. Cover each filled macaron shell with a second shell and press down lightly. Refrigerate the macarons for twenty-four hours.

The following day, remove the macarons from the refrigerator two hours before serving.

Note: "Liquefied" egg whites are egg whites that have been allowed to rest for several days to lose their elasticity. Simply place the egg whites in a bowl, cover with plastic film, pierce a few holes in the film, and refrigerate for five to seven days.

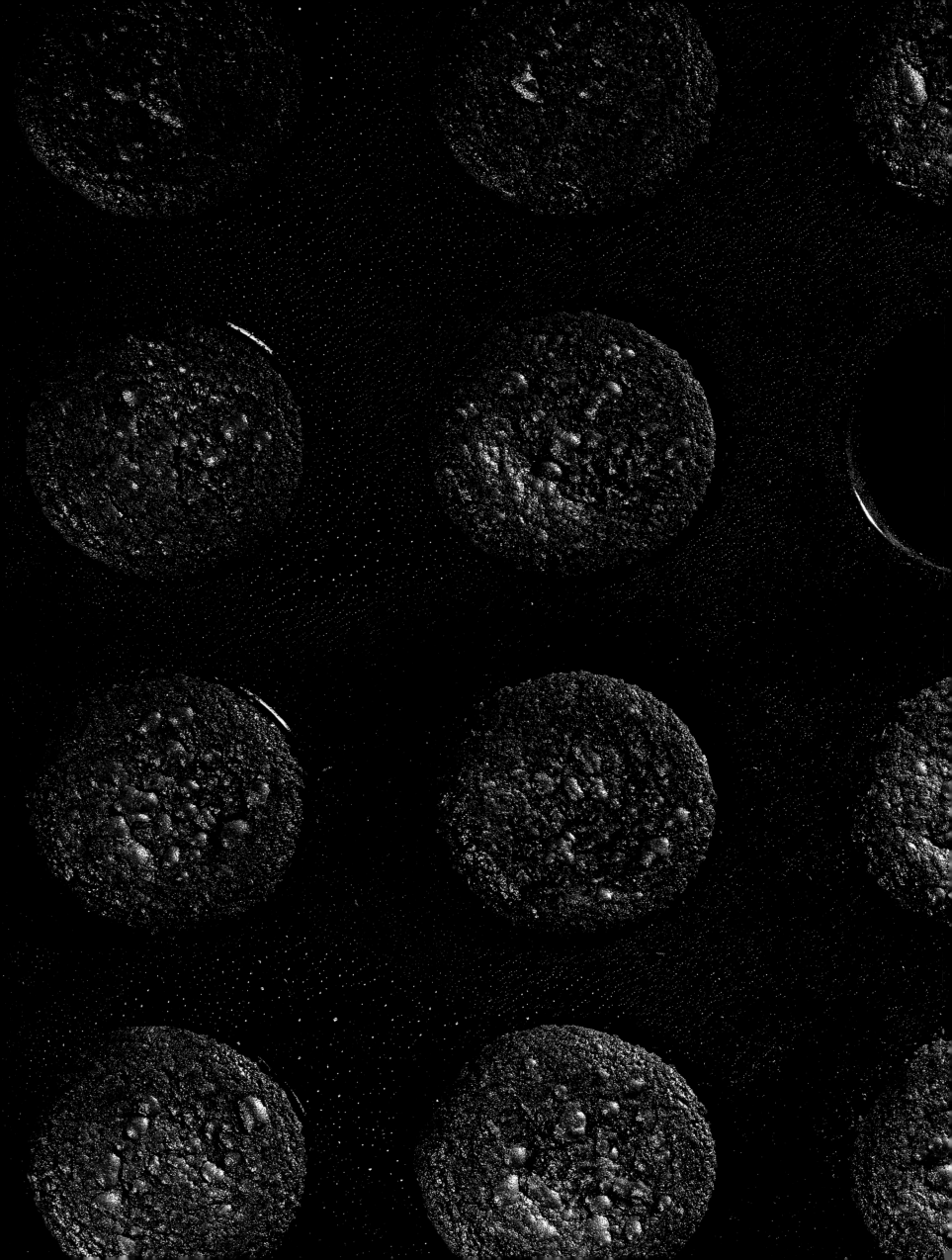

Moelleux Azur

Azur Chocolate Cakes

Makes 20 cakes

Ingredients:

Candied Grapefruit Cubes:

2 pink grapefruit
3/4 teaspoon (2 g) Sarawak
peppercorns
4 1/4 cups (35 1/4 oz./1 liter) mineral
water
2 2/3 cups (17 2/3 oz./500 g)
superfine sugar
1/4 cup (1 3/4 oz./50 g) lemon juice
Star anise (2 g)
Used vanilla bean pods (10 g)

Chocolate and Yuzu Ganache:

4 oz. (115 g) Manjari 64% chocolate
(Valrhona)
2 tablespoons (1 oz./30 g) fresh yuzu
juice
1/2 cup (4 oz./115 g) liquid cream

Chocolate Cake Batter:

5 3/4 oz. (165 g) Extra Amer 67%
dark chocolate (Valrhona)
1/3 cup (1 1/2 oz./45 g) flour
3/4 cup (5 3/4 oz./165 g) butter
3/4 cup (5 oz./145 g) superfine sugar
2/3 cup (4 3/4 oz./135 g) eggs

———

Preparation Time:

15 mins. (1 day in advance);
30 mins. (the same day).

Cooking Time:

1 h. 40 mins. (1 day in advance);
about 20 mins. (the same day).

Resting Time:

1 h.

Freezing Time:

2 h.

Chilling Time:

3 h.

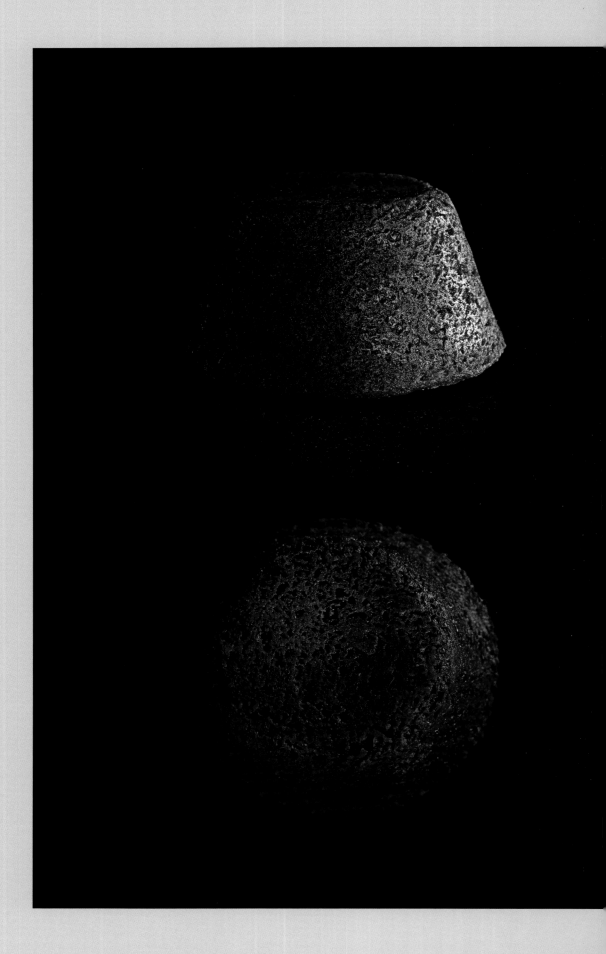

Preparation:

One day in advance, prepare the candied grapefruit:
Brush the grapefruit under cold water. Cut off the ends.
Place the grapefruit upright and with a sharp knife,
cutting from top to bottom, cut wide bands of grapefruit
rind with about 1/4 in. (1 cm) of the pulp. Plunge the
grapefruit bands into a saucepan of boiling water. Let
the water return to a boil and boil for two minutes. Drain
and refresh under cold water. Repeat this operation
two times. Drain the blanched grapefruit.
Crush the peppercorns and place them in a saucepan
with the water, sugar, lemon juice, star anise and vanilla
pods. Bring to a boil and add the blanched grapefruit.
Cover the saucepan partially (about three-quarter) and
simmer over very low heat for one and a half hour. Pour
the grapefruit and syrup into a bowl. Let cool. Cover
with plastic film and refrigerate overnight.

The following day, drain the grapefruit in a sieve set over
a bowl for one hour. Cut the grapefruit rind into
forty cubes of about 1/8 in. (Cover the remaining
candied grapefruit rind with the sugar syrup and reserve
for another use.)

**The following day, prepare the chocolate and yuzu
ganache:** Chop the chocolate with a serrated knife and
place it in a bowl over a bain-marie of simmering water to
melt. Heat the yuzu juice to 113°–122°F (45°–50°C).
Bring the cream to a boil in a separate saucepan. Pour
the cream, one-third at a time, over the chocolate,
stirring from the center out in small, then progressively
larger concentric circles. Incorporate the yuzu juice and
mix with a hand blender until the ganache is smooth and
well mixed. Spoon into a pastry bag and pipe into silicon
dome molds of 3/4 in. diameter, filling each dome about
half-full. Press two cubes of candied grapefruit into the
center of each dome. Cover with enough chocolate and
yuzu ganache to fill the domes. Refrigerate for two hours,
then transfer to the freezer for two hours.

Prepare the chocolate cake batter: Chop the
chocolate with a serrated knife and place it in a bowl
over a bain-marie of simmering water to melt to 113°–
122°F (45°–50°C). Sift the flour. Cut the butter into
pieces and place it in the bowl of a mixer fitted with a
plastic paddle. Beat until the butter is creamy, add the
sugar, beat again, then pour in the melted chocolate,
one-third at a time, taking care not to melt the butter.
Beat in the eggs. Add the flour and beat rapidly. Pour
the batter into a bowl and set aside to rest for one hour
at room temperature.

Preheat the oven on convection setting to 340°F
(170°C/Gas Mark 5–6). Unmold the frozen chocolate
and yuzu ganache domes. Brush a little butter into
tweny silicon mini-muffin molds, 2 in. diameter x 1/2 in.
deep (51 mm x 29 mm).
Fill each muffin half-full with the chocolate cake batter.
Press a dome of frozen chocolate and yuzu ganache
into the center of each, and add enough batter to cover.
Place in the oven and cook for about fifteen minutes.
Remove from the oven and let cool for thirty minutes
before unmolding onto a baking sheet lined with cooking
parchment.

Serve with tea, coffee, or hot chocolate.

Moelleux Chloé

Chloé Chocolate Cakes

Makes 20 cakes

Ingredients:

Raspberry Ganache:

5 1/4 oz. (150 g) fresh raspberries
3 1/2 oz./100 g Manjari 64% chocolate (Valrhona)
2 tablespoons (1 1/4 oz./35 g) liquid cream
Raspberry jam

Chocolate Cake Batter:

5 3/4 oz. (165 g) Extra Amer 67% dark chocolate (Valrhona)
1/3 cup (1 1/2 oz./45 g) flour
3/4 cup (5 3/4 oz./165 g) butter
3/4 cup (5 oz./145 g) superfine sugar
2/3 cup (4 3/4 oz./135 g) eggs

Preparation Time:

35 mins.

Cooking Time:

About 20 mins.

Resting Time:

1 h.

Freezing Time:

2 h.

Chilling Time:

3 h.

Preparation:

Prepare the raspberry ganache: Press the raspberries to a puree in a food mill. Strain through a sieve and heat to 115°F–125°F (45°C–50°C). Chop the chocolate with a serrated knife, place it in a bowl over a bain-marie of simmering water to melt. Bring the cream to a boil and pour over the chocolate, one-third at a time, stirring from the center out in small, then progressively larger concentric circles. Incorporate the raspberry puree, one-half at a time. Mix with a hand blender until the ganache is smooth and well mixed. Spoon into a pastry bag and pipe into silicon dome molds of 3/4 in. diameter, filling each dome about two-thirds full. Cover with raspberry jam up to the rims of the domes. Place in the freezer for two hours.

Prepare the chocolate cake batter: Chop the chocolate with a serrated knife and place it in a bowl over a bain-marie of simmering water to melt to 115°F–125°F (45°C–50°C). Sift the flour. Cut the butter into cubes and place it in the bowl of a mixer fitted with a plastic paddle. Beat until the butter is creamy, add the sugar, beat again, pour in the melted chocolate, one-third at a time, so that the butter does not melt. Beat in the eggs. Add the flour and beat rapidly. Pour the batter into a bowl and set aside to rest for one hour at room temperature.

Preheat the oven convection setting to 340°F (170°C/Gas Mark 5–6). Unmold the frozen raspberry ganache domes. Brush a little butter into twenty silicon mini-muffin molds of 2 in. diameter by 1/2 in. deep (51 mm x 29 mm). Fill each muffin mold half-full with the chocolate cake batter. Press a dome of frozen raspberry ganache into the center of each and add enough batter to cover. Place in the oven and cook for about fifteen minutes. Remove from the oven and let cool for thirty minutes before unmolding onto a baking sheet lined with cooking parchment.

Serve with tea, coffee, or hot chocolate.

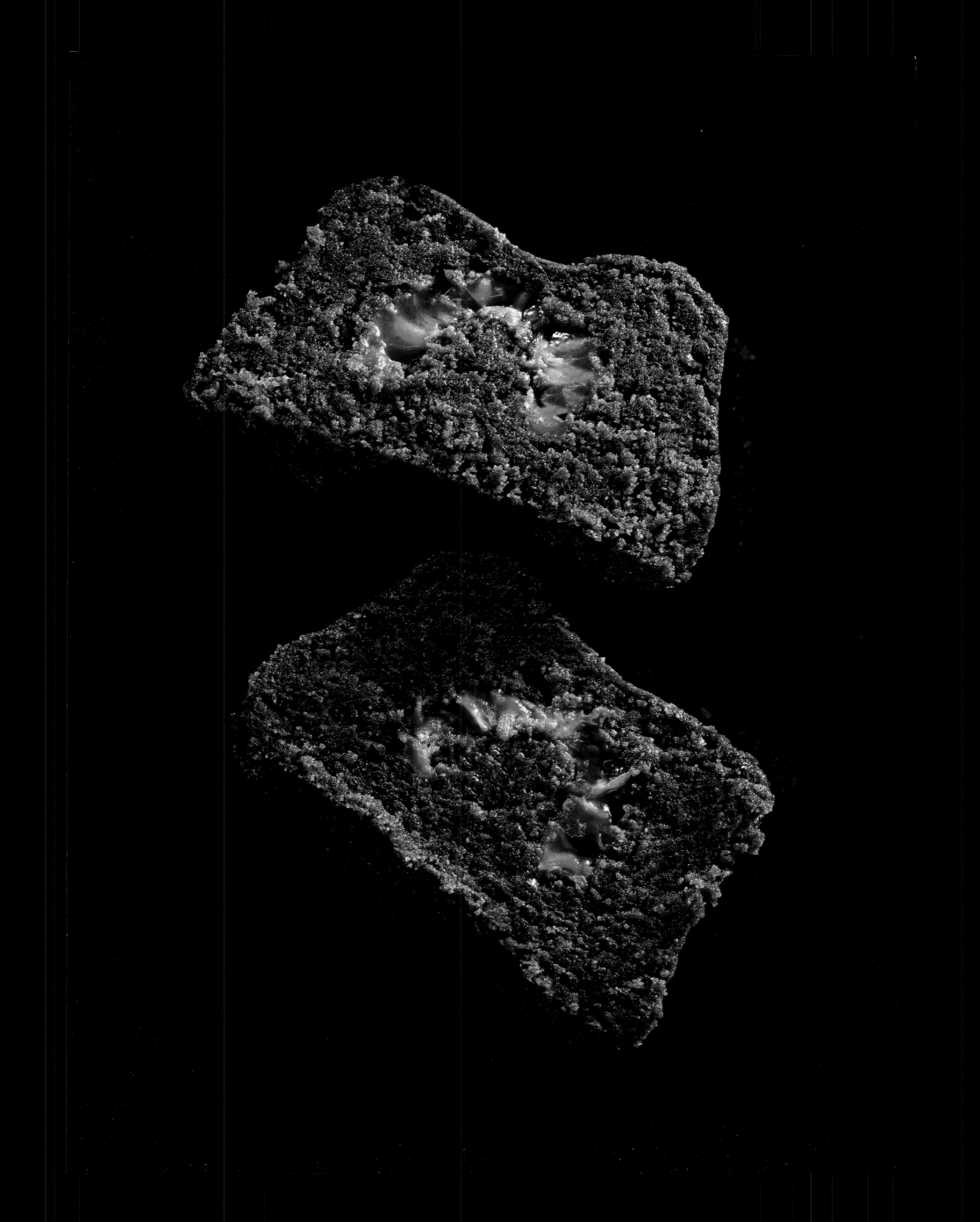

Moelleux Médélice

Médélice Chocolate Cakes

Makes 20 cakes

Ingredients:

Lemon Ganache:

4 3/4 oz. (135 g) Manjari 64%
chocolate (Valrhona)
2/3 cup (5 3/4 oz./165 g) liquid cream
1 teaspoon (1 g) lemon zest (from an
untreated lemon)
40 cubes candied lemon

Chocolate Cake Batter:

5 3/4 oz. (165 g) Extra Amer 67%
dark chocolate (Valrhona)
1/3 cup (1 1/2 oz./45 g) flour
3/4 cup (5 3/4 oz./165 g) butter
3/4 cup (5 oz./145 g) superfine sugar
2/3 cup (4 3/4 oz./135 g) eggs

———

Preparation Time:

30 mins.

Cooking Time:

20 mins.

Resting Time:

1 h.

Freezing Time:

2 h.

Chilling Time:

2 h.

Preparation:

Prepare the lemon ganache: Chop the chocolate with a serrated knife, place it in a bowl over a bain-marie of simmering water to melt. Bring the cream to a boil with the lemon zest. Pour over the chocolate, one-third at a time, stirring from the center out in small, then progressively larger concentric circles. Mix with a hand blender until the ganache is smooth and well mixed. Spoon into a pastry bag and pipe into silicon dome molds of 3/4 in. diameter, filling each dome about half-full. Press two cubes of candied lemon in the center of each dome. Fill to the rim with additional lemon ganache. Place in the freezer for two hours.

———

Prepare the chocolate cake batter: Chop the chocolate with a serrated knife and place it in a bowl over a bain-marie of simmering water to melt to 115°F–125°F (45°C–50°C). Sift the flour. Cut the butter into pieces and place it in the bowl of a mixer fitted with a plastic paddle. Beat until the butter is creamy. Add the sugar, beat again, then pour in the melted chocolate, one-third at a time, so that the butter does not melt. Beat in the eggs. Add the flour and beat rapidly. Pour the batter into a bowl and set aside to rest for one hour at room temperature.

———

Preheat the oven on convection setting to 340°F (170°C/Gas Mark 5–6). Unmold the frozen lemon ganache domes. Brush a little butter into twenty silicon mini-muffin molds 2 in. diameter by 1/2 in. deep (51 mm x 29 mm). Fill each muffin mold half-full with the chocolate cake batter. Press a dome of frozen lemon ganache into the center of each and add enough batter to cover. Place in the oven and cook for about fifteen minutes. Remove from the oven and let cool for thirty minutes before unmolding onto a baking sheet lined with cooking parchment.

———

Serve with tea, coffee, or hot chocolate.

Moelleux Mogador

Mogador Chocolate Cakes

Ingredients:

Passion Fruit Ganache:

About 10 passion fruit for 1/2 cup
(3 1/2 oz./100 g) passion fruit juice
4 3/4 oz. (135 g) Caraibe 66%
chocolate (Valrhona)
1/4 cup (2 1/3 oz./65 g) liquid cream

Chocolate Cake Batter:

5 3/4 oz. (165 g) Extra Amer 67%
dark chocolate (Valrhona)
1/3 cup (1 1/2 oz./45 g) flour
3/4 cup (5 3/4 oz./165 g) butter
3/4 cup (5 oz./145 g) superfine sugar
2/3 cup (4 3/4 oz./135 g) eggs

Preparation Time:

30 mins.

Cooking Time:

About 20 mins.

Resting Time:

1 h.

Freezing Time:

2 h.

Chilling Time:

2 h.

Preparation:

Prepare the passion fruit ganache: Cut the passion fruit in half, scoop out the pulp and press through a sieve to obtain 1/2 cup (3 1/2 oz./100 g) juice. Heat the juice to 115°F–125°F (45°C–50°C). Chop the chocolate with a serrated knife, place it in a bowl over a bain-marie of simmering water to melt. Bring the cream to a boil. Pour over the chocolate, one-third at a time, stirring from the center out in small, then progressively larger concentric circles. Mix with a hand blender until the ganache is smooth and well mixed. Spoon into a pastry bag and pipe into silicon dome molds of 3/4 in. diameter. Place in the freezer for two hours.

Prepare the chocolate cake batter: Chop the chocolate with a serrated knife and place it in a bowl over a bain-marie of simmering water to melt to 115°F–125°F (45°C–50°C). Sift the flour. Cut the butter into pieces and place it in the bowl of a mixer fitted with a plastic paddle. Beat until the butter is creamy. Add the sugar, beat again, then pour in the melted chocolate, one-third at a time, so that the butter does not melt. Beat in the eggs. Add the flour and beat rapidly. Pour the batter into a bowl and set aside to rest for one hour at room temperature.

Preheat the oven on convection setting to 340°F (170°C/Gas Mark 5–6). Unmold the frozen passion fruit ganache domes. Brush a little butter into twenty silicon mini-muffin molds 2 in. diameter by 1/2 in. deep (51 mm x 29 mm). Fill each muffin mold half-full with the chocolate cake batter. Press a dome of frozen passion fruit ganache into the center of each and add enough batter to cover. Place in the oven and cook for about fifteen minutes. Remove from the oven and let cool for thirty minutes before unmolding onto a baking sheet lined with cooking parchment.

Serve with tea, coffee, or hot chocolate.

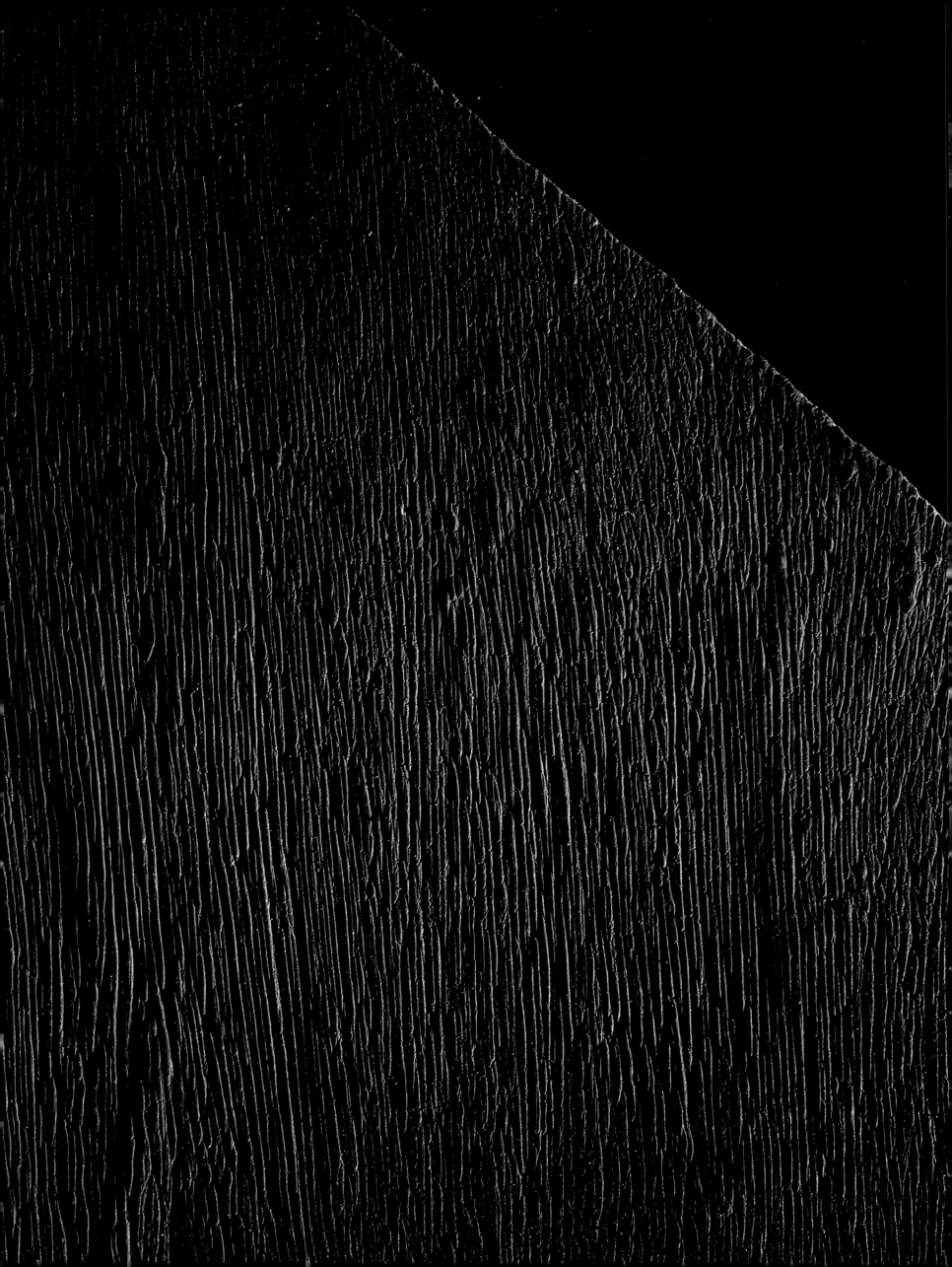

p. 40-41

Bonbon Chocolat au Macaron Chloé

Raspberry and chocolate ganache, smooth raspberry almond paste with macaron biscuit, enrobed in dark chocolate

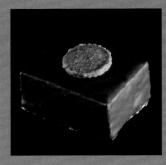

p. 40-41

Bonbon Chocolat au Macaron Infiniment Praliné Noisette

Crunchy, melt-in-your-mouth hazelnut praline, smooth almond paste, enrobed in dark chocolate

p. 40-41

Bonbon Chocolat au Macaron Mogador

Passion fruit and milk chocolate ganache, smooth Passion fruit almond paste with macaron biscuit, enrobed in milk chocolate

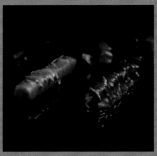

p. 44-45

Orange et Framboise

Candied orange flavoured with raspberry, enrobed in dark chocolate

Orange à la Cardamome

Candied orange flavoured with cardamom, enrobed in dark chocolate

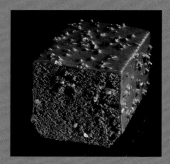

p. 46-47

Cake Chocolat et Praliné

Chocolate pound cake, flaky hazelnut praline, enrobed in dark chocolate with roasted almonds

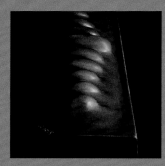

p. 49

Exubérante

Pure Origin Venezuelan dark chocolate ganache, gianduja with corn shortbread, pieces of salted-butter caramel, roasted almonds with salt and pepper, enrobed in dark chocolate

p. 68-69

Croquant au Praliné Chocolat au Lait
Thin nougatine, crunchy, melt-in-your-mouth hazelnut praline,
enrobed in milk chocolate

Croquant au Praliné Chocolat Noir
Thin nougatine, crunchy, melt-in-your-mouth hazelnut praline,
enrobed in dark chocolate

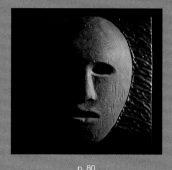

p. 80

Masque de Danse Magar, Népal
Pierre Hermé Paris milk chocolate, 45% cocoa

p. 81

Masque Kényah Kayan, Bornéo
Pure Origin Javanese dark chocolate, 75% cocoa

p. 83

Statuette Précolombienne
Chancay, Pérou
Colombian dark chocolate, 75% cocoa

p. 85

Masque Dan, Côte d'Ivoire
Pure Origin Ghanaian dark chocolate, 75% cocoa

p. 84

Statuette Sénoufo, Côte d'Ivoire
Pure Origin Ghanaian dark chocolate, 75% cocoa

p. 162

Cake Mogador

Passion fruit pound cake, milk chocolate chips with *Fleur de sel*, milk chocolate and Passion fruit ganache

p. 163

Cake Chloé

Chocolate pound cake, pieces of raspberry and dark chocolate, raspberry and dark chocolate ganache

p. 194-195

Galet Chuao

Pure Origin Chuao chocolate ganache with blackcurrant, dark chocolate

p. 194-195

Galet Intense

Bitter dark chocolate ganache, dark chocolate

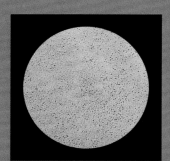

p. 194-195

Galet Infiniment Caramel

Salted-butter caramel, milk chocolate

p. 194-195

Galet Infiniment Café Iapar Rouge du Brésil

Iapar Rouge du Brésil coffee ganache, dark chocolate

p. 211

Caramels Plénitude

Bitter chocolate caramel

p. 125

Truffe Infiniment Caramel

Soft caramel, enrobed in dark chocolate

Truffe Mogador

Passion fruit and milk chocolate ganache,
enrobed in milk chocolate

Truffe Infiniment Praliné Noisette

Crunchy, melt-in-your-mouth hazelnut praline,
enrobed in cocoa

Truffe Intense

Bitter chocolate ganache, enrobed in cocoa

p. 246

Hermé Carré Azur

Yuzu cream, chocolate biscuit, dark chocolate zabaglione
mousse with pieces of dark chocolate with *Fleur de sel*
enrobed in dark chocolate, chocolate shortbread

p. 247-248

Plénitude

Chocolate macaron biscuit, ganache with pieces of caramel,
chocolate zabaglione mousse with pieces
of chocolate with *Fleur de sel*

p. 249

La Cerise sur le Gâteau

Hazelnut dacquoise cake, flaky hazelnut praline, thin layers
of milk chocolate, milk chocolate ganache and Chantilly cream

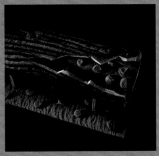

p. 56-57

Perpétua d'après Giuseppe Penone

Chocolate cake imbibed with chocolate syrup, Paineiras
Plantation Pure Origin Brazilian dark chocolate Chantilly cream,
nougatine with cocoa nibs, Infiniment Chocolat shortbread

acknowl edgments charles znaty

Every book has its own story. This one owes a great debt of gratitude to Alain and Suzanna Flammarion. They were kind enough to believe in us and our entrepreneurial project right from the start, when we founded Maison Pierre Hermé Paris. Déborah Dupont-Daguet, who runs the Librairie Gourmande book shop with such boldness and passion, pointed out to me that having a work published by Flammarion is a real honor. This is where successful authors find a home. So it was only natural that, having previously published several dozen recipe books, Pierre Hermé should join such illustrious company. And since we are talking about kindness and friendship, we must also thank Sergio Coimbra, whose affectionate vision, smile, and warmth brightened our Paris winter. He has returned to his native Brazil, leaving us with his magnificent photographs to delight our senses. He was helped every step of the way by the Maison Pierre Hermé Paris pastry chefs, Mickaël Marsollier, Manon Derouet, and Camille Moënne-Loccoz, as well as the indispensable Coco Jobard, who contributes to just about all our publications. Philippe Marchand's expert eye and hand were crucial in designing the best possible showcase for the words and images. He turned the book into a Masterwork. Destiny, ever mischievous, had a hand in the project by bringing together Suzanne Tise-Isoré and Agata Pudelek around the same table. Our thanks also go to Delphine Baussan, Barbara Bartolini, Camille Jeanneau, and Gabrielle Geneste. They worked tirelessly behind the scenes, smoothing out difficulties before they arose and ensuring that harmony reigned over every stage of the production of this book.

Charles Znaty

Co-founder of Maison Pierre Hermé Paris

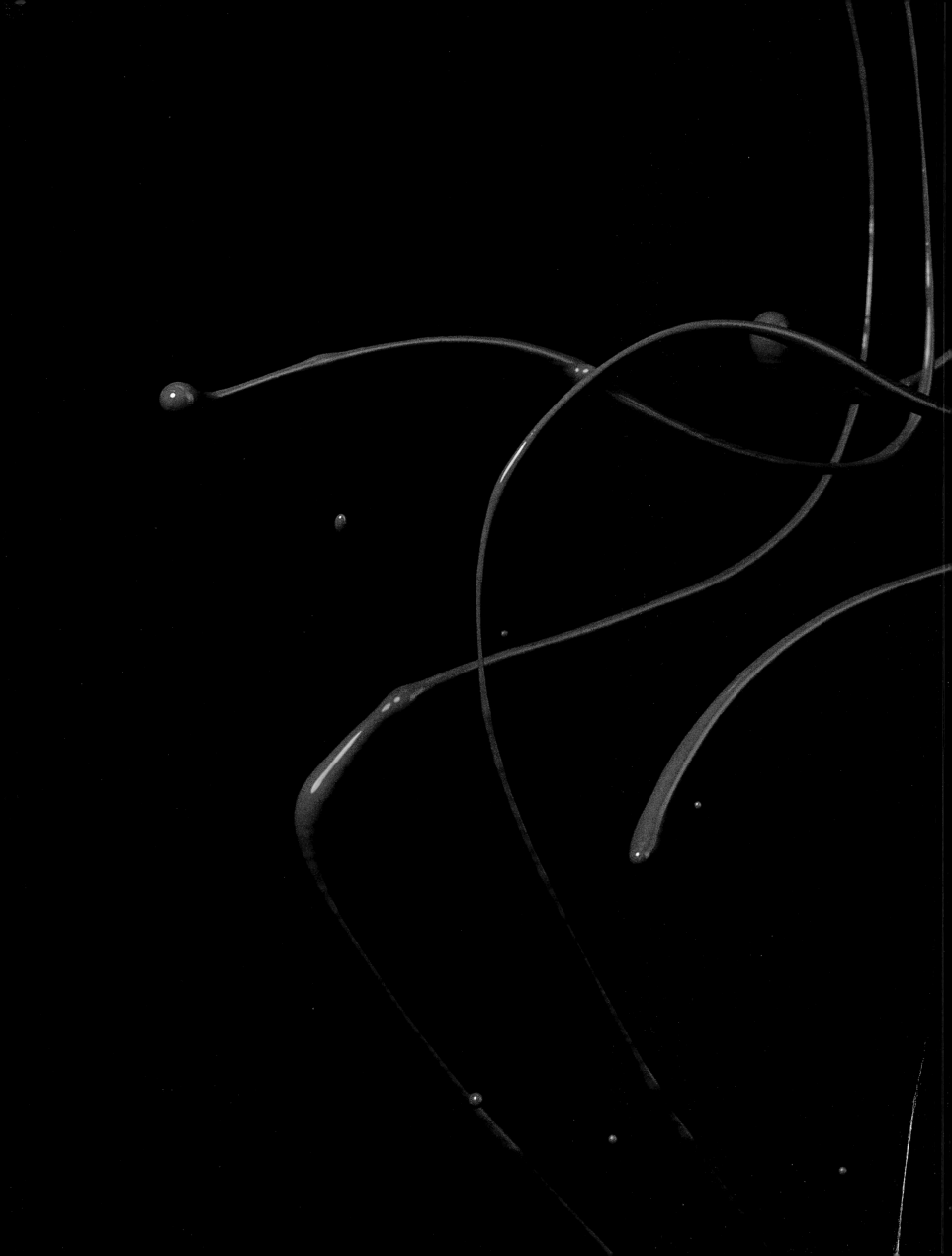

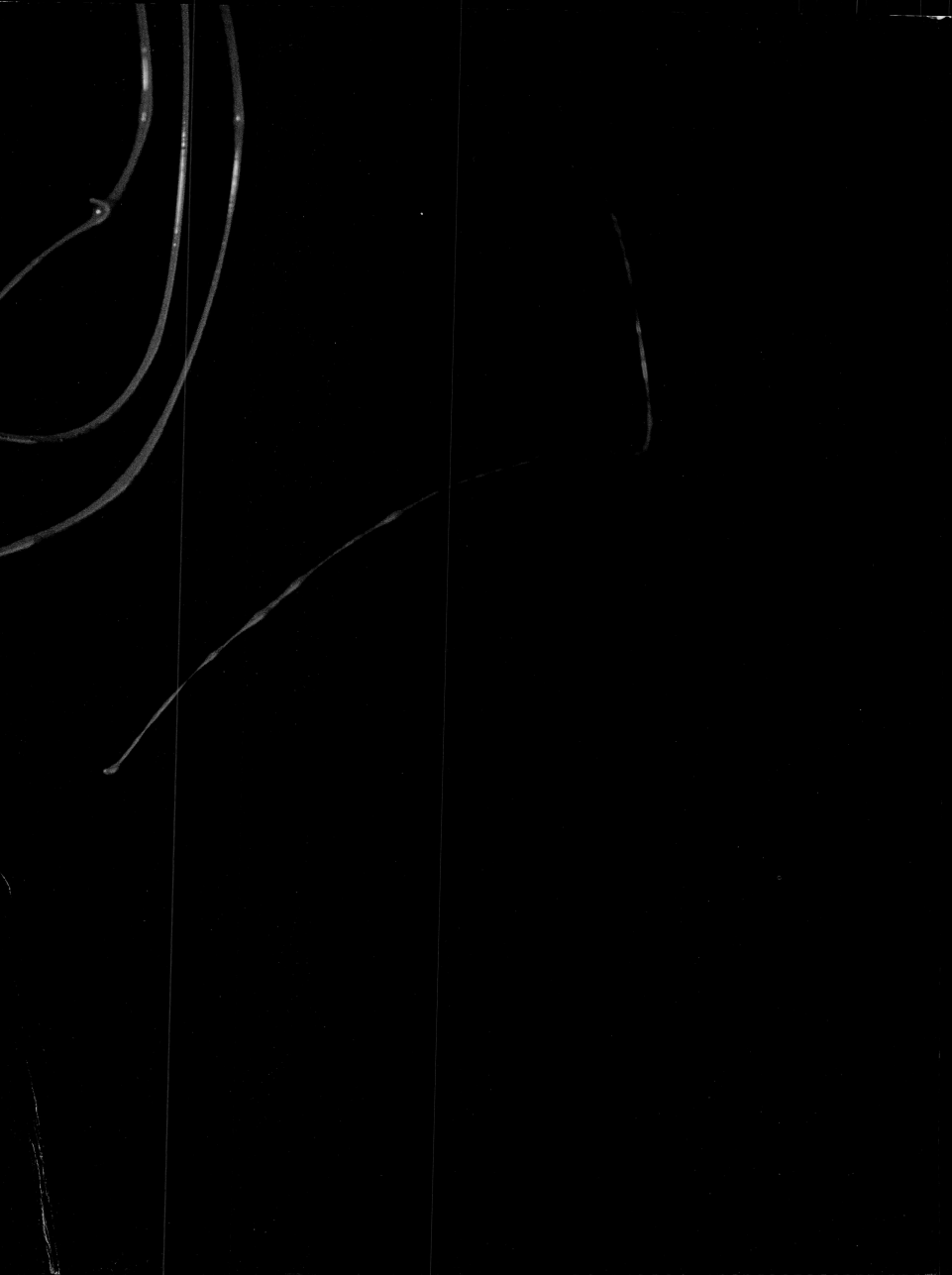

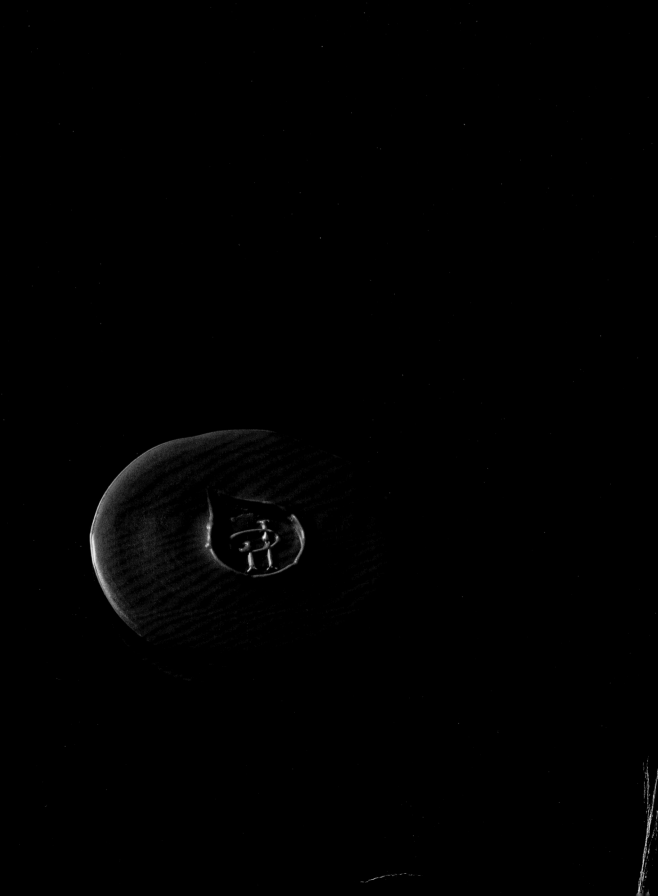